D1474452

Tallahassee

A HISTORY OF TALLAHASSEE AND LEON COUNTY
Revised and Expanded 2nd Edition
by
MARY LOUISE ELLIS and WILLIAM WARREN ROGERS
JOAN PERRY MORRIS,
Photo Editor

*Oak trees at sunset
Photo credit:
Michael Zimny*

FAVORED LAND
Tallahassee

A HISTORY OF TALLAHASSEE AND LEON COUNTY

Revised and Expanded 2nd Edition

by Mary Louise Ellis
and William Warren Rogers

Photographic editor,
Joan Perry Morris

For Gene, who gives much to this place
and to me, and for our son, Taylor.
—M. L. E.

For my grandchildren Elizabeth Ann and
William Arnold Rogers and Madeline
Kate and Caroline Gray Lindsey.
—W. W. R.

For Allen, who permitted me to take over
his "retirement job" and thereby gave me
the rewarding career I enjoy.
—J. P. M.

The Donning Company/Publishers
184 Business Park Drive, Suite 106
Virginia Beach, Virginia 23462

Library of Congress Cataloging-in-Publication Data

Rogers, William Warren.
  Favored Land.
  Bibliography: p.
  Includes index.
  1. Tallahassee (Fla.)—History—Pictorial works.
2. Leon County (Fla.)—History—Pictorial works.
3. Tallahassee (Fla.)—Description—Views. 4. Leon
County (Fla.)—Description and travel—Views. I. Ellis,
Mary Louise. II. Morris, Joan Perry, 1935– . III. Title.
F319.T14R64   1988   975.9'88   88–30975
ISBN 1–57864–064–4 (Revised and expanded 2nd
edition)

Printed in the United States of America

THE
DONNING COMPANY
PUBLISHERS

Sunrise over Lake Hall. Photo credit: Florida Department of State, Florida State Archives, Department of Commerce Collection.

Silhouette of oak tree at Lafayette Vineyards. Photo credit: Ray Stanyard.

One of Leon County's many lovely lakes.
Photo credit: Tallahassee Trust for Historic Preservation.

Aerial view looking west over downtown.
Photo credit: Robert Overton.

Tallahassee City Hall.
Photo credit: Florida Department of State, Florida State
Archives, Department of Commerce Collection, J. L. Gaines.

Florida State University Law School Green.
Photo credit: Florida State University Photo Lab,
Ryals Lee, Jr.

CONTENTS

Buck Lake Road.
Photo credit: Florida Department of State,
Florida State Archives, Department of Commerce Collection.

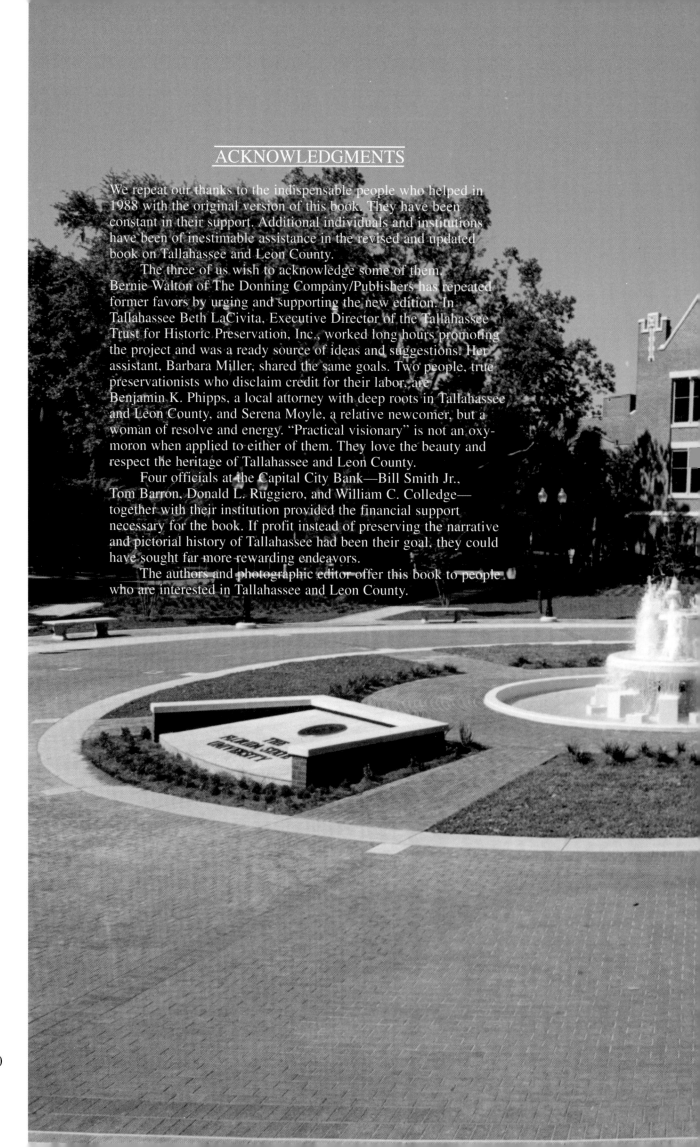

ACKNOWLEDGMENTS

We repeat our thanks to the indispensable people who helped in 1988 with the original version of this book. They have been constant in their support. Additional individuals and institutions have been of inestimable assistance in the revised and updated book on Tallahassee and Leon County.

The three of us wish to acknowledge some of them. Bernie Walton of The Donning Company/Publishers has repeated former favors by urging and supporting the new edition. In Tallahassee Beth LaCivita, Executive Director of the Tallahassee Trust for Historic Preservation, Inc., worked long hours promoting the project and was a ready source of ideas and suggestions. Her assistant, Barbara Miller, shared the same goals. Two people, true preservationists who disclaim credit for their labor, are Benjamin K. Phipps, a local attorney with deep roots in Tallahassee and Leon County, and Serena Moyle, a relative newcomer, but a woman of resolve and energy. "Practical visionary" is not an oxymoron when applied to either of them. They love the beauty and respect the heritage of Tallahassee and Leon County.

Four officials at the Capital City Bank—Bill Smith Jr., Tom Barron, Donald L. Ruggiero, and William C. Colledge—together with their institution provided the financial support necessary for the book. If profit instead of preserving the narrative and pictorial history of Tallahassee had been their goal, they could have sought far more rewarding endeavors.

The authors and photographic editor offer this book to people who are interested in Tallahassee and Leon County.

10

Westcott Building, Florida State University.
Photo credit: Florida State University Photo Lab, Ryals Lee, Jr.

*Lake Bradford.
Photo credit:
R. G. Prophet,
Florida Division
of Tourism.*

*Lake Jackson
Indian Mounds.
Photo credit:
Historic Tallahassee
Preservation Board,*

*Bass fishing on Lake
Jackson. Photo credit:
Florida Division
of Tourism.*

Rolling pasture land near Tallahassee. Photo credit: Florida Division of Tourism

Alfred B. Maclay State Gardens. Photo credit: R. G. Prophet, Florida Division of Tourism.

INTRODUCTION

This book revises and expands the narrative and photographic history of Tallahassee and Leon County first published in 1988. In the interim the city and county have changed in many ways, not all of them good. Old streets have undergone repairs and new ones have been added. There are more houses and subdivisions, fewer trees, old schools have been enlarged and new ones have been built. Businesses have closed only to be replaced many times over, and competition is keen. In religion Protestants are still a majority, but Catholics and Jews are strongly present, as are premillennial churches and non-Western religions.

County and state workers have increased in number to meet the demands of the nation's fourth most populous state. The work ethic of Tallahasseans is as strong as ever, but leisure is a major component of people's lives. Pleasure received and fulfillment derived are the best tests of leisure. Certainly institutional, alumni, and town pride are generated by the athletic success of Tallahassee's three universities and colleges, and that success has an important economic impact on the region.

Racial issues abide, but communication and personal interrelations between blacks and whites are measurably better. In education, in earning power, and as a vital part of life in Leon County and Tallahassee, blacks have earned their right to an equitable place in society. There is much still to be done, but for every step backward, there continue to be many more forward.

A large part of what we are has been determined by what we were. This book recounts how we got here. It relates in words and pictures the past, its present effects, and speculates about the future. In 1824 Tallahassee was deliberately founded as the territorial capital. It had previously been a principal village for the Apalachee Indians and a mission site for Franciscan priests from Spain. The native inhabitants were deprived of their land without just compensation and, often, by force and cruelty. The frontier with its promise of land was irresistible for many

Supreme Court Building. Photo credit: Florida Department of State, Florida State Archives, Jackson Stevens.

whites. It was an area of rolling hills, rich soil, abundant forests, and lakes and streams filled with a variety of fish. There was wildlife of every description. Settlers poured in, and by 1840 Tallahassee and Leon County had 10,713 people (3,461 whites, 7,231 slaves, and 21 free persons of color). Seat of local, territorial, and, after 1845, state government, rough hewn Tallahassee was trade mart for surrounding cotton farms and plantations (the latter were dependent on slave labor). The capital was a frontier town, but it was emerging as Florida's political, economic, educational, and religious center.

Despite a war with the Seminole Indians, yellow fever epidemics, fires, and economic depressions, Tallahassee emerged in 1860 as Florida's most populous county and the state's agricultural leader, particularly in cotton production. There was a rail connection with St. Marks, another line was being built east and west, banks and newspapers flourished, telegraph connections were made, and farm prices were high. Yet, everything changed with the Civil War. Differences over slavery and other issues were now to be settled by combat. The bitter conflict saw heroism and sacrifice, but defeat was the result. There were heavy losses of manpower, the embryonic railroad system was destroyed, and the state's financial and agricultural underpinnings were damaged. The psychological blow was generational.

Mitigating the uncertainties of Reconstruction was the establishment for the first time of universal public education. Women began asserting themselves as teachers and church workers, slowly becoming active in public affairs. The Fourteenth Amendment declared that black and white residents were citizens of the United States and not subject to discrimination by individual states. Jim Crow laws later made blacks second-class citizens, but they were no longer owned, they were free, obeyed no masters, and freedom, once experienced, became the elixir of life.

Agriculture remained dominant after 1880, as the crop lien and sharecropping replaced slave labor. Still, there were "modern" stirrings. Tallahassee dominated the county, as small businesses were established. Stores created a mercantile class. The professions, especially lawyers and doctors, had an impact. Teachers (here was a profession open to blacks as well as whites) grew in number, as public education for the many replaced private education for the few. Professors at the West Florida Seminary (the future Florida State University) and at the black Florida State Normal and Industrial School (later, Florida Agricultural and Mechanical University), influenced society. Public and private morality was upheld by black and white ministers, whose important place in society was both religious and secular.

Despite its horrors, World War I brought patriotism and prosperity. The collapse of the Florida land boom and the banking frenzy of the 1920s were not horrendous in north Florida. The Great Depression of the late 1920s and 1930s was less catastrophic for Tallahasseans than most Floridians. People were brought together, and, some have suggested, hard times gave them the resolve necessary to face World War II. During Franklin D. Roosevelt's New Deal federal buildings built by various agencies (Leon High School for one) revitalized and helped modernize the city.

World War II brought unprecedented prosperity. Combat pilots trained at Dale Mabry Field, and military personnel swarmed to town every weekend. Leon Countians furnished manpower, supported bond drives, and were unstinting in their patriotism. Tallahasseans saved their money and dreamed of spending it in the post-war world. When the war ended, Tallahassee and Leon County shared in Florida's affluence that made possible, for instance, more doctors and dentists and modern hospital facilities. The phenomenon of growth was observable visually and provable by census statistics. There were dramatic and lasting benefits in the new and important places that women assumed in American life and in the civil rights struggles by blacks. Former farmlands were replaced by subdivisions. Growth was east and west, less so in the south, but difficult to control and regulate in the north. The attendant problems resulting from such demographics are frustrating and difficult to solve. Certain

Old Capitol. Photo credit: R. G. Prophet, Florida Division of Tourism.

Battle of Natural Bridge state monument. Photo credit: Florida Division of Tourism.

words—education, drugs, preservation, conservation, environment, pollution, "quality of life," construction—automatically elicited spirited responses and solutions. The compelling facts of growth have called up the efforts of a large number of intelligent and determined people. Their work continues.

In the post-war world, leaders established the United Nations as the guardian of peace. Yet, there was no international abandonment of wars, and actual wars continued. Tallahassee and Leon County became involved in the Cold War, the Korean War, the Vietnamese War, the Gulf War, and various military and political crises around the world.

Locally, post–World War II politics shifted dramatically away from the dominance of the Democratic party. A two-party system at every level of government became a fact of life. Recently, Republicans have held every major political office from United States senator to governor, and various lower-ranking elective positions. Both parties share the many offices of government and both parties now battle for supremacy on a comparatively even basis.

The civil rights revolution that began in the 1950s saw the rectification of past wrongs and injustices. Many whites protested federal laws and court decisions, but there was limited violence in Tallahassee and Leon County. With the twenty-first century the people of Tallahassee and Leon County see it as a time of unequaled prosperity when realism demands an honest reckoning of what needs to be done in numerous areas. If that is accomplished, contemporary citizens can add their contribution to the cherished legacy of the favored land.

FROM ANTIQUITY TO ANDREW JACKSON

Drawing depicting Juan Ponce de León at the Fountain of Youth.

Florida's first human occupants were groups of hunter-gatherers who arrived roughly twelve thousand years ago. The Paleoindians found a much larger and drier region than the present state as the phenomenon of the Great Ice Age resulted in considerably lower sea levels. The Paleoindians depended on game large and small, some of which later became extinct, such as the mastodon, and others which are still common today. These early people moved about in search of food and sources of water, camping near lakes and springs.

The pattern of hunting and gathering continued as the climate altered at the end of the Ice Age (around 9000 B.C.), although with modifications in the kinds of animals hunted as some species became extinct, and in the types of stone tools, and locations of camps. As the millennia slowly passed, Florida's first people changed, developing new and distinct cultures. The climate moderated, becoming warmer and wetter. By about 3000 B.C. the climate was not unlike that of the present. The resulting increase in the supply of freshwater sources meant that there was more livable space, and the population increased accordingly, spreading throughout what is now Florida. By about 2000 B.C. the practice of making fired clay objects tempered with plant fiber was wide spread. The native people comprised a number of cultures, shaped in part by the particular conditions in their area, and had developed a variety of customs, dietary practices, and distinctive styles of ceramic work. These cultural groups were distributed across Florida, with many concentrating along the coast and the river systems where shellfish and other food sources were most abundant.

Evidence indicates that some limited agriculture existed in the late Archaic period (3000 B.C.–500 B.C.), but by about 800–1000 A.D. farming was of considerable importance. More concerted agricultural efforts brought more settled ways, an increased food supply, and more growth in population. It was in this period that some groups began to build large ceremonial earthen mounds at permanent village sites.

In the region that includes Tallahassee and Leon County the native culture that gradually developed was what archaeologists have named the Fort Walton culture. This group spread across much of the Panhandle, from the Aucilla River (in present-day Jefferson County) westward, and has been described by Jerald T. Milanich as among the "largest and most politically complex" of Florida's pre-Columbian cultures.

The Fort Walton culture eventually gave rise to the next definable cultural group that would inhabit the Tallahassee region, the Apalachee. The mounds that can be seen today at the Lake Jackson Mounds State Archaeological Site were part of a once larger group of ceremonial mounds that were begun before 1000 A.D. Archaeologists believe the Lake Jackson site was abandoned sometime between 1200 and 1500 A.D., when the major Apalachee settlement was established on the hills where Spain's Hernanado de Soto would set up camp in 1539, just east of the present state capitol building. It was the Apalachee who inhabited the region when the first Europeans began to explore Florida.

Throwing sticks, called atlatls (left and right) were used for launching darts (center) by prehistoric Indians in Florida.

Daniel T. Penton excavating a cache of Swift Creek period (circa 3000 B.C.–200 A.D.) ceramics at mound 1 of the Block-Sterns site in eastern Leon County, in 1973. This site is said to be one of the most significant in this area.

Pottery from an Indian burial mound.

Apalachee Indian village near Tallahassee about 1000 A.D., complete with a plaza and as many as seven dirt mounds. Photo credit: State of Florida, Mark Foley.

Apalachee Indians climbing stairs to a plateau at the top of a large mound on the shore of Lake Jackson. Photo credit: State of Florida, Mark Foley.

Drawing of a copper breastplate recovered from a Lake Jackson mound. Photo credit: State of Florida, Mark Foley.

THE SPANIARDS ARRIVE

The European discovery of Florida dates from the spring of 1513. Juan Ponce de León, who accompanied Columbus on his second voyage and served as governor of Puerto Rico, came with three ships seeking the magical islands of Bimini and their precious metals and jewels and youth-restoring fountain. The expedition landed in early April probably between the mouth of the St. Johns River and present Saint Augustine. Ponce de León carried out the ritual of planting a flag and a cross and taking possession in the name of King Ferdinand V. The discoverer named the land "Pascua Florida" because it was the time of the "Feast of Flowers."

By the time Ponce de León arrived, Florida had fifteen or twenty distinct Indian tribes. Those in the north lived by farming and were more advanced than the southern groups. The indigenous population was about 350,000. As discussed by John H. Hann and Bonnie G. McEwan in *The Apalachee Indians and Mission San Luis*, this number included approximately 50,000 to 60,000 Apalachee, the largest and most important of Florida's native groups. The Apalachee lived in the region stretching from the Aucilla River on the east to the Ochlockonee on the west, and from the Gulf to about where the Georgia line is today.

Living in permanent locations with a fairly stable village life, the Apalachee in the northwest (along with the Timucuans of central Florida) had reached an impressive level of social, political, and economic organization. Their large villages were distinct, protected units. An agricultural people, the Apalachee grew various crops, including corn, and domesticated animals. Important in itself, Apalachee was also a beginning point for military, commercial, and exploratory expeditions to the west and northwest.

Ponce de León did not find the riches he sought, but it was soon apparent that he had discovered more than an island. To the Spanish, Florida stretched westward to Texas and northward to the Chesapeake region. Spain concentrated on exploiting the fabulous wealth of Mexico and Peru, but Florida was not forgotten. In 1528 Pánfilo de Narváez landed near Tampa Bay. With over three hundred men and forty-two horses he moved north, seeking the purported treasures of the Apalachee country. He found no gold but encountered hostility from the Indians. The beleaguered Spaniards fashioned rafts near what is now Saint Marks and started westward along the coast. Narváez and all but four of his men perished. Alvar Nuñez Cabeza da Vaca, one of the survivors, left an anguished account of wandering for seven years before reaching safety in Mexico.

Hernando de Soto, age thirty-nine, a companion of Pizarro in Peru and the wealthy governor of Cuba, made the next attempt. His fleet put into Tampa Bay in May 1539, landing 600 men and 250 horses. Like Narváez, de Soto pushed north in search of riches. The conquistador and

San Luis de Talimali was governmental and religious headquarters for the Spanish in Apalachee. It also served as the capital for the Apalachee Indians.

his men passed through what would become Leon County and possibly celebrated Christmas there.

De Soto's winter camp evidently was located on a wooded hillside a short distance east of the present capitol. Artifacts discovered there in 1987—including scraps of chain mail, pottery, glass beads, and coins—indicated that the area probably was the site of the main Apalachee town where the explorer and his followers settled in October 1539.

The expedition passed into Georgia and the Carolinas, then doubled back across Alabama and into Mississippi. The Spaniards encountered and some-times fought Indians, but never found the mythical caches of precious metals and jewels. De Soto died and was buried near the banks of the Mississippi. Only half of his original company reached safety.

Other Spanish incursions into Florida followed. Between 1559 and 1561, Tristán de Luna y Arellano and his successor Angel de Villafañe tried but failed to establish colonies in the Alabama country, at Pensacola, and on the coast of South Carolina. They were the victims of storms, bad luck, and their own inefficiency. Half a century had passed since de León's discovery but, stymied by nature and Indian resistance, Spain possessed Florida only in name.

The need to convert the Indians was not sufficient motive to push colonization in Florida, and the area had no mineral riches to develop. Although Spain could afford to wait, she could not afford to let Florida fall to another country. Florida was an elongated land mass that threatened the main routes of Spain's colonial commerce. If colonization was not necessary, control was vital.

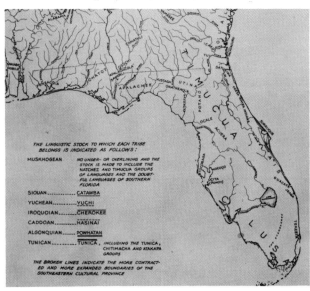

Map showing location of Indian tribes in the Southeast.

FRANCE CHALLENGES SPAIN'S AUTHORITY

A French challenge to Spanish hegemony came on May Day 1562, when Jean Ribaut and a group of French Huguenots discovered a majestic river on the coast which the Protestant leader named the River of May (now the Saint Johns). They were part of Catholic France's attempt to combine a religious settlement with a commercial settlement. Ribaut claimed the land for King Charles IX,

Hernando de Soto landed at Tampa Bay in 1539.

made friends with the Indians, and sailed north along the Atlantic coast, naming rivers. He established Port Royal, a short-lived outpost in South Carolina. In 1564, Rene de Laudonnière led a group of 300 settlers (among them Jacques LeMoyne, his geographer) back to the River of May, where they built Fort Caroline. After a difficult beginning, the colonists regrouped and welcomed the arrival of Ribaut, who appeared in 1565 with provisions and reinforcements.

That same year, Pedro Menéndez de Avilés, a nobleman and proved soldier, landed 35 miles to the south. Menéndez had orders from Philip 11 of Spain to explore the eastern coast and to destroy alien settlements. The Spanish arrived on the feast day of Saint Augustine, and the future settlement would be named in his honor. After moving against Fort Caroline but finding the French forces too strong, Menéndez returned to Saint Augustine. There on September 6, 1565, he began to build a fort at the settlement.

A storm wrecked Ribaut's counterattacking fleet, and his soldiers became lost south of Saint Augustine. Menéndez made a forced march against Fort Caroline, where he put to death the French (sparing women and children). Returning south, he rounded up the scattered and starving Frenchmen. In two operations, he managed to capture and kill his enemies, including Ribaut. A nearby inlet was named Matanzas—"Slaughters."

Led by Menéndez, Saint Augustine became a pioneer village whose settlers farmed the surrounding land. Indians were held in check by treaties and by force. The coast from South Carolina to Tampa Bay was explored, and forts or blockhouses were erected and garrisoned at strategic points. Jesuit priests (the Society of Jesus) came to the forts to convert the Indians. They worked to learn the Indian languages and to accommodate their services to the needs of a different people. Yet the Indians, even when converted, were often little better than slaves. They fought back, killing priests and threatening the existence of the Spanish forts and missions. In 1572, the Society of Jesus withdrew, shifting its activities from Florida to Mexico. The Jesuits had laid the foundation for others.

After 1573, the Franciscans moved in. By 1595, they had extended their missions up the Georgia coast. Despite Indian massacres, they also advanced westward past the Suwannee River, entering the Apalachee region by 1633, partly in response to earlier requests from the Apalachees for missionaries. By 1655, the Franciscans claimed 26,000 Christian converts, and by 1683, fifteen missions had been established in the Apalachee Province. Like other missions, those in the Apalachee region usually had only one friar, sometimes two. From time to time a few soldiers were present, although the military influence was not paramount. Outside the missions were probably 30 "satellite" villages where religious services were conducted by friars from the main settlements. Apalachee's Indian population during the mission period was about 10,000—down from the pre-Spanish figure of approximately 30,000.

On the western edge of present Tallahassee stood the important mission of San Luis de Talimali, probably established shortly before 1656. Set on a high hill, San Luis was the governmental and religious headquarters for the Spanish in Apalachee. It also served as the capital for the Apalachees, whose chief moved his village there. By 1675, approximately 1,400 Christianized Indians lived in the immediate vicinity. A few Spanish families settled near San Luis and produced corn, vege-

French geogapher Jacques LeMoyne's drawing of the building of Fort Caroline.

tables, cattle, and chickens. The agricultural commodities and livestock were transported overland to Saint Augustine or were carried to Saint Marks and shipped to Saint Augustine or to Havana, Cuba. By 1639, Saint Marks, with its outlet to the Gulf via river and bay, was used as a trading port: deerskins, wild turkey, corn, and beans were loaded on ships there. A wooden fort was built in 1679, and the town of Saint Marks was established in 1718. Within a short period, the chain of missions along the Gulf coast and up the Apalachicola River numbered 52. They became outposts of Spain's empire in the New World.

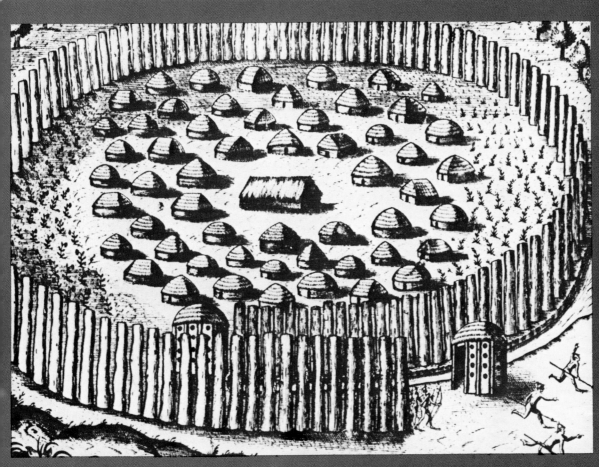

A fortified Timucua village.

Rene de Laudonniere, French explorer and governor of Florida, founded Fort Caroline with 300 colonists in 1564.

THE ENGLISH ENTER THE NEW WORLD

Even as the Franciscans secured Florida for Spain, the government in Madrid grew weaker and was unable to withstand English and French encroachments down the Atlantic seaboard and the Mississippi River. The far-flung area of Spanish Florida was being reduced to the peninsula. How could Spain contend with England? Seafaring adventurers such as John Hawkins looted Spanish treasure galleons and laid a foundation for English commerce. Pirates during the reign of Elizabeth I (1558-1603) portended permanent English colonists in the seventeenth century. England defeated the Spanish Armada in 1588, but failed to colonize the coast of North Carolina. The setback proved temporary. British raiders burned Saint Augustine in 1586, and an English company colonized Jamestown, Virginia in 1607. Spain could not counter English successes. In 1670, Charles II granted Carolina to several favorites, and the British claimed that the colony extended south to Saint Augustine. Spain belatedly agreed to recognize England's North American claims, and England promised to curtail southern threats—a promise she had no plans to keep.

A desperate Spain moved to make the Franciscan missions militarily—as well as spiritually—strong.

Alliances were sought with the Indians, and immigration was encouraged. Trying to hold Florida, Spain enlarged and reinforced the Castillo de San Marcos at Saint Augustine. The European powers soon drifted into the War of the Spanish Succession (Queen Anne's War, 1702-1714), involving Spain and France against England. In 1702, Governor James Moore of South Carolina sacked Saint Augustine, but failed to capture the Castillo and left in disgrace. Moore took steps in 1704 to regain his honor by leading a military expedition against the mission settlements in the Apalachee region. With 1,500 Creek Indians and some 50 Carolina ruffians, Moore looted, burned, and murdered. Spanish Florida was devastated, and never recovered from the raid. Afraid of the invaders, the people of the San Luis mission and the nearby village burned their dwellings and structures. Some who escaped capture fled to Saint Augustine, and others reached safety at Pensacola and Mobile. By 1708, the Apalachee missions had been destroyed or abandoned, and several thousand Indians were carried off to slavery in the Carolinas.

In the seventeenth and eighteenth centuries, France and England engulfed section after section of the huge area called Florida. From Québec (settled in 1608), French explorers, fur traders, and woodsmen moved up the Saint Lawrence River, through the Great Lakes, and down the Mississippi River. Reaching the mouth of the Mississippi, the French claimed the area and named it Louisiana for the Sun King Louis XIV.

Spanish military leader and explorer Pedro Menéndez de Avilés entered the harbor which he called San Augustine on August 28, 1565. Later, his forces cap- *tured Fort Caroline, which was then renamed San Mateo, and massacred the shipwrecked French forces of Admiral Jean Ribaut on Anastasia Island.*

Fort Matanzas was built in the inlet named for the massacre of Ribaut's forces.

Spain countered French incursions into the Gulf region by establishing Pensacola in 1698. Yet the action at Pensacola Bay by Andrés de Arriola did not prevent France from founding Biloxi (1699) and Mobile (1702), or from temporarily occupying Pensacola in 1719. As France gouged Florida property in the west, England cut large slices on the Atlantic side.

Carolinians claimed that Spain encouraged Indian raids on British property and that the invaders made hasty retreats to the sanctuary of Florida. In truth, both the English and the Spanish mistreated the Indians. British settlers demanded protection: the mother country should create a buffer area against unruly Florida. King George II listened to his colonists and in 1732 granted Georgia to James Oglethorpe. The humanitarian turned soldier, Oglethorpe, and his associates founded Savannah and built forts to back their claim that Georgia extended south to the Saint Johns River.

During much of the next 30 years, the three major powers were at odds in Europe and in the new world. The conflict, known as the Seven Years' War in Europe, culminated in the colonies as the French and Indian War (1754-1763). France, with Spanish and Indian help, fought the British. When the struggle ended, the English emerged as the dominate presence in North America. Spain was forced to yield Florida to Great Britain. As compensation, France passed Louisiana to Spanish hands, thereby surrendering her North American empire. After more than two centuries of control, Spain had lost Florida. The Spanish and French were left with a strong taste for revenge, and Florida was still a pawn in the game of imperial rivalry.

ENGLAND RULES THE FLORIDAS

With the Proclamation of 1763, England revamped her North American colonial system. As applied to Florida, the proclamation divided the colony into British West Florida, with its capital at Pensacola, and British East Florida, where Saint Augustine became the seat of government, the whole administered by crown-appointed officials. The Apalachicola River was the dividing line between the Floridas, and West Florida extended to the Mississippi River. Spanish residents in Florida moved out as British subjects moved in. The British bribed the Indians into treaties, and agriculture expanded as a plantation economy took shape—including the institution of slave labor.

Elsewhere in the American colonies, England tightened her imperial control. The seaboard colonies resisted, and the ultimate result was the Declaration of Independence in 1776 and the American Revolution. During the conflict, France, Spain, and Holland rendered valuable military and economic aid to George Washington's struggling Continental Army. Moving from bases at New Orleans and Havana, Cuba, Spain captured Mobile in 1780, Pensacola in 1781, and West Florida ceased to exist. East Florida remained an unconquered British colony, furnishing Loyalists (Tories) to fight the crown's foes, and serving as a refuge for Tories fleeing from other colonies. When George III agreed to grant the Americans their freedom in 1781, the treaty that followed also awarded both Floridas to Spain. The English moved out.

SPAIN HAS A SECOND CHANCE

During its second possession of Florida—1783 to 1819—Spain attempted to rectify past mistakes. Religious policies were liberalized, immigration was encouraged, and the British firm of Panton, Leslie and Company was permitted to continue its Indian trade. Florida's expansionist neighbor to the north spoiled the plan. Once encouraged, Americans—especially southerners—came roaring into the colony from Georgia and lands bordering West Florida. They wanted the rich plantation lands and the potential ports, and they wanted Florida to become part of the United States.

Map showing Franciscan missions up the Florida and Georgia coast, circa 1674-1675.

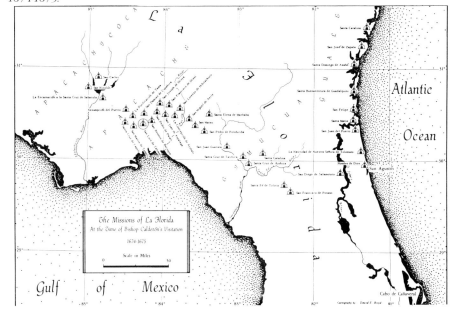

Gradually, the United States exerted pressure on Spain. The Pinckney Treaty of 1795 forced the Madrid government to accept the American version of Florida's northern boundary: Spain further agreed to control Indian outrages and to shut the border door to runaway slaves. The purchase of Louisiana—which Spain secretly had returned to France—in 1803 only whetted the American desire to secure Florida. Unsuccessful efforts to purchase the peninsula in 1803 and 1805 led to American encroachments in West Florida, from the Mississippi River to the Pearl River in 1810.

Fort San Juan de Pinos (Fort San Marcos) as it appeared in 1671.

THE BATTLES BEGIN— AND ANDREW JACKSON ARRIVES

The United States also had difficulties with Great Britian. Locked in combat with Napoleon, England angered the United States by its policy of impressment of American sailors and the violation of America's neutral rights. An added fear was that England might annex Florida. A group of militant young congressmen, the war hawks, clamored for military reprisal. John Bull would be put in his place, and the United States could claim both Canada and Florida. James Madison acceded to their wishes, and the unpopular War of 1812 began. During the conflict, Great Britian used Florida as a supply base. Spain never declared war on the United States, but was too weak to control British activities. Andrew Jackson of Tennessee emerged to challenge the English and their Indian allies. Old Hickory, with his mixture of regulars, militia, volunteers, and Indians, moved south into Alabama and crushed Creek Indian power at the Battle of Horseshoe Bend in 1814. Next, he moved into previously occupied Mobile to defend it from a Pensacola-based attack by the British. He threw the redcoats back, marched on Pensacola—which he captured—and went on to his great victory at New Orleans in early 1815. The war wound down with neither power scoring a decisive victory, but in Andrew Jackson—destined to cast a long and controversial shadow over Florida—the United States had a genuine national hero.

As a nonbelligerent, Spain stood aside during the peace negotiations, but the United States had not forgotten about Florida. As the war progressed, the United States occupied West Florida from Pearl River to the Perdido River near Pensacola, and never gave up the area. Southerners raised anew their complaints at the war's end: Spain could not govern Florida; Indian encroachments were getting worse; the number of runaway slaves was increasing. The complaints brought Jackson back to Florida in 1818 in the First Seminole War.

Clashes between Indians living along the Florida-Georgia boundary and federal troops stationed in forts along the Flint and Chattahoochee rivers led Jackson across the international border of Florida. Whether he was granted proper authority from President James Monroe for his military foray remains an unsettled question. In any case, Jackson marched into Florida with his familiar mix of regulars, militia, and Indians. Apparently authorized to chastise the resident Indians, Jackson came down the Apalachicola River, pushing the Indians before him, and paused to construct Fort Gadsden. The post was located at the site of Negro Fort, a haven for escaped slaves that had been destroyed in 1816. In March, Jackson swung east and, violating a flag of truce, captured the Spanish fort at Saint Marks. There he hanged two Indian leaders. From Saint Marks, Jackson's questionable expedition continued east to the Suwannee River, chasing the elusive Seminoles. To his disappointment, Jackson found Billy Bowlegs' town (the Alachua branch of the Seminoles) practically

General James Edward Oglethorpe, head of the English colony of Georgia, led several expeditions against the Spanish colony at Saint Augustine in 1740.

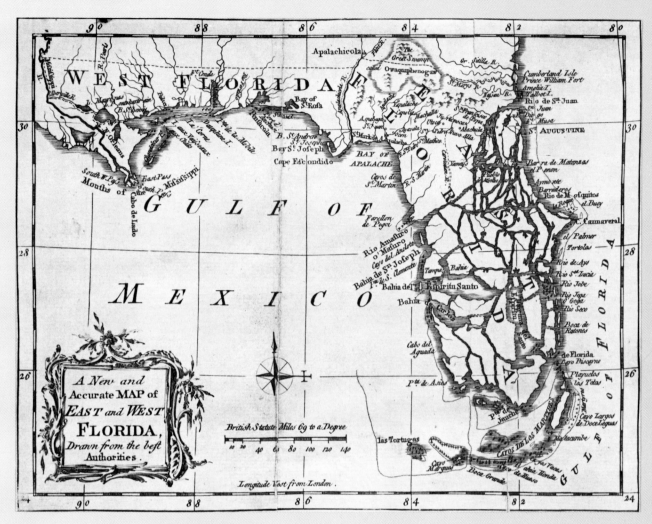

Map showing division of colony into British West Florida and British East Florida in 1763.

The United States obtained Florida from Spain by assuming Spanish debts to U.S. citizens of approximately $5 million during President James Monroe's administration.

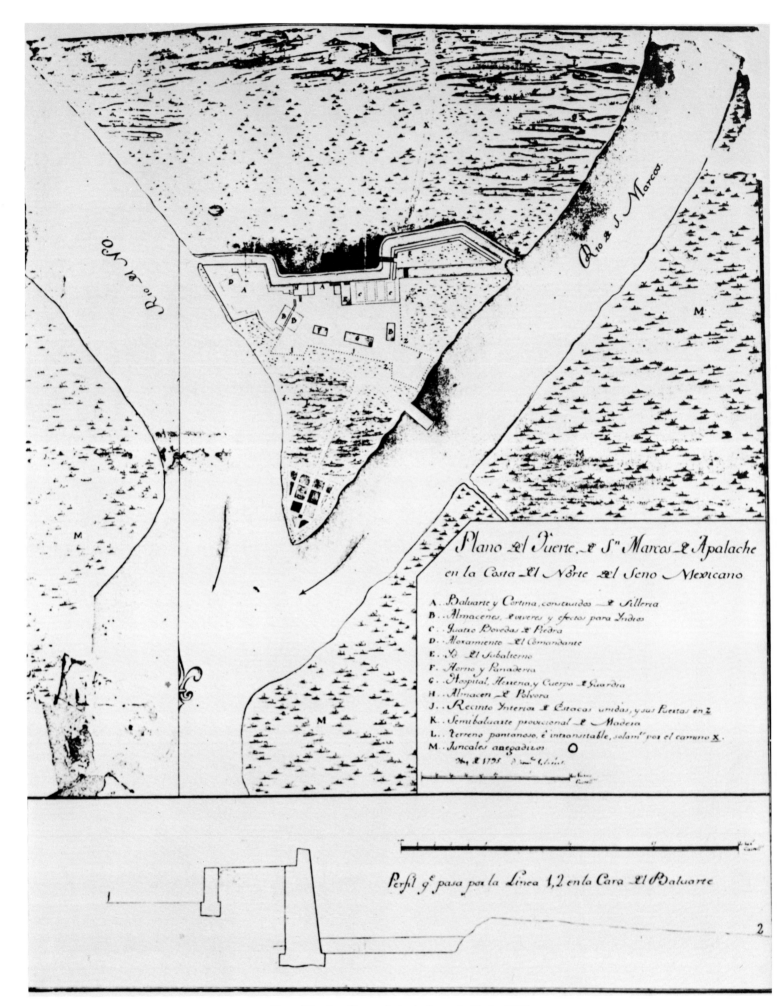

Plano del Fuerte, de Sn Marcos de Apalache
en la Costa El Norte del Seno Mexicano

A .. Baluarte y Cortina, construidos de Sillería
B .. Almacenes, de viveres y efectos para Indios
C .. Quatro Bovedas de Piedra
D .. Alojamiento del Comandante
E .. Do del Subalterno
F .. Horno y Panadería
G .. Hospital, Herrería, y Cuerpo de Guardia
H .. Almacen de Polvora
J .. Recinto Interior de Estacas unidas, y sus Puertas en Z
K .. Semibaluarte provicional de Madera
L .. Terreno pantanoso, é intransitable, solamte por el camino X
M .. Juncales anegadizos

Perfil 9º pasa por la Línea 1,2 en la Cara El Baluarte

Plan of Fort San Marcos de Apalachee at St. Marks, 1795

*Capture of Pensacola by
the Spaniards in 1781,
from a contemporary
print.*

WITH JACKSON IN THE APALACHEE COUNTRY

John Banks, militia volunteer from Georgia, rode with Andrew Jackson's force during the controversial Florida expedition, and gave this account of the episode in his memoirs.

"On the 25th [of March, 1818] we drew what provisions we could carry on our backs and set out in an eastern direction toward the Mackasooky town. The next Sunday following (the 29th) we came to the Oconochy [Ochlocknee] river. All hands set to building canoes, the river being very high that night, and the next day we crossed the river. On Tuesday, the 31st, arrived at a town called Tallahassee. The Indians had abandoned it before we got there. We passed an old Indian lying near a pond, dead. She had not been dead long from her appearance; she had been left there to die by the Indians who fled before us; she was lying on the ground by some ashes and a dirt pot. We burnt the town (this is the present capital of Florida). We found some cattle that day which were distributed among the soldiers.

On Wednesday, the 1st of April, we arrived at the Mackasooky town at 2 o'clock P.M., 78 miles from Fort Gadsden. The day before we reached this place, the Tennessee horsemen joined the army. We had a battle here with the Indians. They met us a mile from town. They fled before us, but continued to fire back. The Tennesseeans, being mounted, pressed them through the town. They took to a swamp. Eleven Indians were found dead on the ground. We took some more prisoners. One of the Tennesseeans was killed and five wounded. We got between four and five hundred cattle, some horses, hogs, poultry and about one thousand bushels of corn. Here we had a plentiful feast. The cattle were put in a pen near the encampment. I shall never forget the melancholy effect produced on me by the simultaneous lowing of the cattle, howling of the dogs and chirping of the chickens."

[From A Short Biographical Sketch of the Undersigned by Himself, *a memoir and journal written by John Banks from 1830-1865, and published circa 1936.*]

deserted. The route east took Jackson's men through the old Apalachee country, now the home of the Seminoles, who had drifted into the practically deserted area in sporadic movements. After the earlier invasion by Governor James Moore in 1704, the region largely had been abandoned. The Indians gave the now desolate area the name of *Tallahassee*, which meant the land of the old fields or abandoned villages.

Life returned first in the form of vegetation and trees. Within a dozen years, cattle and buffalo grazed the area, and within 30 years of Moore's invasion, Creek Indians from the North (both Upper and Lower Creeks) and Seminoles migrated into the area. The Tallahassee and Micasukis were among their tribes. The Seminoles were Creek in their culture, but they broke away from the Creek Confederation as independent units and came south. Their name meant *runaways* or *seceders*. Later, all Florida Indians came to be called Seminoles. The country thus had become populated again by the middle of the eighteenth century. British mapmakers (George Gauld in 1767 and Joseph Purcell in 1778) charted the area. Each map showed an Indian town in the old fields, spelled variously as Tallahassee and Tallahassa Taloofa.

In 1818, Jackson's forces marched through the Indians' *fowl town* villages (named for the chickens the Indians kept) clustered around the lakes. John Banks, a militia volunteer, recalled that his unit entered a recently abandoned town called Tallahassee. Meeting no resistance, Jackson's men burned Tallahassee and marched east to the larger village of Mackasooky, where they defeated the Indians who mounted a brief defense.

Returning to Saint Marks from his unproductive raid to the Suwannee, Jackson ordered two captured British citizens, Alexander Arbuthnot and Robert Ambrister, court-martialed and summarily executed. Next, Jackson marched west, where he captured Pensacola and deposed the Spanish governor. The United States was not at war with Spain or Great Britian. American public opinion favored Old Hickory's action, but it could have resulted in war with England, and Jackson narrowly missed censure by Congress and the cabinet.

President Monroe placated the Spanish by restoring the captured forts, but Spain realized that the United States was determined to take Florida, one way or another. Negotiations for the transfer, already under way, continued. The result was that on February 22, 1819, Luis de Onís, the Spanish representative, and John Quincy Adams, the American secretary of state, signed the Adams-Onís Treaty. Spain gave up its claims to Oregon and ceded East and West Florida to the United States without payment. The United States assumed $5 million in claims against Spain by American citizens and surrendered all previous claims to Texas. The Senate ratified the treaty immediately, but Spain delayed carrying it out for almost two years. Although the transfer was frustratingly slow, the fact remained that the United States now owned Florida.

Trial of British citizen Robert Ambrister, 1818.

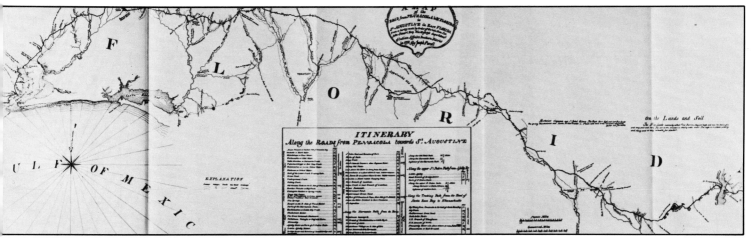

A British map of the roads from Pensacola toward Saint Augustine, circa 1778, shows "Tallahassa."

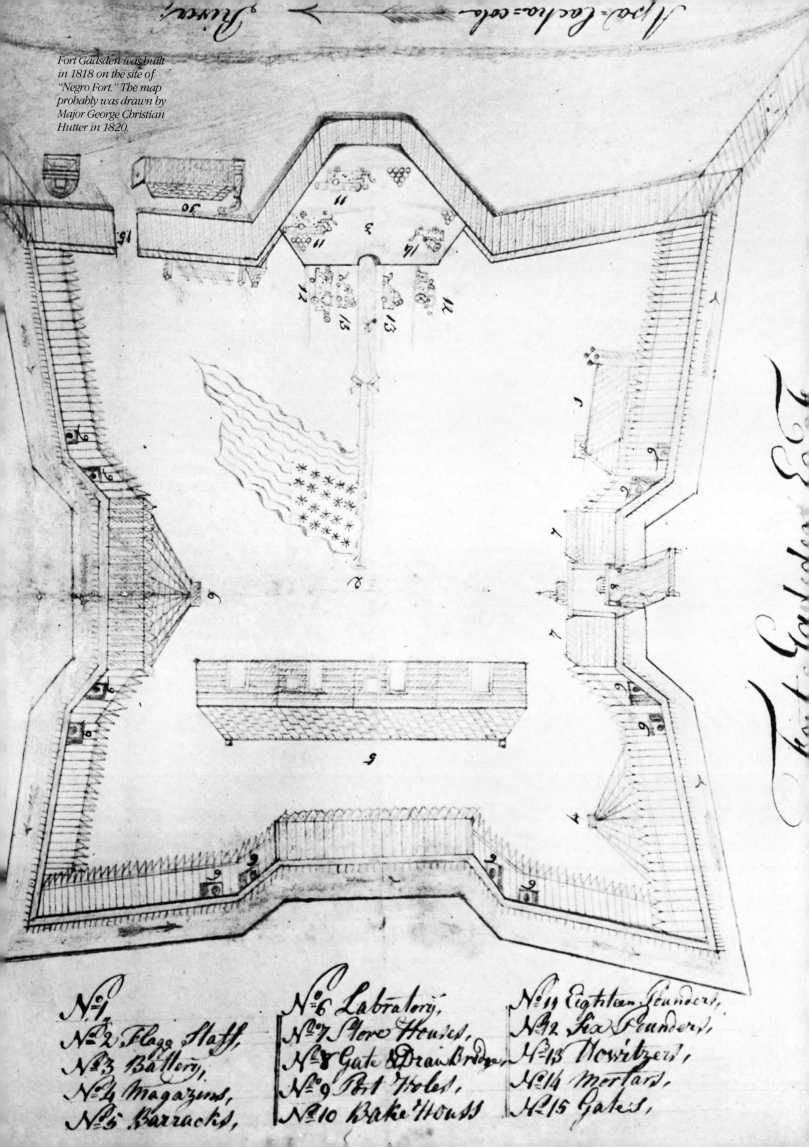

Fort Gadsden was built in 1818 on the site of "Negro Fort." The map probably was drawn by Major George Christian Hutter in 1820.

Nº 1.
Nº 2 Flagg Staff,
Nº 3 Battery,
Nº 4 Magazins,
Nº 5 Barracks,

Nº 6 Labratory,
Nº 7 Store Houses,
Nº 8 Gate & Drawbridge,
Nº 9 Port Holes,
Nº 10 Bake Houss

Nº 11 Eighteen Pounders,
Nº 12 Six Pounders,
Nº 13 Howitzers,
Nº 14 Mortars,
Nº 15 Gates,

FLORIDA
TERRITORY AND STATE

Map of Florida

2.

In his journal, John Lee Williams described his first meeting with Neamathla, who gave the commissioners a courteous but wary reception.

October 28 [1823] . . . we proceeded eastward [from the Ochlockonee River]. The land continually improving, in about an hour it rose into a delightful high rolling country, clothed with excellent oak, hickory and dogwood timber on a soil of chocolate colored loam. We here often observed traces of the old Spanish highway, which we had also seen on the west side of the Ochlockney river . . . . At one o'clock I arrived at the new Tallahassee village. Seeing a fine, stout Indian in a nut patch, I left my horse and accosted him, asking for information where the chief of the village might be found. He very sternly demanded what I wanted and said he was Neomathla. I told him we were sent to him by Governor Duval to inform him that he wished to build a house in which he might meet his council . . . . he [Neamathla] was requested to assist us with his advice and counsel . . . . After satisfying his curiosity and suspicions, by several pertinent questions, he said he would consider the matter. He then took me to his shed and offered me cigars and roasted nuts . . . . Neomathla directed our horses to be turned loose in his field and our baggage deposited in one of his council houses, which we afterwards occupied.

October 29 . . . Neomathla called very early with an interpreter, and desired us to state to him before his chiefs distinctly what our object was in visiting his country . . . . Neomathla said that he was much annoyed by people from Georgia, who endeavored to get his land away from him. But at length he told us to go and do as we pleased, but not to tell anybody that he sent us, and not to tell the Indians that he had given us permission to select a site for the seat of government. We paid him two dollars for our horses ranging in his fields . . . and the charges of his people were enormous for corn and potatoes. We, however, left them in friendship and in passing through the numerous villages which abounded in the woods for more than twenty miles we were not molested. Neomathla is a shrewd, penetrating man; he evidently feels no affection for the white man. His interest restrained him at this time, so that he wished not to obstruct our progress, but he feared that his lenity would render him unpopular with his people.

[From "The Selection of Tallahassee as the Capitol: Journal of John Lee Williams, Commissioner to Locate the Seat of Government of the Territory of Florida," Florida Historical Quarterly, I (July 1908), 19-21.]

The Spanish cession of 1821 was a turning point for Florida. For more than 300 years, she had been claimed by European powers. Now a continental nation—the United States—had possession. Partly to vindicate previous criticism, Jackson accepted President James Monroe's appointment as provisional or military governor. On July 17, "Old Hickory" received West Florida from the Spanish at Pensacola (earlier ceremonies had taken place at St. Augustine on July 10). Despite the heat, the audience cheered as the American flag was raised and band played the patriotic song, "The Star-Spangled Banner."

After serving as governor for only 80 days, Jackson resigned. In October, he and his wife Rachel returned to the Hermitage, their home near Nashville. The fiery general may have abbreviated his tenure because President Monroe made various civil appointments without consulting him.

An act of Congress officially created the territory of Florida on March 30, 1822. William P. Duval of Kentucky was appointed as the first civilian territorial governor, a post he held for twelve years. The act provided further for a court system, an appointed delegate to Congress, an appointed legislative council (later enlarged, made elective, divided into a bicameral body, and called the general assembly), and an appointed territorial secretary. That office was filled by George Walton, a disciple of Jackson, who served as acting governor before Duval arrived.

The territory's two largest towns, Pensacola and Saint Augustine, alternated as meeting places for the legislative council. Logistical difficulties involving time, transportation, and even physical danger (ships sank, land routes were hazardous)—not to mention local jealousies—soon made obvious the critical need for a permanent capital. The legislative council passed an act in June 1823, authorizing the governor to appoint two commissioners to select the site for a territorial capital. It was to be located somewhere between the Ochlocknee and Suwannee rivers. The commissioners, one from East Florida and one from West Florida, were to rendezvous at Saint Marks in the fall to carry out their mission.

Dr. William Hayne Simmons, a doctor of medicine and a native of Charleston, South Carolina, was picked to represent the Atlantic side. A lifelong bachelor, Simmons was an author *(Notices of East Florida, with an Account of the Seminole Nation of Indians)* and a member of the legislative council. He left Saint Augustine on September 26, took an overland route, and arrived eventually at Saint Marks on October 10.

John Lee Williams was in charge of the Gulf region's interests. A native of Massachusetts who grew up in New York, Williams migrated to Spanish Florida for his health in 1820 and settled in Pensacola. There he engaged successfully in law, business and politics. Williams and his party left Pensacola on September 24, in a small open boat and without a chart or map. The disastrous trip lasted more than a month. Williams' group endured a punishing amphibious journey that included bouts with mosquitoes, swamps, a storm, and fierce personal quarrels. They were shipwrecked and marooned on Saint George Island. Much the worse for wear, they reached Saint Marks in late October. There Simmons and Williams regrouped, obtained supplies and guides, and headed north. Simmons had heard that the red hills of the future Leon County were "high,

Neamathla, Seminole chief of a settlement a few miles north of Tallahassee

Andrew Jackson served less than three months in 1821 as military governor of Florida.

This view by Francis, Comte de Castelnau, shows Jefferson Street in the 1830s, looking east from Adams.

healthy and well watered."

The explorers pushed through the forests and came first to the New Tallahassee village of Neamathla, a bold and intelligent Seminole chief. Neamathla was angry at the intrusion, but did not resist. The chief had his people entertain the Americans with a ball game and a dance (among the participants were a few blacks), and permitted the whites to spend the night. The next day Williams and Simmons found fields covered in peach trees, and came to Old Tallahassee town, where they encountered the chief, Chifixico. No hostilities erupted, but Chifixico voiced strong disapproval of the invasion. In late September 1823, Neamathla and other chiefs had signed the Treaty of Moultrie Creek (near Saint Augustine), exchanging their northern lands for territory in south Florida and a monetary compensation. The treaty had been weighted heavily in favor of the United States.

Williams and Simmons explored the surrounding countryside before returning to Saint Marks and departing in early November for their homes. The men recommended Tallahassee to Governor Duval as the best location for the state capital. Endorsing the selection, the governor instructed the legislative council to meet at the new capital in November 1824.

TALLAHASSEE IS ESTABLISHED

Absolute documentation of Tallahassee's first settlers is unavailable, but on April 9, 1824, John McIver of North Carolina, accompanied by a party of six, including a mulatto man, staked camp halfway down the hill from the present capitol building. The settlers unloaded their wagon and set up tent shelters. The same day, Judge Jonathan Robinson and Sherrodd McCall brought slaves from

their coastal property to clear land. They made a clearing at the top of a hill, and erected a two-story log structure where the legislative council held its first session in the new capital in November and December 1824.

A new resident himself, Governor Duval built his home near a clear cascade of water on Houstoun's Hill (named for an early settler). The raw village became home to several close associates of Andrew Jackson. Robert Butler, a comrade in arms, was appointed surveyor general, and gave the name Lake Jackson, to the large body of water north of Tallahassee. A Jackson man, Territorial Secretary George Walton, chose the prime meridian marker: the southeast corner of Tallahassee's first quarter section (160 acres). Future land surveys in Florida were based on that point. The area that became Tallahassee was granted by the federal government and reserved from public sale.

On December 11, 1824, the lawmakers officially named the village "Tallahassee." According to one story, the name was suggested by Walton's fourteen-year-old daughter, Octavia. The town was incorporated December 9, 1825, and would have additional incorporations in 1827, 1831, and 1840. Originally one-fourth of a square mile, Tallahassee assumed its square-mile area (640 acres) in 1840 and kept it until well into the twentieth century.

Colonel Butler submitted the winning plans for a capitol building, and a two-story wing was completed in 1826. The cornerstone was laid by Jackson's Lodge No. 1, the first Masonic group in Florida. Construction money was to come from the "Tallahassee Fund" (fed by the sale of lots within the town). Completion was delayed by disputed contracts, lawsuits, and financial problems. The small town had difficulty in maintaining the partial structure. A congressional appropriation in 1839 permitted the two-story wing to be demolished, and a new brick building was begun. Additional delays followed; another grant from Washington was needed before the three-story building was completed in 1845, just before the territory achieved statehood. The 1845 capitol remained basically unchanged until 1891, when a cupola was added.

The town plan, devised by Governor Duval, centered on Capitol Square. Benjamin F. Tennille was the surveyor who laid out the streets, squares, and lots. Monroe and Adams were the two principal north-south streets; Pensacola and Saint Augustine went east and west. Bronough, Gaines, and Gadsden were named for Jackson compatriots. Boulevard, corrupted in pronunciation and spelling from Bolivar (the South American hero), would be changed in 1980 to honor Martin Luther King, Jr. Other thoroughfares were Lafayette, Jefferson, and Duval.

Richard Keith Call, Jackson's close personal friend (he and Mary Kirkman had married in 1824 at the Hermitage), arrived in the 1820s and along with Joseph

Francis, Comte de Castelnau, depicted the cascade which helped determine the site of the Florida capital.

George Walton was acting governor of West Florida in 1821-1822.

William P. Duval was territorial governor of Florida from April 17, 1822, to April 24, 1834.

Robert Butler, former military aide to Andrew Jackson, was named surveyor general for the territory of Florida by Jackson and conducted the survey of Tallahassee.

A replica of Florida's first capitol, in which the third session of the territorial council was convened in November 1824.

Rachel Donelson Jackson in 1815, from a miniature which Andrew Jackson wore over his heart for 30 years.

M. Hernandez, served as an appointed congressional delegate. In 1825, Joseph M. White became the territory's first elected delegate. The legislative council provided for Tallahassee's town government in December 1825. An intendant (mayor) and five-man city council—all unpaid—were to be elected annually. In 1826, Dr. Charles Haire was chosen first intendant. Salaried officials included the dual post of clerk and treasurer ($57.50 annual salary); town marshal, who doubled as tax collector; and two tax assessors.

News of the new country caught the attention of planters and farmers in Georgia, the Carolinas, Virginia, and Maryland. Cabins, most of them with chimneys, and more legislative buildings of logs were built, giving Tallahassee the trappings of a town. Town lots were auctioned. As 1825 ended, Tallahassee had a church, school, seven businesses, two hotels, a printing office, apothecary, two shoemakers, two blacksmiths, three carpenters, a tailor shop, three brickyards, and various bright-colored houses. James Cameron, receiver of taxes, took the census in 1825. Leon County had 996 people: 608 whites, 387 slaves and one "free person of color."

Set in the wilderness amid unhappy Indians, Tallahassee was only semicivilized. A law provided bounty payments for the pelts of wolves, bears, tigers, and panthers. In 1826, a town ordinance levied a five-dollar fine on offenders guilty of discharging firearms or racing a horse or carriage within the corporate limits. A plea based as much on preserving order as on raising revenue came from the grand jury for a tax on all retailers of "spiritous liquors." Ralph Waldo Emerson, the New England essayist and poet, described Tallahassee as "a grotesque place . . . rapidly settled by public officers, land speculators, and desperadoes." Comte Francis de Castelnau, a fastidious French naturalist who visited Tallahassee in the late 1830s, noted with horror that "the habit of carrying arms is universal. Every man has constantly on him a bowie knife, and when he is on horseback he has a long rifle in his hand." Yet proof existed of better thing to come. As early as 1826, a town ordinance established the City Library and Museum of Tallahassee. Operating expenses were to come from the collection of certain fines and an annual appropriation of two dollars.

THE AGRICULTURAL KINGDOM BEGINS

Outside Tallahassee, Leon County developed an agricultural economy that was profitable and diversified. Tallahassee was important as the county seat and as the territorial and, later, state capital. The town's politicians, professional men, merchants, and workers—skilled and unskilled—were significant. Yet the land and what it produced determined the area's well-being. Leon County quickly became a region of farms and plantations, planters and their families, independent yeoman farmers, and black slaves.

The county's rich lands caused the area to boom. From a population of 996 in 1825, the country grew to 11,442 (3,451 whites, 7,231 slaves) in 1840, an expansion in fifteen years of 1,049 percent. The Second Seminole War and the Panic of 1837 halted the process, and from 1840 to 1860 the county reached a plateau of prosperity and relative growth (7.9 percent).

By 1860, Florida had a population of 140,424, and Leon's 12,343 people made it the state's most populous county. It was easily the most important farm county, leading the state in total acres in farmland, cash value of farmland, and worth of farm machinery. Near the top in all areas of farm production, Leon County was number one in mules, sheep, swine, and total value of livestock. It held first place in sweet-potato production and in the all-important crop of corn. The South's money crop, its uncrowned king, was cotton. Leon held premier ranking in Florida in 1860 with its 16,686 bales of ginned cotton.

Planters moved in from the upper South, coming overland in caravans and bringing their families, slaves, household supplies, and farm animals. They purchased Florida land and established, almost overnight, a plantation system. Less affluent white farmers were much more numerous; they bought small homesteads and became an important part of the agricultural system. The independent farmers who worked their own acreages did not obtain the best lands. Such properties—the red clay fields of the lake country in the county's northern and eastern areas—were appropriated by the planters. Leon County's southern portions were flat, sandy, unproductive, and studded with pines and black-jack oaks.

Major planters, numbering around 75, dominated the county and town's political, social, and economic life. A few lived in Tallahassee, but most resided in the country. Their prominence and means of production were not unlike those of broadcloth aristocrats in the

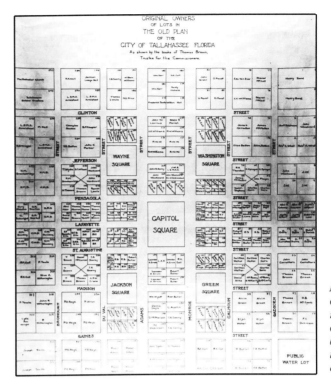

Names of the original owners of lots are shown in the old plan of the city of Tallahassee, from the books of Thomas Brown, trustee for the commissioners.

The second capitol, built in 1826, was one wing of a plan by General Robert Butler. After additional construction in 1828 and 1832, the building resembled this view by Francis, Comte de Castelnau.

State capitol, as it appeared between 1845, when the main building was finished, and 1891, when the cupola was added.

black-belt and delta regions of Georgia, Alabama, and Mississippi. A number of them combined planting with politics, medicine, law, and merchandising.

The leading planters included Robert Butler. More than six-feet tall and weighing 300 pounds, Butler idolized Jackson and Sir Walter Scott, and was himself a poet. He had a 900-acre plantation on Lake Jackson. Richard Keith Call, another Jackson protégé, held various civil and military appointments. He was most prominent as territorial governor, a position he held twice (1836-1839 and 1841-1844). Call owned two plantations: Orchard Pond and, nearer Tallahassee, the Grove. The mansion, which still stands as an enduring example of Greek Revival architecture, became a focus of the capital's social life. The aristocratic Gamble brothers, John Grattan and Robert, came from Virginia. Like other planters, the Gambles owned land in neighboring Jefferson County to the east. John Grattan owned Waukeenah and, later, Neamathla plantations. Robert was master of Weelaunee. The North Carolinian

DOROTHY O'CANE— AN ATYPICAL SOUTHERN PLANTER

Dorothy O'Cane, a free mulatto, was a dramatic exception to Leon County's usual type of planter, male or female. She was 59 and a native of South Carolina. Little is known about her, including when she came to Florida. In 1860 she had a personal estate valued at $12,000 and real estate worth $2,000. She owned 400 acres of land, 160 of them improved, and produced eighteen bales of cotton and 700 bushels of corn. O'Cane's labor force consisted of ten slaves (five females and five males). Besides cotton, she raised Irish potatoes, sweet potatoes, and produced butter, syrup, and meat. Her livestock included a horse, three mules, five milk cows, four other head of cattle, and 30 hogs.

BENJAMIN CHAIRES— "USEFUL CITIZEN AND GOOD MAN"

Benjamin Chaires, although perhaps not typical, exemplifies Florida's planter class at its zenith. Born in North Carolina in 1786, he grew to adulthood in middle Georgia, where he married and became a plantation owner, surveyor, and minor political figure before he was 30. In 1818, Chaires bought his first Florida property: a one-third share in a plantation on Amelia Island, completely furnished with slaves, tools, canoes, and other necessities. Eventually he bought as many as 30,000 acres in Saint Johns, Alachua, and Duval counties. In addition to his responsibilities as planter and landowner, he served as alderman and judge in Saint Augustine and Jacksonville, and helped in the original survey of Jacksonville, as control of Florida shifted from Spain to the United States.

In 1823, the Treaty of Moultrie Creek set aside lands between Ocala and Tampa for resettlement of the Indian population. The following year Chaires bid on—and won—a federal contract to furnish the Indians with rations on a regular basis as they adjusted to their confinement. During the year or so when he was involved with the Indian contract, he made several trips to Tallahassee on business. Evidently he liked what he saw of the area, for sometime during the late 1820s he settled his large family there permanently.

For the next ten years or so, until his death in 1838, Chaires amassed great wealth through his involvement in farming, banking, building, and brickmaking. He also helped form the first railroad company to serve Tallahassee. His home, Verdura, a few miles east of town, was an elegant Greek-revival mansion of thirteen rooms, wide verandas, and towering columns. At his death at age 52, Benjamin Chaires owned more than 9,000 acres and 80 slaves in Leon County, and was said by some people to have been Florida's first millionaire. He embodied the characteristics of the aggressively entrepreneurial southern frontiersman, always ready for a new opportunity in the volatile environment of the early nineteenth-century South. Chaires was eulogized in the newspapers of Saint Augustine, Apalachicola, and Tallahassee as a "useful citizen and a good man," and it was clear that "Florida. . . sustained a loss by his death which cannot soon be supplied."

Castelnau's drawing of an 1830s plantation on Lake Lafayette.

An artist's conception of Verdura, Benjamin Chaires's mansion, southeast of Tallahassee.

Richard Keith Call, was Florida's governor from 1836 to 1839 and 1841 to 1844.

The Grove, residence of Richard Keith Call, was begun in 1824.

Bryan Croom owned Goodwood plantation. His brother, Hardy Bryan Croom, also a planter, perished tragically at sea with his wife and family in 1837.

Prince Achille Murat was a planter, but not a typical one. He was the nephew of Napoleon (his mother was Caroline, the emperor's sister, and his father was Joachim Murat, marshal of France and ruler of the kingdom of Naples). Dispossessed when Napoleon fell, Murat emigrated to America. He eventually settled in Florida, and in the mid-1820s married Catherine Daingerfield Willis Gray, widowed great-grandniece of George Washington. Murat was a linguist, skilled writer, bizarre chef (he prepared baked owl with the head on, cow's-ear stew, tails of hogs, and rattlesnakes), and successful planter. He and his wife became prominent social leaders in territorial Florida, and owned Lipona and Econchatti plantations, both in Jefferson County. Until his death in 1847, Prince Murat added a Gallic flavor, a spicy mixture of French sophistication and earthiness, to Tallahassee and Leon County. Princess Murat move to Bellevue plantation near Tallahassee, and lived there until her death in 1867.

Slaves provided the labor that sustained the plantation system. Without counting slaves, Leon County ranked eighth in Florida in white population. The county's front rank in 1860 was caused by the presence of 9,089 slaves and 60 "free persons of color." Most of the latter lived in Tallahassee and worked as dairymen, carpenters, seamstresses, and washerwomen. Never considered first-class citizens, they found their limited rights restricted even more with the sectional crises of the 1850s.

Tallahassee and Leon County had 515 slaveholders, or about 16 percent of the population. Yet the planters dominated every facet of life. The largest slaveholder was Joseph John Williams, whose five plantations totaling 7,000 acres, were worked by 245 slaves. Williams was hardly representative; generally the largest number of slaves held by one owner ranged from ten to fifteen. In Leon County, 76 slaveholders were in that category.

As property, slaves were inherited, exchanged, presented as gifts and, mainly, bought and sold. In 1860, Tallahassee had five slave auctioneers, some doubling as commission merchants. By definition, slavery was an evil system. Throughout the South a special set of laws, the slave code, controlled the bondsmen in their movements, their religious privileges, and forbade them to possess arms or to be taught to read and write. Because the slave code bestowed on the masters absolute control, they treated the slaves badly or well, depending on individual judgment. In Tallahassee, slaves were whipped publicly; the intent was to punish them and to set examples of obedience for other slaves. That the bondsmen longed for freedom was evidenced by frequent advertisements in the papers for runaways.

Wedding certificate of Prince Achille Murat and the widowed Catherine Willis Gray, July 11, 1826.

Prince Achille Murat, Napoleon's nephew by marriage, settled in Florida in the mid-1820s.

Princess Catherine Daingerfield Willis Gray Murat was a great-grandniece of George Washington.

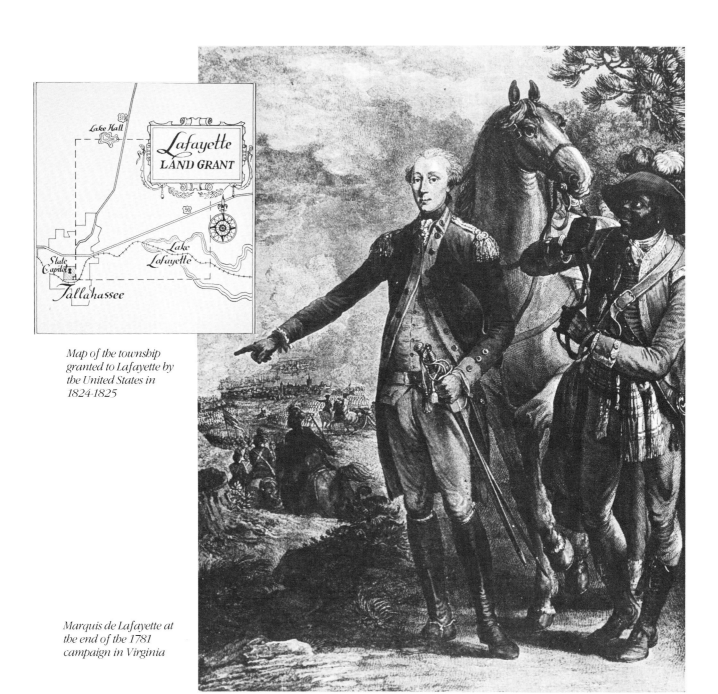

Map of the township
granted to Lafayette by
the United States in
1824-1825

Marquis de Lafayette at
the end of the 1781
campaign in Virginia

A EUROPEAN EXPERIMENT FAILS

The Lafayette land grant was an unsuccessful attempt to challenge the planter-dominated system of landholding and labor. A grateful United States had granted back pay in 1794 to the impoverished Marquis de Lafayette for his gallant services during the American Revolution. In 1803, he was given land in the Louisiana Territory, and in 1824 the Frenchman made a triumphant tour of the United States. Honored everywhere, the foreign hero received a congressional grant of $200,000 and a township of land (36 square miles) in Leon County. While in Washington, Lafayette met Richard Keith Call, who, desiring to promote the territory, urged him to settle in Florida. An abolitionist, Lafayette declined, but decided to found a free colony on his land. In 1831, three of the marquis' friends arrived with some 60 Norman peasants. They formed a slaveless agricultural community incongruously located on Lake Lafayette in the heart of plantation country.

The ill-fated colony did not rise and fall—it never rose. The orchards of lime and olive trees never matured. Even if they had time to grow, the capricious north-Florida weather would have intervened. The same was true of the mulberry trees planted to furnish leaves for silkworms as the basis of a projected silk industry. Without a physician, the settlers fell victim to diseases, and struggled with additional problems of culture, religion, and language. Lafayette never visited his colony, and eventually it collapsed. A few settlers remained in Leon County, some returned to France, and others migrated to New Orleans. Lawsuits over ownership of the property lasted until the Civil War.

Kept busy by the world they had fashioned, Leon County planters scarcely noticed the Lafayette experiment. They owned large tracts of land, built classic Greek-revival homes, marketed their cotton through their Gulf ports of Saint Marks and Newport, and followed a life-style which they would have exchanged for no other on earth.

Hardy B. Croom was lost
at sea with all his family
in the wreck of the steamer Home in 1837

The establishment of churches helped turn Tallahasseeans and Leon countians away from their brawling frontier ways. Through the years, ministers had been important in the community. The first Protestant church was Trinity Methodist, although the Franciscan missions dated to the seventeenth century. Itinerant Methodists gave occasional sermons—probably in the log capitol—before Josiah Evans became the first regular pastor in 1825. By 1827, Tallahassee had two churches: a public church and the Methodist, at the corner of Park and Boulevard. The church was wooden, had shutters instead of windows, and a gallery for slaves. Growth was slow, but a brick house of worship was completed in 1846. A Sunday school was flourishing by the mid-1840s when the church had 131 white and 168 black members.

After the American Revolution, Virginians established the Episcopal church to replace the Anglican church. Those Old Dominion planters who migrated to Leon County brought their religion with them. Parkhill, Brown, Call, DeMilly, Kirksey, and other pioneer-family names were added to the roll of Saint John's, which was incorporated in 1829. The members met in the capitol and the courtroom. Saint John's was first a mission, but in 1837 the church building was completed. From the beginning, its members were civic leaders in Tallahassee. In 1854, Trinity Chapel at Bel Aire (south of Tallahassee) was opened.

The Presbyterian Church, at the northwest corner of Park and Adams, was completed in 1838 at a cost of $13,000. The church was organized in 1832 by Joseph Styles, an active Presbyterian. Incorporated in 1833, First Presbyterian was not far behind the Methodists in

First Baptist Church, on the south side of College just west of Adams, was completed in 1853. The "Pawn Shop" at right was a fenced corral that held wandering animals until they were redeemed by owners.

The first Saint John's Episcopal Church cost $10,000 when built in 1837-1838.

First Presbyterian Church at the northwest corner of Adams and Park, begun in 1835 and dedicated in 1838, is the city's oldest house of worship.

A PRIMITIVE BAPTIST PATRIARCH—
THE FIRST SETTLER?

*M*ost accounts of the first American settlers to arrive in the Tallahassee hill country after the Spanish cession begin with John McIver of North Carolina. A competing claimant for that honor was introduced in the early 1900s, with the publication in a Tallahassee newspaper of a remarkable tale.

"Henry Crawford Tucker, who was born in South Carolina in 1805, came to Georgia in 1814, and moved down to Florida in 1823 and built a log cabin near where the capitol building now stands. He was the first white man that ever cut a stick on the hills where the city of Tallahassee now flourishes.

"Mr. Tucker was a primitive Baptist preacher and was in the ministry 46 years; was married three times and when he died was the father, grandfather, and great-grandfather of 714 descendants. He first married Nancy Capp in 1823, she was the first white woman in Tallahassee, and brought forth seven boys and one girl. He next married Peggy Ann Watson, and added three boys and eight girls to his little family; after the death of Peggy, he married Becky Bryant and this union added eight boys and five girls, making a total of eighteen boys and fourteen girls, or in all thirty-two children.

"One of the boys proved to be a drunkard, while fourteen of them are members of the same church, nearly all are preachers, and all are noted for piety, except the usual one black sheep."

The second Trinity Methodist Church building was constructed on the northeast corner of Park and Duval in 1846.

43

membership or the Episcopalians in influence. The church building is Tallahassee's oldest public structure.

The Baptists, who experienced great expansion after the Civil War, worshiped first at Enon Church at Lake Bradford. Although membership was small, the Tallahassee Baptists raised the necessary funds and built a church which was dedicated on July 4, 1859.

When the Right Reverend Michael Portier came through Tallahassee in 1827, the town's small number of Catholics had no place to worship. The situation was remedied when Bishop Portier bought property in 1845, and Saint John the Evangelist was completed in 1846. It burned in 1847 and was replaced in 1853 by the Church of Saint Mary. Tallahassee had no priest until 1860, when another church was built.

The Church of Saint Mary, circa 1870-74, at the northeast corner of Park and Gadsden, later the site of the George Lewis home.

Before the Civil War, no black churches were permitted in the town limits—the fear that the blacks would plot up-risings under cover of religious services was too strong. Some white churches had galleries for slaves to sit in during regular services. Others had afternoon sessions at which white ministers preached, sometimes with black assistant pastors. A few black churches existed in the country.

The ritual counting by the federal government every ten years of people and property gave Leon County a good showing in 1860. Yet the census—which listed 27 churches (property value of $41,900) attended by 5,800 members—greatly underestimated the actual figures.

EDUCATION IS PUBLIC AND PRIVATE—BUT FOR WHITES ONLY

Tallahassee's first school began as early as 1825, on the lower floor of a two-story log building on the corner of Duval and Park. It was conducted by the Masons, Tallahassee's first fraternal order, who were established locally on December 18, 1825, and met on the second story of the building. The schoolroom also may have been used for church worship on Sundays.

Education was for the white population. The slave code prohibited blacks from classroom instruction. Numerous violations of the statutes occurred but 74 percent of the population was kept legally illiterate.

Structured education began in 1827 when Leon Academy, a public city school, was opened for boys. It was incorporated in 1831 and a "female department" was added. Controlled by the Tallahassee City Council, Leon Academy struggled along with inadequate funding and a constant turnover of teachers until it closed in 1836. Reopening as a private seminary for boys, it functioned until 1840.

For the next ten years, Tallahassee had several private schools for boys. The Reverend William Neil operated his Male Academy in the basement of the courthouse. Later in the 1840s, he moved the school to the corner of Park and Bronough opposite his wife's school, the Leon Female Academy. These and other private schools existed on tuition fees. They were one-room affairs, poorly equipped, and often taught by northerners (and sometimes southerners) who had moved to Florida for their health. The Female Academy of Leon, incorporated by the town in 1845 and succeeded by Mrs. Neil's school, was taught by Jane and Agnes Bates, young sisters from South Carolina. The idea of coeducation rarely was considered. The separate schools for males and females had fixed curriculums. If they were from wealthy families, young women often were educated at home by tutors or governesses.

Under the Reverend Neil's leadership, Tallahassee voted in 1850 to have a public school. The Free School that was established admitted males above the age of seven free, and it was hoped that facilities for females could be added later. County children who wished to attend had to pay tuition. The Free School lasted from 1850 to 1853.

Higher education became possible in 1851 when, the legislature provided for the establishment of seminaries east and west of the Suwannee River. Hoping to be selected, Tallahassee took money from its "fire fund" and the city council and erected a building on Gallows Hill, near the present Westcott Building on the campus of Florida State University. Completed in 1854, the building was opened as a school in 1855. Under its able principal, W. Y. Peyton of Virginia, it was known by several names, usually Florida Institute or the Tallahassee Seminary. In 1857, Tallahasseean Medicus A. Long, saw his bill become law: the capital city was awarded the state school. It opened that year with Peyton as principal. Most of the students came from Tallahassee. In 1858, the Leon Female Academy became part of the college as the Female Branch of the West Florida Seminary. The city council paid most of the tuition for Tallahassee students. In 1859, military training was added, and in 1860 the institution was authorized to confer bachelor of arts degrees.

On the eve of the Civil War, 200 students were enrolled in the West Florida Seminary, and others attended several private secondary and elementary schools in the county.

The first building on what is now Florida State University campus, which opened as the Florida Institute in 1855. Built as an inducement for the state to designate Tallahassee as the site for an institute west of the Suwannee River, the school became West Florida Seminary in 1857.

The First Leon County Courthouse was built on the north side of Park between Monroe and Adams in 1832-1833. For a time, the basement was used for Reverend William Neil's Male Academy.

*Castelnau's drawing of
the Tallahassee railroad
depot shows bales of
cotton being readied for
shipment to Saint Marks.*

TRANSPORTATION AND COMMUNICATION
LINK TALLAHASSEE WITH THE WORLD

*A*s the capital city, Tallahassee needed adequate
transportation and communication facilities.
The dirt road became the single most important link to the outside. In the 1820s, Congress
funded the Federal Road to replace the old Spanish
road connecting Saint Augustine and Pensacola. John
Bellamy, a planter who lived near Lake Miccosukee,
was awarded the $13,000 contract to construct the
regional section of the Federal Road. Using slave labor,
Bellamy began the project in 1825 and completed it in
1826. The road, fifteen to twenty feet wide, was full
of stumps (none more than two feet high). Crude
bridges were built, although major streams were
crossed by ferries. Old Indian paths, such as the
one to Saint Marks were widened into roads. As time
passed, other connectors, including plank and toll
roads, were constructed.

Various plans for canals—including an early
cross-Florida canal—were proposed, but little was
done about the proposals. Although the Ochlocknee
River was navigable only for commercial travel near the
coast, Governor Duval wanted to build a canal from the
river to Lake Jackson, making Tallahassee a seaport.

Tallahassee had the territory's second railroad.

The first, completed in 1836, connected Saint Joseph and Lake Wimico in Franklin County. The Tallahassee Railroad Company, after two false starts, was chartered in 1834. It connected the capital with Saint Marks, 21 miles to the south, and opened in December 1837 (officially in May 1838). Passenger service was $1.50 to Saint Marks, 75 cents for children, and 75 cents for a bale of cotton. The mule-drawn trains ran on wooden tracks topped by thin iron straps. The railroad was "certainly the very worst that has been built in the entire world," according to Castelnau.

The line was extended to Port Leon, two-and-a-half miles below Saint Marks, although the new town was destroyed by a hurricane in 1843. Port Leon's inhabitants moved upstream and established Newport, but it had no rail connection. The Tallahassee Railroad remained a profitable venture and did not add steam engines successfully until 1856. By 1861 another line, the Pensacola and Georgia Railroad, linked Tallahassee with Quincy on the west and Lake City on the east.

A telegraph line was opened in 1859, connecting Tallahassee with the rest of the nation. Local citizens communicated with one another by conversation and, although the area boasted some gifted talkers, general news was circulated by newspapers. The capital's first newspaper was an irregularly published journal called *The Florida Intelligencer.* Established in 1825, it was owned by Ambrose Crane, Ede Van Evour, and Cary Nicholas. Crane was the first court clerk and Tallahassee's first postmaster. One early paper was the *Florida Courier* (1830-1832). It was notable because the first novel published in Florida came from its press. *An Historical Novel Founded on Facts, Connected with the Indian War in the South, 1812 to '15* by Don Pedro Cassender (a pseudonym for Wiley or Willie Conner).

The major spokesman for the Democratic party was Charles Edward Dyke's Tallahassee *Floridian.* A native of Canada, Dyke served as editor from 1847 to 1883. The outspoken and brilliant Cosam Emir Bartlett made the Tallahassee *Star of Florida* the chief advocate of the Whigs. Even Tallahassee's most successful newspapers did not exceed 500 or 600 in circulation, and subscription rates averaged about five dollars a year. Even so, individual issues were circulated through several hands. The papers were influential, and few readers complained about not getting their money's worth.

WAR AND FINANCIAL PANIC BRING CRISIS

The Second Seminole War combined with the financial Panic of 1837 to destroy Florida's prosperity. The war resulted from the whites taking over Indian lands. The federal Indian Removal Act of 1830 provided for the exchange of Indian lands east of the Mississippi River for grants in the West. Subsequently, the Seminoles signed the Treaty of Payne's Landing (1832) and the Treaty of Fort Gibson (1833), agreeing to leave Florida within three years and to accept land and cash indemnity. As usual, the terms favored the whites, and Indian leaders such

as Osceola and Coacoochee (Wildcat) rose in revolt. The Second Seminole War began in 1835 and lasted until the early 1840s. It was a dress rehearsal for the Mexican War—Winfield Scott, Thomas Jesup, and Zachary Taylor saw service in the Florida peninsula.

Osceola was betrayed, captured, and died in 1838 at a military prison in Charleston, South Carolina. The Seminoles fought bravely, although both sides resorted to savage acts. Not much fighting took place in Leon County, but its militia companies saw combat, and a few local massacres occurred. Tallahassee became panic-stricken when one attack was rumored. Roads into the capital were barricaded with cotton bales, and women and children were sent to the town's center. The intermittent war ended with some Seminoles going into the Everglades of south Florida. Almost 4,000 were shipped West.

William Williams, known as "Money Williams," was Tallahassee's first banker. He migrated from North Carolina to the capital about 1830 and built a two-story red brick home known as the Columns. The bricks, which cost five cents each, gave rise to a legend that each brick contained a nickel. The Williams family lived on the upper floor and used the lower story as a bank. Later, a bank building was added adjacent to the house. There Money Williams operated the Bank of Florida from 1830 to 1832. The Tallahassee Chamber of Commerce now occupies the Columns, which was moved to its present site in 1971.

The Bank of Florida was absorbed by the Central Bank, with Benjamin Chaires as president. In that same year, 1833, the Union Bank was chartered. Unlike the Bank of Florida and the Central Bank, which had merchants as directors, the Union Bank was an institution for planters, and only planters could buy stock in it. Governor Duval supported the bank, believing it would attract northern and foreign capital. President John Grattan Gamble borrowed the idea from a bank in Louisiana, and the Union Bank, with the Bank of Pensacola, and the Southern Life Insurance and Trust Company of Saint Augustine comprised the "big three" of Florida's territorial banking system.

The Union Bank's capital stock was backed by "faith bonds" issued by the territory of Florida. In turn, planters subscribed to shares by mortgaging their slaves and property. A planter could sign interest-bearing notes to borrow money up to two-thirds of his stock. Poor administration, a nationwide depression (brought on by President Jackson's fiscal policies), and the Second Seminole War sent the delicate edifice crashing down. Interminable state and congressional investigations followed, and the Union Bank was ordered closed in 1843.

After 1845, Tallahassee's banking was handled by agents of a northern bank. In 1851, the State Bank of Florida was incorporated with the four-time Tallahassee

Coacoochee (Wild Cat) was one of the Seminole leaders who revolted against the unfair terms of the Paynes Landing and Fort Gibson treaties.

Osceola, great chief of the Seminoles

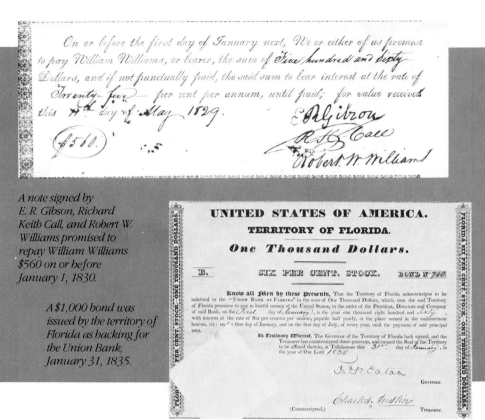

A note signed by E. R. Gibson, Richard Keith Call, and Robert W. Williams promised to repay William Williams $560 on or before January 1, 1830.

A $1,000 bond was issued by the territory of Florida as backing for the Union Bank, January 31, 1835.

intendant Leslie A. Thompson as president. In 1856, a druggist named B. C. Lewis and his three sons founded a bank later known as the Lewis State Bank and today as First Florida Bank. The family bank's directors were mainly local merchants.

EPIDEMIC RAGES IN FLORIDA

In 1826, Tallahassee had seven practicing physicians, or one for every 100 individuals. By 1860, fourteen doctors practiced in Tallahassee and seventeen more in Leon County. As early as 1826, physicians in the area, lacking a formal organization, established rates for their services.

Lewis Willis, whose sister married Prince Achille Murat, was among the first doctors. His father, Byrd Willis, was also a physician but gave up medicine to become a planter. Dr. W. W. Waddell, an honor graduate of the University of Pennsylvania, took care of the medical needs of the Murat family and its slaves, charging $331 in 1839. Dr. Miles N. Nash not only kept office hours but also operated a drugstore and served as a Methodist preacher. He was called sometimes from the pulpit to deliver a baby. Dr. Henry Randolph doubled as a successful planter, as did Dr. Edward Bradford, antebellum Tallahassee's most noted physician. A native of North Carolina, Bradford brought his family to Leon County in 1831. He owned 3,200 acres—Pine Hill and Horseshoe plantations—ten miles north of Tallahassee. His daughter, Susan Bradford Eppes, wrote two local histories, *The Negro of the Old South* and *Through Some Eventful Years*.

Although some doctors cared for their patients' teeth, a few dentists also practiced in Tallahassee.

Nonresident dentists such as Dr. J. H. C. Miller arrived during meetings of the legislative council to solicit additional business and take advantage of all the social life. Another wandering dentist with the appropriate name of Dr. S. W. Comfort treated diseased gums and extracted old roots (described as "fangs") with "caution and skill." Dr. W. Cross became the town's first permanent dentist in October 1838. When Dr. P. P. Lewis opened his practice in 1850, he employed the latest dental techniques. By using chloroform and ether, he was the capital's first modern dentist. Dr. Lewis produced a local anesthetic with electrical charges and noted that his patients "experienced little or no pain."

In an age when doctors had no knowledge of antibiotics, death was often the result of illnesses. It was ironic that in Leon County's humid and hot climate the biggest killer in 1860 was pneumonia.

The yellow-fever epidemic of 1841 was the biggest crisis faced by the area doctors, and one they could do little about. From the beginning, Tallahassee was considered an unhealthy place. With summer heat came fevers and closed shops. The wealthy left for the mountains. The deadly epidemic began in June 1841 at Saint Joseph, when two infected men from Havana, Cuba were brought ashore. No one knew yellow fever was caused by a virus transmitted by mosquitoes. The disease soon spread to Tallahassee, where doctors were kept busy. The populace tried home remedies. They applied hot water and cayenne pepper to their feet and legs, reduced their eating and exercise, guarded against exposure, and abstained from alcohol. Some took enormous doses of calomel and were said to "look like walking skeletons more than like live persons."

In July the death toll rose, and the town was in a

Susan Bradford Eppes was the author of The Negro of the Old South *and* Through Some Eventful Years.

state of helpless fear. A night watch went into effect, and regulations for burial were strictly enforced. A board of health was appointed, but could do nothing. One family of five died within a week, and the epidemic did not end until November, when the first frosts came. Tallahassee lost about ten percent of its summer population of 800.

Some people saw the hand of God at work in the death toll. Tallahassee was being punished for its wickedness. One observer believed the tragedy was worthwhile because it killed "most all the Gamblers & Blacklegs of the place and now they have a chance to begin anew." Many churches held prolonged revivals. The epidemic slowed Tallahassee's growth. Yellow-fever epidemics occurred in 1853 and 1867, but neither was as serious as that of 1841.

SALTS AND SNAKEROOT

Charles Hutchinson, a native of Connecticut who worked as a clerk, attempted to ward off yellow fever with heroic medications. He wrote on July 5, 1841:

"I am 'chawed up'—Last Friday & Saturday, I did not feel quite as well as usual (but in healthy times I should not have minded it) so Saturday night I was persuaded to go to work Florida fashion & took 25 Grains of calomel & Castor Oil. It worked finely, today I have been drinking salts and snakeroot, a wine glass full every two hours—I feel first rate now, or as near so as a man can feel who has hardly strength to blow his nose—I shall be well tomorrow—already my mouth begins to water for its accustomed dose of Boiled ham."

"TESTED BY FIRE"

On Thursday, May 25, 1843, Tallahassee saw almost its entire business district destroyed by fire. The conflagration began in a house just southeast of the capitol at about 5:00 p.m. The flames traveled quickly up the east side of Monroe Street towards the Leon County Courthouse and beyond, jumping across Lafayette, Pensacola, and Jefferson streets, and present College Avenue. The courthouse was saved, but nearly all the other buildings on the eastern side of Monroe were consumed.

The stores on the opposite side of the main street fared no better. The flames leaped to the rooftops of buildings between Monroe and Adams streets. Within three hours the blaze had leveled almost every structure from the capitol to Park Avenue—or "200-Foot Street" as it was called then. By 8:00 p.m. the individual efforts of citizens (Tallahassee had no fire department) and the natural firebreak of Park Avenue stopped the advancing flames.

Over the next few days, a "Committee on losses" attempted to assess the extent of the damage. Reporting to Intendant (Mayor) Francis Eppes, the committee revealed that losses were well over a half million dollars, including buildings, merchandise, and furnishings. Very little was covered by insurance. A contemporary

newspaper reported that a number of Tallahasseeans "lost their all."

Mayor Eppes appointed a relief committee to find ways to alleviate the suffering of those most affected by the disaster. At the committee's suggestion, Eppes sent an appeal to a number of newspapers around the country. He emphasized the commercial importance of the city as a cotton-exporting center and a vital market for goods from northern merchants. It is not known how much money was collected, but the response was gratifying, and funds were distributed over the next three years.

Many of Tallahassee's merchants and businessmen gamely set up shop within two days of the fire, operating in temporary shanties near their former locations. They offered for sale whatever goods they had managed to salvage from their ruined establishments. By early June, city officials enacted an ordinance which approved the use of such temporary structures for one year and which prohibited construction of any wooden buildings in the downtown area.

Some merchants gave up on the capital city, but most stayed to rebuild. One editor observed just a few weeks after the fire: "As gold is tested by fire, so are the qualities of a man tried by adversity."

TALLAHASSEE SURVIVES ITS WORST FIRE

As if bank failures, Indian wars, and yellow-fever epidemics were not enough, Tallahassee was hit in 1843 by a devastating fire. It began late in the afternoon of May 25 at a hotel near the capitol. No rain had fallen in more than two months, and the town had no fire department, fire engine, or organized plan for fighting fires. Most of downtown Tallahassee was destroyed in the three-hour tragedy— the worst fire ever in Tallahassee. Few property owners carried insurance.

The fire's cause never was discovered, although many people believed it was an act of arson. Intendant Francis Eppes called out the Tallahassee Guards to protect the town, and presided over a pubic meeting the next day. An ordinance was passed requiring future buildings to be fireproof and to have alleyways between them. Nearby towns contributed funds to help the stricken capital, and the money along with local allocations and donations, became a "fire fund." The fire probably eradicated the source of the yellow-fever epidemic and the new brick buildings that rose made the capital, with its abundant live oaks and other trees, a beautiful town by 1860.

POLITICS AND STATEHOOD KEEP CENTER STAGE

Governor Duval worked hard to promote the new capital, and was succeeded as territorial governor in 1834 by John H. Eaton, a Jackson man and "Old Hickory's" secretary of war. Eaton's wife, Peggy O'Neal, was more famous than her husband. Peggy's good looks and questionable behavior earned her the ostracism of proper Washington society. In the cabinet crisis that followed, Jackson defended her honor privately and publicly. The president appointed Eaton governor of Florida to let the crisis simmer (after his appointment, Eaton took seven months to reach Florida). The Eatons did not particularly like their new assignment, although Mrs. Eaton wrote later of the capital, "We had two happy years in Florida. To me, it was the land of flowers as Washington had been the land of briars."

Richard Keith Call succeeded Eaton in 1836, just as the war with the Seminoles was beginning. As the third governor, Call became bitterly involved with Washington authorities over proper procedures of carrying on the war, and was asked to resign. Still, Call had played a major role in the territory's development. The fourth governor was Robert Raymond Reid (1839),

John H. Eaton served as secretary of war under Andrew Jackson, who later appointed Eaton as the second territorial governor of Florida. The appointment was made partly to quiet a cabinet crisis involving Eaton's wife, Peggy O'Neal Eaton.

Peggy O'Neal Eaton was first lady of Florida, 1834-1836.

Robert Raymond Reid, Florida's fourth territorial governor, served from 1839 to 1841.

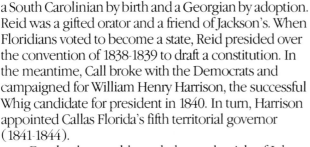

a South Carolinian by birth and a Georgian by adoption. Reid was a gifted orator and a friend of Jackson's. When Floridians voted to become a state, Reid presided over the convention of 1838-1839 to draft a constitution. In the meantime, Call broke with the Democrats and campaigned for William Henry Harrison, the successful Whig candidate for president in 1840. In turn, Harrison appointed Call as Florida's fifth territorial governor (1841-1844).

Few leaders could match the credentials of John Branch, Florida's sixth and last territorial governor. Branch had served as state senator, governor, member of the United States Senate and the House of Representatives. He was Jackson's secretary of the navy. His well-kept plantation in Leon County was called Live Oak.

In 1845, Florida became the twenty-seventh state. In the elections for state offices, William D. Moseley, a North Carolina politician and lawyer who had moved to Jefferson County, Florida, in the 1830s, became the state's first governor. A Democrat, Moseley defeated Call, the Whig nominee. The inauguration on June 25, 1845, took place amid elaborate festivities in the newly opened state capitol. The occasion was marred only by the news that Jackson had died at his home near Nashville.

Thomas Brown, elected governor in 1849, was

Florida's only Whig chief executive. A compassionate and capable man, Brown brought his family from Virginia to Leon County in 1828. His dreams of being a sugar planter were destroyed by a disastrous freeze. Undeterred, he entered the hotel business and was active in civic affairs. Brown was succeeded by a Democrat, James Emilius Broome of South Carolina. A resident of Tallahassee since 1837, Broome was governor during the national crisis from 1853 to 1857. He was a noted speaker who never hesitated to use his veto power, and was married five times. Madison Starke Perry was an Alachua County planter. Governor from 1857 to 1861, Perry favored secession from the Union. He left office in the fall of 1861 and served as colonel of the Seventh Florida Regiment until illness forced his retirement.

Francis Eppes was Tallahassee's most notable—and its most cultured—local politician before the Civil War. As the grandson of Thomas Jefferson, Eppes benefited from his distinguished kinsman's personal direction of his education. Eppes knew French, Spanish, and German as well as English, and read the Scriptures in the original Latin and Greek. Eppes and his family came to Leon County from Virginia in 1828. He engaged in planting and built an excellent reputation as intendant of his adopted Tallahassee.

John Branch, sixth territorial governor of Florida, had served as a United States senator and as governor of North Carolina. He was Andrew Jackson's secretary of the navy before assuming his Florida duties in 1844.

Live Oak plantation, Governor John Branch's home, burned in 1894.

When speaking of the Tallahassee area and all of Florida, John Randolph, the caustic Virginia congressman, said, "It is a land of swamps, of quagmires, of frogs, and alligators, and mosquitoes! A man, sir, would not immigrate into Florida. No sir! No man would immigrate into Florida—not from hell itself!"

The Pensacola Gazette *and* West Floridan Advertiser *had a totally different view. In 1827 the paper described Tallahassee and the nearby countryside: "In appearance it is entirely unlike any part of the United States, so near the seaboard yet it resembles the high land above the falls of the rivers in the Atlantic States. . . . The natural open groves of hickory, beech, oak and magnolia surpass in magnificence the proudest parks of the English nobility. . . . In the valleys there is a much heavier growth of timber and frequently deep cane brakes. There are also grassy ponds surrounded by glades. The soil of the uplands as well as in the valley is adapted to the culture of sugar cane, rice, Sea Island cotton and Indian Corn. . . . the Strawberry, the wild grape and plum are found everywhere. . . . [It is] an oasis which appears to have been formed by nature in one of her most sportive and fantastic humors."*

THE GOOD LIFE REIGNS

For a town so new, Tallahassee developed a sophisticated society. Thomas Brown owned the Marion Course, a racetrack that flourished in the 1830s and early 1840s. Circuses included the town on their circuit, and local citizens gave their enthusiastic patronage to such shows as Robinson and Lake's Great Southern Menagerie and Circus. Leon County had local fairs beginning in 1852.

The Tallahassee Tournament Field was the site of ring contests—tamer imitations of medieval jousting events. The object was for a horseman to spear a ring with a lance at full gallop. The tilts were heavily competitive, and were followed by awards to the victorious knights by maids of honor. The tournament's activities ended with a grand ball, usually at Brown's Hotel.

Dramatic productions were all the rage. Emanuel Judah, an actor turned manager, and his wife and two sons performed at the Planters' Hotel in 1839. Judah opened a permanent theatre in Apalachicola, but he and his family were lost in a shipwreck before he could build a theatre in Tallahassee. W. R. Hart took over the operations in 1840 and established several theatres in Georgia, Alabama, and Florida. In the capital, he built a playhouse adjoining the Planters' Hotel. The performances were timed to coincide with the lawmakers' sessions. Usually a "mainpiece" was followed by a shorter "afterpiece," most often a farce. Hart and his wife were accomplished players. In Tallahassee it became socially significant for well-dressed society people to see the plays and, equally important, to be seen at them. Financial difficulties set in by the mid 1840s, and the theatre closed.

More modest forms of entertainment attracted Tallahasseeans and Leon countians. Individual performers—phrenologists, travelling singers—appeared briefly and departed. Permanently based and permanently important were clubs, church socials, charity fairs, and temperance societies. Portrait painters appeared, solicited customers, and left, but Tallahassee also had local painters of talent. With so much going on, it was hard to keep up with the developments of the nineteenth century. In 1860, all of Tallahassee turned out to marvel at a balloon ascension.

By 1860, Tallahassee and Leon County were prosperous. The sense of well-being that pervaded town and country was taken for granted, at least outwardly. Even so, a feeling of apprehension, of uncertainty, existed. The nation was divided bitterly over the question of slavery in all its moral and political implications. The North and South seemed to be on a collision course. As the locals went about their daily routines, many feared that a disruptive future (they called it "squally times") lay ahead. If the North could not accept the South—of which Tallahassee and Leon County were so inextricably a part—then profound changes would have to be made.

William Dunn Moseley, Florida's first governor after statehood, was inaugurated on June 25, 1845, in the newly opened state capitol.

Thomas Brown, Florida's only Whig governor, served from 1849 to 1853.

GEORGE PROCTOR—A FREE BLACK BUILDER

George Proctor, a free black, worked as a contractor in Tallahassee through the 1830s and 1840s. He built many of the city's finest homes during that period, some of which still grace the streets of the downtown area. Among these are the Randall-Lewis house and the Rutgers house, now the home of the Tallahassee Garden Club.

Proctor left Tallahassee—and his family—in the late 1840s to seek his fortune in California. His wife, whose freedom he had purchased, and several of his children subsequently were sold into slavery to cover debts he owed in Tallahassee. Proctor died in California in 1862. John Proctor, one of George's sons, served in the Florida legislature in the 1870s and 1880s.

"RIOTOUS, IMMORAL, AND DISORDERLY PROCEEDINGS"

Disorderly conduct in Tallahassee prompted the Leon County grand jury in 1827 to complain: "We are sorry to find that in Tallahassee, a horrible state of things has existed for some time. The most flagrant breaches of the laws have taken place. The civil authorities have in many instances been set at defiance; and the most riotous, immoral, and disorderly proceedings have constantly taken place. It is truly lamentable to see such occurrences in any civilized country but that it has occurred at the capital of our Territory, where it is so particularly desirable to establish a character for morality and good order, is the more to be regretted."

Francis Wayles Eppes came to Tallahassee in 1828. He served three times as mayor before moving to Orange County in 1869

Brown's Inn, on the west side of Adams between Lafayette and Pensacola, was built in 1834 by Thomas Brown, later governor.

THE CIVIL WAR
AND RECONSTRUCTION

The secession convention of Florida met at Tallahassee in January 1861.

3.

A series of sectional crises—the Compromise of 1850, the Kansas-Nebraska Act and "Bleeding Kansas," the birth of the Republican party, the Dred Scott decision, John Brown's raid on Harper's Ferry, and the publication of Harriet Beecher Stowe's *Uncle Tom's Cabin*—propelled the South toward secession. Abraham Lincoln's victory in 1860 seemed to confirm all fears of northern domination. Lincoln did not even appear on the ballot in Florida, as the citizens cast a majority vote (8,453) for the southern Democrat John C. Breckinridge. Even so, John Bell, the moderate candidate for the Constitutional Union party, captured a strong vote (5,437), and Stephen A. Douglas, a northern Democrat, received 363 votes. In the race for governor, Democrat John Milton won over Edward A. Hopkins, a Constitutional Unionist, 6,994 to 5,248. Leon County gave Milton 400 votes and cast 352 for Hopkins. The closeness of the election indicated that Florida was not rabid for secession.

John Milton was elected the fifth governor of Florida, defeating Edward A. Hopkins in 1860.

Yet the highly articulate Floridians who wanted to secede were known as "fire-eaters," and they were a majority. Among them were outgoing Governor Madison Starke Perry and Charles E. Dyke, editor of the Tallahassee *Floridian and Journal.* Dyke reacted in his newspaper to the Republican triumph: "WHAT IS TO BE DONE? We say *Resist*.... 'Who would be free themselves must strike the blow.'"

Florida's general assembly set December 22, 1860, as election day for delegates to a convention to decide what course Florida should follow. The convention was to meet at Tallahassee on January 3, 1861. The major question would be whether to take separate state action or wait and see what neighboring southern states would do. In the meantime, South Carolina had seceded on December 20, an action that brought out the Unionism in Tallahassee's Richard Keith Call. He hoped that "reason may not be dethroned by passion

...that no attempt will be made to declare Florida a Nation alien and foreign to the American people."

The majority of the delegates elected were "immediate secessionists," and of the 69 elected, 51 were slaveholders. More moderate delegates were called "cooperationists." The delegates and interested persons swarmed into Tallahassee, filling the hotels and boardinghouses, staying with friends, searching all over for lodging. As the largest county, Leon had the most delegates: John Beard, a fire-eater; William G. M. Davis; James Kirksey, a lawyer; George W. Parkhill, a prominent planter and owner of 172 slaves; and George T. Ward, a conservative planter and businessman who had 170 bondsmen.

During its sessions, the convention heard many speakers. Among them were the Right Reverend Francis Huger Rutledge, the Episcopal bishop of Florida, and Edmund Ruffin of Virginia. Both were secessionists. Rutledge lived in Tallahassee, where he had been the rector at Saint John's before becoming bishop. Ruffin, a scientific agriculturalist of international renown, yielded to no one in his hatred of the North. The secessionists' strength was revealed early with the election of John C. McGehee of Madison as convention president. McGehee had been a leader in the secessionist movement since 1851.

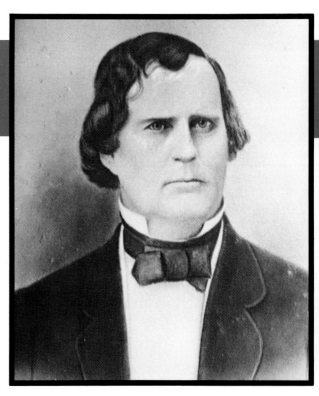

Madison Starke Perry, fourth governor of Florida, served from 1857 to 1861. He was among the "Fire-eaters," Floridians who favored secession.

Spectators packed into galleries watched futile delaying tactics by the cooperationists. On January 5, a resolution declared the right of secession and the necessity for it. Commissioners from other states spoke, and at night restless crowds held impromptu parades that climaxed with spontaneous speeches. A correspondent from Charleston sent stories to South Carolina describing the scenes. Captain H. R. Amaker's Tallahassee Guards and Captain P. B. Brokaw's Leon Cavalry marched and countermarched. At evening gatherings illuminated by burning torches, the speakers "talk SECESSION *straight, immediate.* Great tumultuous applause greets each orator as he utters the word SECESSION, certainly indicative of the popular feeling on the subject."

FLORIDA SECEDES FROM THE UNION

On January 9, a special committee called for immediate secession, brushing aside George T. Ward's attempt to require statewide popular approval. On January 10, the ordinance of secession passed by a vote of 62 to seven (no dissenting votes came from Leon County), and at 12:22 McGehee declared the ordinance adopted. Florida was the third state to secede (Mississippi had left the Union on January 9). Governor Perry appointed delegates to the regional convention to be held at Montgomery, Alabama.

On January 11, 1861, a huge crowd gathered at the Florida capitol's east portico to witness the formal signing of the secession ordinance. State officials and dignitaries mixed with the populace as the document was read. As each delegate's name was called, he approached the convention secretary and affixed his signature. Before signing, Ward held his pen aloft and said, "When I die I want it inscribed upon my tombstone that I was the last man to give up the ship." When another, the Reverend James B. Owens, signed, he declared, "Unlike my friend Colonel Ward, I want it inscribed upon my tombstone that I was the FIRST man to quit the old rotten hulk." Finally, convention President McGehee proclaimed to the cheering audience that Florida was "a free and independent nation." Cannons boomed; Kate, Prince Murat's widow, fired one of them. Governor-elect Milton presented the convention "a beautifully wrought flag of three stars." Amid the speeches that followed, few noticed the 65-year-old Call, who cried bitter tears at what he had witnessed.

Florida's role in the Civil War hardly matches that of Virginia, but it has been neglected badly in general and specialized accounts. With a population of only 140,424 (61,745 of them slaves), not many male whites were of fighting age. Yet at least 15,000 Floridians served the Confederacy, 13,800 of them seeing service outside the state. At least 1,200 whites were in the Union armies, a number almost matched by blacks. Some 5,000 Floridians died from wounds or diseases. The encounter at Olustee (or Ocean Pond) in February 1864 was the only major battle fought within the state. Yet almost 140 military events occurred in Florida. They included evacuations, occupations, expeditions, seizures, engagements, reconnaissances, raids, skirmishes, bombardments, naval actions, captures, coastal raids, recaptures, reoccupations, and attacks.

Perez B. Brokaw, captain of the Leon Cavalry, led his troops in torchlight demonstration during the secession convention.

Monroe Street, looking north from Pensacola, much as it appeared when Florida seceded in 1861.

The flag of three stars was adopted at the end of the secession convention.

Leon County was among the state's leaders in furnishing men for the war effort. The county supplied six companies of infantry, three of cavalry, and two of light artillery. Three locals served in the Confederate States Navy and six surgeons went to the front. About 1,450 men enlisted directly from Leon County, and numerous residents volunteered at other places. Leon County supplied 30 captains, a lieutenant colonel, ten colonels, and two generals, T. W. Brevard and W. G. M. Davis.

Emotionalism and patriotism gave Floridians confidence in the face of overwhelming odds. The state had practically no industry; the anticipated exchange of cotton for British manufactured products was negated by an effective blockade of the coast. Transportation was hampered by inadequate roads, and the state had only 400 miles of railroads, none connected to lines in nearby states. In addition a 1,200-mile coastline had to be defended.

Still, Florida had an outstanding governor, John Milton (1807-1865). Born in Georgia, Milton practiced law in several southern states before moving to Jackson County, Florida. He served in the Second Seminole War and later established Sylvania, his plantation near Marianna. Milton served in the Florida house of representatives and was elected governor as an advocate of secession. A superb wartime leader, Milton was one of the few southern governors able to work with the enigmatic Jefferson Davis, selected by the Montgomery convention as president of the Confederate States of America. In February 1861, the Florida convention unanimously approved the state's membership in the new nation.

"WEAVILS" AND SAND FLIES

James Jewel served in the Confederate Army as a private. Much of his time was spent in the various camps, especially Brokaw and Leon, around Tallahassee. He wrote many letters home to his family in Oglethorpe County, Georgia. Most of the letters, including the excerpts included here, were to his sister Sallie. Jewel recounted conditions in north Florida:

[April 15, 1863] "Our Quartermaster went up to Tallahassee Monday to get our rations for this week but he came back yesterday without anything at all the excuse was the Quartermasters wife was sick and he would not attend to giving out our rations. There is at least four companies that draw rations there the same day with ours and if they are like ours they were out of some thing to eat. So we shelled some corn yesterday and sent to the mill and got a little meal. I reckon we will have to live on dry bread till the Quartermasters wife gets well or steal some hogs. He promised to send our rations down today. I think it very hard that four or five hundred men should be put off in such a manner as that through the carelessness of one good for nothing scamp. For he is not worthy of a home in the confederacy let alone an office in the army. . . . Well I reckon I had just as well stop writing such as this for fear I will make you think we are suffering for something to eat. I had got so I have cornbred and can eat it without any thing else and it is very sorry at that, the corn is half eat up with the weavils.

[March 23, 1863] There is a new fashion telegraph from Tallahassee to St Marks from any thing that I have ever seen before. The news is carried by sentinels or watch man posted abord the rail road in little houses and some of them have tent as far a part as they can see each other and they have flags of different kinds and by the wave of the flag they under stang each other. At night they use lights in the same way. So they can operate at any time except foggy or rainy weather they all have spyglasses to look through. Such a thing as that would be expensive in our country as it is so hilly they could not see far. Here they are near two miles apart.

[May 3rd, 1863] I recon you have heard of the sand fly. What sort of things do you think they are. I thought before I came down here that they were something like a house fly but they are nothing more than a gnat you have no idea how bad they bit. They were worse here yesterday evening and last night than I have every seen before and in fact they were so bad this morning that any one could hardly [stand it]. But it is raining now and they dont bit. You may think when the black gnats bit they hurt but these are the worst. I have often thought of the fellow that was asked if the mosquetoes were bad and as knocking as hard as he could to keep them off but sayed just below here they are pretty bad. That is the way here if you say the sand flies are bad here some body will say that they are worse down below here.

The east portico of the Capitol, where the formal signing of the secession ordinance took place, on January 11, 1861.

Richard Keith Call, second congressional delegate and third and fifth territorial governor (1836-39, 1841-44).

THE CIVIL WAR ERUPTS

Florida had prepared for war in the fall of 1860 by appropriating military funds and reorganizing the state militia. Action followed. The United States arsenal at Chattahoochee in Gadsden County was seized by the Quincy Guards on January 5, 1861. Next, Fort Marion (the Castillo de San Marcos), the Federal garrison at Saint Augustine, surrendered on January 7. In the extreme northeast, Fort Clinch on Amelia Island was strategically important. Nearby was Fernandina, crucial as a rail connection with Cedar Key on the Gulf Coast. Both the fort and the town were occupied by Florida troops a few days after Fort Marion was taken. In addition, the Floridians removed the lenses from the lighthouse at Saint Augustine and Jupiter (north of Fort Lauderdale), deactivating them and hampering night operations by Federal naval forces.

The Confederates wanted to take possession of strategically important Key West, guarded by Fort Taylor and by Fort Jefferson in the Dry Tortugas. Alert action by the Federals prevented Confederate success. Despite yellow-fever epidemics, the citizens and soldiers survived on quinine—and whisky—and Key West remained secure for the duration of the Civil War.

What rightfully has been called the "American tragedy" almost began at Pensacola. With 2,876 people, Pensacola was Florida's largest town and had important federal installations—Fort Barrancas, Fort McRee, and an extensive navy yard, all on the mainland, and Fort Pickens on Santa Rosa Island, a narrow strip of land fronting the city. Fort Pickens commanded the entrance to Pensacola Bay. By January 12, Floridians had control of Pensacola and the mainland forts, but Lieutenant Adam J. Slemmer moved his men to the sanctuary of Fort Pickens. Lieutenant Slemmer refused to surrender, and a southern assault threatened to trigger the war— an event not yet desired by either side. Major Robert J. Anderson was involved at the same time in a similar standoff at Fort Sumter in the harbor at Charleston, South Carolina. Union forts on southern soil challenged the independence of the Confederacy. Sympathetic to the South and hoping to avoid war, Democratic President James Buchanan maintained a precarious status quo until the Republicans took over in March. Lincoln's decision to reinforce Forts Sumter and Pickens led to the crisis of April 12, 1861, when the first shot was fired at Fort Sumter.

The South concentrated troops at Pensacola— including two companies from Leon County—but no immediate action followed the bombardment at Fort Sumter. However, events in South Carolina galvanized

Theodore Washington Brevard was one of two Confederate generals from Leon County.

the North and the South. Lincoln called for volunteers, and the Upper South joined the Lower South in secession. The Confederate capital was shifted from Montgomery, Alabama to Richmond, Virginia, to be near the center of action. The waters of Pensacola Bay became the scene of thrusts and counterthrusts, and the first shedding of blood in Florida occurred on September 16, 1861. On October 9 the Confederates attacked Fort Pickens. They withdrew from Santa Rosa Island without taking the fort, but got the better of the fighting. The engagement resulted in the first two casualties from Leon County, Captain Richard H. Bradford and Private William Roth. Bradford, a member of an important planter family, lay in state in the Madison County courthouse and in Tallahassee before being buried in the family cemetery. Governor John Milton gave the eulogy, and in December the name of New River County (established in 1858) was changed to Bradford County in the captain's honor.

Throughout the fall and winter of 1862, artillery

duels took place at Pensacola, but when Confederate troops were needed in the Upper South, General Braxton B. Bragg ordered the town evacuated. On May 10, Union forces received the surrender of the city. The South lost an excellent port, and Pensacola remained in Union hands throughout the war.

To Governor Milton's anguish, the pattern of removing troops from the state had been set. The Richmond government considered Florida's defense relatively unimportant. General Robert E. Lee assigned priority only to holding Apalachicola, gateway to the Lower South via the Apalachicola-Chattahoochee river system. As soldiers were withdrawn, disaster struck. In January 1862, a Federal amphibian force staged a devastating raid on Cedar Key, and in March a Union land and sea operation easily recaptured Fernandina. For the remainder of the war, Fernandina remained an outpost populated by contrabands—blacks who escaped into the protection of United States forces.

An expedition from the South Atlantic Blockading

The railroad between Cedar Key and Fernandina was a vital supply line.

William Denham, a West Florida Seminary cadet and soldier, was captured near Jacksonville after the Battle of Olustee.

Squadron captured Saint Augustine on March 11, 1862. The city stayed under Union control, although the garrison was confined largely to the town limits by Confederate guerrillas who waited at the outskirts. Part of the same Federal force took temporary command of Jacksonville—adding insult to injury, a band played "Yankee Doodle." Jacksonville was taken again in the fall of 1862, and would be occupied by Union forces four times during the war.

As Florida's chief port, Apalachicola was important for blockade runners. The East Gulf Blockading Squadron soon appeared, effectively preventing ships from entering and leaving Apalachicola and Saint Marks, where inbound goods were transported to Tallahassee by rail and carried in wagons to the nearest Georgia railroad at Thomasville. At Apalachicola, defensive positions were erected around the town and on Saint Vincent Island in the bay. The lighthouse lenses of the beacon on nearby Saint George Island were removed, but Confederate requisitions of troops rendered the

A five-dollar and a ten-dollar bill issued by Florida in 1861.

United States gunboat Mohawk *chases the Confederate steamer* Spray *into the Saint Marks River, 1862.*

town defenseless. In March 1862, an invasion force captured the town and left. From then on, Apalachicola existed in a twilight zone—from time to time both Confederate and Union forces appeared. Meantime, the Confederates who had moved out placed obstructions in the Apalachicola River to prevent Union gunboats from going upstream. The blockading squadron became ever more effective and performed important work in breaking up and destroying Confederate saltworks on the Gulf.

THE CONFEDERATES WIN AT OLUSTEE

The battle of Olustee (Ocean Pond) on February 20, 1864, had a background both military and political. The military objectives included confiscating cotton, lumber, and turpentine; recruiting blacks for soldiers; reoccupying Jacksonville; and moving into the interior—perhaps slashing to Tallahassee and cutting off the important supply routes of

cattle and agricultural produce for the Confederate armies. Politically, the idea was to establish a civil government in Florida. A victory would look good and—since it was an election year—would earn votes (including Florida's) for the Lincoln administration or for Lincoln's rival, Salmon P. Chase, secretary of the treasury.

Jacksonville fell, but as the Union force of about 5,000 men commanded by General Truman A. Seymo[ur] moved into the interior, it encountered problems of supply and communication. It also encountered the Confederates. For once, the southern personnel equalled the numbers of their foes. The opposing forces met at Olustee, thirteen miles from Lake City. The gray-clad troops were commanded by General Joseph Finegan. The ensuing engagement began sho[rt]ly after noon and lasted until after 6:00 p.m. when the Union forces retreated. A tune some of the Federal soldiers had sung ended on a sour note: "We're boun[d] for Tallahassee in the morning." Confederate casualtie[s] came to 946, while the Federal total was 1,861. It was [a] rare Confederate victory, although the Federal troops withdrew into Jacksonville without a massive sur-

ender. The southerners managed to capture a wide variety of military arms and supplies.

Other action in 1864 took place in the panhandle area of west Florida. In September and October, Brigadier General Alexander Asboth led a raid of about 700 men from Pensacola to Marianna. Skirmishing along the way, the invaders found brief but furious opposition at the Jackson County seat of government. Fighting from Marianna's streets and buildings, the rebel force of 150 was made up of young boys and old men fittingly called the "Cradle and Grave Company." Finally, the Union soldiers prevailed and took away contrabands, horses, mules, and cattle.

A desperate Governor Milton called for the massive arming of every male who could lift a gun. Yankee raids continued, with destruction and loss of life. Tallahassee lived in fear of a Union attack. Logic dictated that the move would come first against Saint Marks and would be followed by a march against the capital. Governor Milton was so fearful that he kept his family at the safer refuge of Sylvania—he even employed an English governess to live at the plantation and tutor his children. The long-dreaded thrust came in March 1865.

A UNION INVASION FAILS

In the fog-shrouded waters of Apalachee Bay, a Union fleet—some of the ships bearing black soldiers and a scattering of white officers— rendezvoused in late February. Authorities in Washington knew nothing about the expedition until it was over. Various objectives were involved. An attempt by the rebels to run the blockade at Saint Marks, where 2,000 bales of cotton were stored, could be thwarted. Saint Marks and the fort there could be secured, and a march against Tallahassee then would be possible. The capital was known to contain contrabands and cotton. Its surrender would deal Floridians a telling psychological blow and would lower their will to fight. Beyond that, it was a chance to win glory by mounting a last large-scale military operation in Florida.

Commander R. W. Shufeldt and General John Newton, the ranking navy and army officers, devised a five-part strategy. They would land a party at Saint Marks lighthouse and take possession of the East River bridge. Simultaneously, they would land a larger force

Drawing of the battle of Olustee, February 20, 1864.

and be ready to march the following morning. On March 4, they would move to Newport, cross the Saint Marks River at the bridge there, destroy any Confederate works, and take the town of Saint Marks from the rear or strike the connecting railroad to Tallahassee. They would move the gunboats upriver, dropping off a force to cover the land expedition and prevent an attack from the rear, and would capture the batteries at Saint Marks. Then they would land other units to destroy bridges and trestles over the Ochlocknee and Aucilla rivers.

The East River bridge was taken, but the main force was delayed when two vessels ran aground. Not until the morning of March 5 was the march begun. By then Tallahassee had been alerted and troops were rushing south to meet the invasion. Lieutenant Colonel George W. Scott and his men skirmished with the Yankees as they moved north. Newton's men found Newport in flame and smoke—the Confederates had fired warehouses, foundries, and mills—and they discovered that the bridge had been dismantled. The Confederates peppered the black troops with rifle fire. Plainly, it was impossible to cross the river. Newton left a contingent of men at Newport, and that night marched six or eight miles north to a place called Natural Bridge. He expected to take the Confederates by surprise.

Tallahassee received news of the landing at 9 p.m. Saturday, March 4, and the whole city and county responded, including a number of cadets from the West Florida Seminary. Some youths who wanted to board the train for the fight were denied permission because they did not have notes from their parents—the Civil War had its share of strange moments and the participation of Tallahassee's "Baby Corps" was one of them. The Confederate defense was coordinated by Major General Samuel "Sam" Jones, who assigned battlefield command to Brigadier General William Miller.

Natural Bridge lay in a swampy area of southern Leon County where the Saint Marks flowed through a series of underground passages, emerging, disappearing, and emerging again in short channels. The Federals reached the spot on March 6, only to find the Confederates waiting. The fighting began almost at daybreak and lasted until 10 p.m. or later. Two Union attacks were repulsed, as Confederate reinforcements arrived throughout the day. The Yankees fell back, pursued by rebel cavalry, retracing their route to the Saint Marks lighthouse and to their ships. The gunboats slated to ascend the river were unsuccessful. One floundered and went aground, and by the time they were ready to resume the attack, the fighting at Natural Bridge was almost over. The Union invasion had failed.

Out of about 700 troops involved, the southerners had three killed and 23 wounded, while the northerners, with about 500 soldiers, suffered casualties of 21 killed, 89 wounded, and 38 missing in action. Two Confederate deserters were caught and executed shortly afterwards.

Joyful celebrations were held when news of the victory reached Tallahassee. Susan Bradford, nineteen-year-old daughter of the county's most prominent physician, wrote, "God has been good to us and the enemy completely routed. . . . After the terrific excitement of the last forty-eight hours Tallahassee should sleep well tonight." When the soldiers returned to the capital, Governor Milton spoke to them in the house of representatives chamber, citing their courage and fighting skill. General Samuel Jones permitted the men to keep their arms and equipment. Soon many Leon countians descended on Natural Bridge to picnic and search for souvenirs.

TALLAHASSEEANS FIGHT DAILY "BATTLES" ON THE HOME FRONT

Tallahassee was the center of Florida's war effort; it housed state government and was Governor Milton's base. As such, the town was a military target, although the citizens exaggerated its importance. Outlying Leon County and Gadsden and Wakulla counties were protected by small garrisons. A number of units were stationed at Quincy, which was considered by soldiers as a much better "duty" than at Camp Leon, about six miles south of Tallahassee, or Camp Brokaw, three miles from Saint Marks. The old outpost at Saint Marks was converted into Fort Ward. Except for the Battle of Natural Bridge, the troops saw little action. An exception came in 1862 when Captain George Scott led his company against a small Union supply base at the mouth of the Aucilla River. The Confederates destroyed the encampment and returned to Tallahassee with twelve prisoners.

Tallahasseeans, for all their apprehension, never erected adequate defenses for the capital. No follow-up occurred to a letter from "Prudence" in the *Florida Sentinel:* "If this city is attacked, shall we run off like so many stampeded mules, or stay and defend it . . .? Let us be prepared at any rate, to give them a warm reception, and to defend the place to the last." The Union move against Saint Marks and the threat posed to Tallahassee caused the citizens to throw up breastworks south of town. The never-used defensive post was euphemistically called Fort Houstoun.

Like other Floridians, the people of Leon County struggled with the problems of health, food, finance, clothing, and shelter. They objected to various levies—general taxes, taxes in kind, impressment taxes—but

Some Union prisoners were held in the yard of the Leon County jail.

Map at the Natural Bridge State Monument showing the movement of Confederate and Federal troops that preceded the March 6, 1864 battle.

Brigadier General William Miller was the battleship commander for Confederate troops at the battle of Natural Bridge.

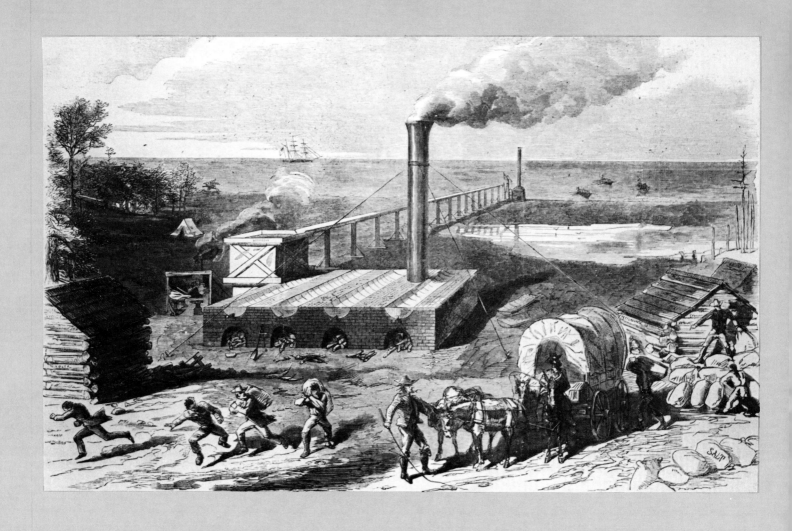

Destruction of a Con-
federate salt factory on
the Florida coast by the
crew of the United States
bark Kingfisher.

Abraham Kurkindolle
Allison, as president of
the Florida senate,
became Florida's sixth
governor when John
Milton, unable to face
the fall of the Confed-
eracy, shot himself to
death on April 1, 1865.

supported programs that provided food and relief for the families of soldiers. They also supported the manufacture of salt which, along with food, was a major contribution of Florida to the Confederacy. In summer 1862, a Tallahassee editor wrote, "Our eyes are now and then gladdened by seeing a parade of [salt] wagons pass by on their way to the coast but we confess we should like to see them pass more frequently." The editor added a poem that made up in earnestness what it lacked in talent:

> Make salt! Make salt!
> Let all make salt who never made before;
> those who have made now only make more—
> Your bread crop now is pretty sure of mankind—
> Your next care be to *save your bacon!*

Prices rose and shortages developed. The women of Leon County proved inventive in devising ersatz products, particularly substitutes for coffee. Home-front residents drank "coffee" made from okra seed, pumpkinseed, acorns, rye, cottonseed, and grits. Children played with homemade dolls and stuffed animals. Christmases were sad times, and some slaves were told that Santa Claus had been killed by Yankees when he tried to run the blockade. One Tallahasseean devised a novel Christmas present: a foot-high rooster made entirely of watermelon seed.

Providing medical care was a major problem. The civilian population—whites and blacks—had to be tended. Wounded Confederates were brought in from time to time, and Tallahassee had the double responsibility of housing and hospitalization for healthy and injured prisoners of war. The City Hotel served as a makeshift hospital, and Dr. Edward Bradford used four small houses on his Pine Hill Plantation as emergency wards. Northern prisoners were held in the city jail yard, the City Hotel, the Masonic-Odd Fellows Hall, and even the Baptist Church. Apparently no one escaped, although security was light and, by the war's end, young boys from the West Florida Seminary were serving as guards.

Tallahasseans showed no lack of patriotism. Early in the war, the carpets from the state capitol were made into blankets and sent to Florida troops. The women from town and country gave silverware to aid in building a gunboat for the state, and donated tablecloths, old linen, and napkins for the Florida hospital in Virginia. Tallahassee had a Ladies' Aid Society, which met in the capitol's house of representatives chamber and made bandages from cherished sheets, tablecloths and petticoats. Throughout the county, women brought out spinning wheels and looms. The resulting homespun was too coarse for bandages, but with it the women proudly clothed their families. A group of Tallahassee women made hats from cotton cloth and palmetto leaves. Called "Dixie Bonnets," they sold for five dollars for men and ten dollars for women.

The citizens staged numerous tableaux, fairs, and suppers. One combination fair and supper in 1863 raised $1,450 for the war effort. In May 1863, the women of Leon, Jefferson, and Madison counties sponsored three nights of theatre at the state capitol. Ticket sales went to "the cause," and the patrons enjoyed *King Lear,* a burlesque entitled *Bombastes Furioso,* and an original melodrama called *Tampa.* Ironically, on the day Lee surrendered—April 9, 1865—a musical concert was staged at the capitol to raise money for the Confederacy.

During much of the war, the citizens held daily prayer meetings at various churches. But by 1864, the belief in military victory had declined drastically. Governor Milton and his administration faced the growing problem of "layouts," men who avoided military service. A serious menace was posed by deserters, who formed a fifth column and cooperated with Union raiders. Bands of deserters attacked the plantations in neighboring counties; the problem was especially bad in Taylor County. The families of some Taylor County deserters once were interned south of Tallahassee. They were transferred later to blockading ships. Although some slaves made successful escapes, most remained and farmed the land. No slave uprising occurred, although many whites lived in fear of such a revolt. The people of Leon County did not look forward to 1865.

THE CONFEDERACY FALLS

After the Battle of Natural Bridge in March 1865, military operations in Florida and on the Gulf coast virtually ceased. Informed of General Ulysses S. Grant's relentless wearing down of Lee's forces in Virginia, Governor Milton became increasingly depressed. He knew the Confederacy he had worked so hard to sustain could not survive. Late in 1864, Milton had addressed the Florida legislature: "If we ever return [to the Union] we shall be compelled to submit to their government and placed in bonds to endure their loathsome embrace. Death would be preferable to reunion! This is the sentiment of all true Southern men." The prospect was one Milton could not face. The despondent governor had his son take him to Sylvania plantation, and there on April 1, Milton shot himself to death. In every way, he was a true casualty of the war.

Abraham K. Allison, the president of the Florida senate, succeeded Milton as governor. Lee surrendered on April 9 and by the middle of the month, Tallahassee was the only Confederate state capital east of the Mississippi River still flying the Stars and Bars. General Joseph E. Johnston surrendered his command to General William Tecumseh Sherman at Durham Station, North Carolina, on April 26. Because Florida was in Johnston's

Major General John G. Foster was military governor of Florida from 1865 to 1867.

View of Tallahassee from the southwest, 1868, shows the United States flag flying over the Union soldiers' camp.

A composite photograph shows members of the Tallahassee Ladies' Soldiers Friend Sewing Society, 1861.

Colonel John Titcomb Sprague was military governor during Reconstruction from April 1, 1867, to July 4, 1868.

department, the general informed Allison of his capitulation. In the meantime, Confederate President Jefferson Davis had fled Richmond and was making his way south toward Florida. Davis and his party were captured at Irwinville, Georgia, on May 10. In separate ventures, other high-ranking Confederates—Secretary of War John Breckinridge and Secretary of State Judah P. Benjamin—escaped the country by way of Florida.

Major General James H. Wilson, with headquarters in Macon, Georgia, was responsible for accepting the surrender of Florida. Delegating the role to Brigadier General Edward M. McCook, Wilson ordered the cavalry officer to "receive the surrender of Confederate and other troops at Tallahassee . . . and its vicinity, together with all public stores." McCook, with 500 men of the Second Indiana Cavalry and the Seventh Kentucky Cavalry, and five staff officers, moved south from Thomasville, Georgia, reaching Tallahassee on May 10.

McCook left the main body of his men four miles north of town and rode into the capital with his officers. Ellen Call, whose father had opposed secession, was a young girl at the time. She remembered being "startled . . . by a cry from our little 'black boy,' of 'Yankees! Yankees!' and I found myself running with the 'rest of the children' to the front to see General McCook and staff enter to take command of our little city." She reported that McCook "made a very modest entrance, respecting the humiliation of our people . . . The General was very properly received by representative men of the place, and the courtesies due him were gracefully extended." The Union officers raised the American flag without any special ceremony and established headquarters at the present Knott home on the corner of Calhoun and Park. The remainder of the Federal troops entered town the next day.

The transition was painful for Floridians, but it took place without incident. Even so, Mary Brown Archer and her younger sister, Margaret, removed the

William Marvin was named provisional governor in July 1865.

state's battle flags from the capitol and hid them in the ceiling of their home—where they stayed until 1878. McCook paroled Confederates and received property, including quartermaster's stores. He exchanged older horses and mules for corn or, in some cases, he loaned livestock to local farmers. Fort Ward at Saint Marks surrendered on May 12, and the formal ceremony at Tallahassee occurred on May 20. State officials, Union soldiers, and a number of newly freed blacks (most white Tallahasseeans remained at home) assembled for the flag raising. A band played "The Star-Spangled Banner" as the ensign unfurled, and a salute was fired for every state in the Union. At sunset a 100-gun salute was fired. McCook had explained to the former slaves that they were now free. Having accomplished his mission, McCook left Tallahassee on May 21. Although a few units did not surrender until June 8, the Civil War ended for Florida on May 20, 1865, when the United States flag floated over Tallahassee.

RECONSTRUCTION BEGINS

The era known to history as Reconstruction derives its name, of course, from the controversial decade during which the states of the Confederacy were brought back into the Union. The process was slower and more painful in some states than in others, but in all of them, it forced the acceptance of profound changes. The South was defeated militarily, devastated economically, and exhausted spiritually and emotionally. Not the least of events was a complete change in the labor system—the former slaves were now free. Their work no longer could be commanded. Since no constitutional provisions existed that dealt with a state's leaving or being readmitted to the Union, complexities abounded and mistakes were made. The problems were exacerbated by the length

The first page of the 1865 Florida Constitution.

David S. Walker was elected eighth governor in December 1865.

and bitterness of the war. Thus, the "new South" inherited legacies from the old South and was confronted with new challenges and realities.

Tallahassee and Leon County adjusted to the new order, and to the social, political, and economic changes that were part of Reconstruction and the following decades. Political reconstruction in town and county and in the rest of Florida needs to be put in proper perspective. Scholars and students of the era see Reconstruction as a time of significant transition, with good and bad results. On an individual basis they point out rogues and heroes, but neither the Republican nor the Democratic party emerges as having a monopoly on good or evil, on accomplishment or failure.

When the war ended, Governor Allison set about to restore civilian peacetime elections. He moved too rapidly, however, and Allison's administration ended abruptly on May 22, 1865, when Florida was put under martial law. The governor was imprisoned for a brief period. Five companies of Federal troops—many of them blacks—were stationed at Tallahassee, and other units were scattered around the state. Soldiers under the overall command of Major General John S. Foster played a large role in maintaining law and order. Although their presence was resented by white Leon countians, the military officials were neither harsh nor unfair. On July 23, President Andrew Johnson, who had succeeded the assassinated Lincoln, appointed William Marvin of Key West as provisional governor. While Marvin had opposed secession, he was not widely disliked by white Floridians.

Working with General Foster, Governor Marvin called for the election of delegates to the constitutional convention and went across the state preaching moderation. No blacks participated, and fewer than 7,000 whites cast ballots. The low turnout stemmed from the unsettled times and the requirement that voters take the oath of loyalty to the United States or

Harrison M. Reed, ninth governor, served from July 4, 1868, to January 7, 1873. He was impeached four times but not convicted, and served his full term in office.

Ossian B. Hart, tenth governor, served from January 7, 1873, to March 18, 1874.

have a special presidential pardon.

The convention met in Tallahassee in the fall of 1865; it ratified the Thirteenth Amendment, declaring slavery unconstitutional; repealed the ordinance of secession; and repudiated the Confederate war debt. The constitution which emerged from the convention failed to grant blacks the right to vote. In the elections that followed, David S. Walker—a Whig, former legislator, and state supreme-court justice—was elected governor without opposition. Subsequent laws passed in 1866, known collectively as the black code, were aimed specifically at the former slaves, and narrowly and harshly circumscribed their civil and political rights.

The events in Florida were duplicated in other parts of the South in the period immediately after the war. Former rebels were elected to office (Alexander Stephens, vice-president of the Confederacy, was elected United States Senator from Georgia), and blacks were restricted severely in the enjoyment of their newly won liberty. The actions of a seemingly unrepentant South, particularly the black codes, stirred a strong negative reaction in the North. Florida's elected representatives to Congress, like those of other former Confederate states, were refused their seats by the Republican majority. Congress strengthened the Freedmen's Bureau (a federal agency created earlier to aid the newly freed bondsmen), passed a civil-rights law, and drafted the Fourteenth Amendment. The lenient Reconstruction policies of Lincoln and Johnson were abandoned in favor of what became known as Radical (more punitive) Reconstruction, as crafted by Congress.

All the former Confederate states except Tennessee rejected the Fourteenth Amendment. They acted on the advice of President Johnson, who had broken openly with Congress, and—in the case of Florida—on the advice of Governor Walker. In response to what northerners construed as Florida's defiance, lack of cooperation, and racial tension, the state, along with the rest of the South, faced a series of acts that instituted Radical—or Congressional—Reconstruction. Colonel John T. Sprague, commander of the district of Florida, established headquarters in Tallahassee and declared martial law on April 1, 1867. The state was once again under military rule.

FLORIDA'S POLITICAL ALIGNMENTS EMERGE

Florida's basic political alignments became the Conservative Democrats (mostly native whites) and the Republicans. The latter had three components: native whites, who were scornfully labeled "scalawags"; whites recently arrived from the North ("carpetbaggers"), who were divided into two rival groups; and blacks, who were loyal to the party that freed them and comprised the majority foot soldiers of the party. Further distinctions existed among the Republicans which included the Freedmen's

Josiah T. Walls was elected to the United States House of Representatives in 1870 and 1874.

Jonathan C. Gibbs was secretary of state from 1868 to 1873 and superintendent of public instruction from 1873 to 1874.

Bureau, important politically because of its connection with the blacks; army personnel and federal office-holders; and some private businessmen. The Lincoln Brotherhood and the Loyal League were two organizations led by carpetbaggers who sought black support. The scalawags were directed by a moderate, Ossian B. Hart of Jacksonville.

Few white Democrats participated in the November 1867 election for delegates to a new constitutional convention. It met at Tallahassee in January 1868, under highly charged and confusing circumstances. The Loyal Leaguers took temporary control and, turning the meeting into a nominating convention, named a candidate for governor. The Lincoln Brotherhood seceded temporarily from the convention, only to return and claim control. The episode deteriorated into a standoff. Governor Walker could do little until General George C. Meade arrived and recognized the legitimacy of the seceders—The Lincoln Brotherhood. That faction drafted the constitution of 1868. Its most important provision awarded the right to vote to black males. Overall, it was a good document which provided—for the first time—for a public-school system, and for a homestead exemption.

In the governor's race, the seceders' faction nominated Harrison Reed, a carpetbagger from Wisconsin. Samuel Walker, a Florida Unionist who had opposed secession, was picked by the regular Radical Republicans. The Conservative Democrats named George W. Scott, a Civil War hero. When the votes were counted, Reed emerged victorious, and the Republicans gained control of both houses of the legislature. The party of Lincoln took power on June 8, 1868; Florida ratified the Fourteenth Amendment on June 9; civil government was resumed and on July 25, Congress accepted Florida into the Union.

Reed faced bitter opposition, but despite being impeached four times, he served his four-year term. Nothing the Republicans accomplished suited the Conservative Democrats, who were determined to regain political control and to reestablish white supremacy. Some whites attacked what they considered Republican excess and corruption with violence. The Ku Klux Klan terrorized blacks and Republicans in the state, especially in Jackson County, in an effort to reduce their participation in government. Blacks never received equitable compensation for their contribution to the Republican party. Josiah T. Walls, a black, was elected to the national House of Representatives, although he lost his office in two contested elections. Jonathon Gibbs, a black, was appointed as Florida's secretary of state. The Republicans kept their organization together long enough to elect moderate Ossian B. Hart, the scalawag leader, as governor. His Democratic opponent was Leon County planter William D. Bloxham.

Hart died in office in 1874 and was succeeded by Lieutenant Governor Marcellus L. Stearns, another moderate. As a carpetbagger from Maine, Stearns faced a united Democratic party in the 1876 election, which

Governor Marcellus L. Stearns greets Harriet Beecher Stowe (lady in black on sixth step) at the Capitol.

73

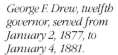

Members of the Florida legislature assemble on the capitol steps, circa 1875.

George F. Drew, twelfth governor, served from January 2, 1877, to January 4, 1881.

combined a presidential contest with the gubernatorial race. By then the Democrats had ceased Klan activities and had learned more subtle ways of influencing black voters, especially by economic coercion.

The Democrats met at Quincy and nominated George F. Drew, a former Whig from New Hampshire who had moved to Georgia and later had established a large sawmill at Ellaville, Florida. Drew was a Unionist during the war, but Florida's white voters supported him. The Republicans were split, but finally named Stearns to succeed himself.

FLORIDA CASTS A DECISIVE VOTE

At the national level, the Democrats nominated Samuel J. Tilden of New York to oppose the Republican choice, Rutherford B. Hayes of Ohio. As the votes came in, it appeared that Tilden had won, but the Republicans contested the returns from Florida, Louisiana, and South Carolina. If

Hayes received all the electoral votes from those states, he would be the president. Since so much was at stake, Tallahassee occupied the center stage of national attention, and officials of both parties, known as "visiting statesmen," descended on the capital to witness the vote count. To prevent possible violence, twelve companies of federal troops, including an artillery unit, were sent to Tallahassee. The state canvassing board gave Hayes a slight edge. Some counties contested the returns, and the board declared a second time that Hayes had won. Angry Democratic electors certified that Tilden had been elected. Thus, two sets of returns were forwarded to Washington.

The state election also was contested. Again, claims and counterclaims were made. Without going behind the returns in disputed counties, the Florida Supreme Court decreed that Drew and the Democrats had narrowly defeated Stearns and the Republicans (24,179 to 23,984). After some tense moments, Drew was sworn in on January 12, 1877.

Unable to decide who should count the electoral votes for president, Congress appointed a fifteen-member federal commission comprised of five senators, five representatives, and five Supreme Court Justices. The vote was eight to seven for Hayes in Florida, and that majority held in the other two contested states as well. Hayes was declared the winner, with Florida's official vote set at 23,849 for Hayes and 22,923 for Tilden. By accepting the verdict, the South supposedly would receive internal improvement funds, a place in the presidential cabinet, and the removal of the last federal troops.

Republican Reconstruction was over in Florida. Historians still speculate over who really carried the state elections in 1876. It would be 90 years—1966—before the Republicans elected another Florida governor. The party had continued to nominate candidates for the office; sometimes they ran well, but they never won. Conservative Democrats, known as Bourbons, solidified their power with a pledge of honesty in government, limited spending of state moneys, and white supremacy. The Democrats demonstrated their mastery of the state's political environment in 1885, when they wrote a conservative constitution. The new document provided for the enactment of a poll tax and other devices to control the black vote.

"TALLAHASSEE. . . A MILITARY CAMP"

*T*allahasseeans doubtless were enthralled by the attention directed toward their town during the "disputed election" of 1876. One editor expressed his contempt for the proceedings —and for the Republicans:

Tallahassee has been converted into a military camp. Two generals, some forty captains and lieutenants and 500 and odd private soldiers garrison it. Shame upon the man who represented to the general government that there has been or is the slightest necessity for any such thing. Pity for the country that has a government knowing so little about its real condition. Forgetting for a moment the enormous expense incurred in bringing these troops here, and the bad purposes of Governor Stearns in procuring their presence, it appears farcical. It looks as if Stearns had perpetrated a huge joke on the President or Secretary of War. And we have really laughed over the thought. We doubt not that officers and men have wondered time and again why such a farce should be enacted. But there is a method in all this madness. Governor Stearns knows he has been defeated by a large majority of the honest voters, and he has played upon the authorities at Washington to get these troops here, hoping that their presence would deter our people from insisting upon an honest count and that the troops would thereby aid him. He did not think General Grant would issue the

instructions found in his telegram of the 10th inst. to General Sherman. Ah, Governor, our people knew as soon as they saw this telegram that you had been badly beat at your own little game. You are mistaken, Governor, if you think they are frightened. So far as you and your feelings and purposes are concerned there is not a Democrat in Florida who does not feel that each soldier here is a better friend to Florida and the rights of honest men than you are. They had rather entrust their lives, liberty, property and bacon to any honorable soldier than to you. Many of our citizens were desirous before the election that troops should be had on election day, as they knew what teachings the colored people had received from your supporters. None of them will find their presence objectionable now. In fact, they will enliven our town, increase trade and be a source of entertainment and interest. We bespeak the kindest treatment at the hands of our people, and know they will receive it.

[From the Tallahassee Weekly Floridian, *November 14, 1876]*

FROM RECONSTRUCTION TO THE JAZZ AGE

Workers at the Wahnish Cigar Factory on south Macomb Stret, now the site of McGowan Lighting Center.

Postwar landowners in Leon County adjusted to a free labor force and an economy largely void of liquid cash. In Tallahassee, the Lewis State Bank continued to operate, and a Freedmen's Bank functioned briefly in the old Union Bank building before failing in 1874. The 766 black depositors lost a little more than $30,000. In 1895, George W. Saxon converted his private facility into the Capital City Bank, and by 1912 four banks were in operation.

During the 1870s, former planters retained land ownership but divided their acreages into small farms. They could not pay cash wages and their workers could not pay rent, so the sharecropping or tenant-farming system was worked out. A tenant signed a lien note in the winter, agreeing to supply his labor in return for a portion of the crop. The owner agreed to furnish the tenant with supplies, directly or through one of numerous small crossroads stores owned by commission or "furnishing" merchants. When the crop—invariably cotton because it could be converted immediately into cash—was harvested and sold, the proceeds were divided. It was a bizarre credit system, prompting a long, pitiless chain of debt which doomed the South's sharecroppers to a cruel bondage. Under the system, prices went down, surpluses piled up, and the soil was depleted. Firmly entrenched by 1880, the tenant-farming system worsened by 1920 and would not be broken until after World War II.

Until 1920, white Leon countians sought to improve matters by attracting white immigrants. Small, independently owned farms would, it was believed, make the county wealthy. Yet the area had little in-dustry, commercial transportation was lacking, and only a few new settlers came in. With rare exceptions, hard economic times haunted the countryside until the prosperity brought on by World War I. In 1890, Leon County's population had declined from its total in 1880, although the black population steadily increased, with a ratio of approximately five to one over whites.

Community leaders preached the gospel of agricultural diversification. A variety of vegetables supported truck farming on a modest scale. Orchards were established; the LeConte pear was especially popular. Oil from the nuts of tung trees—referred to locally as "Chinese varnish trees"—was used in the manufacture of paints and varnishes. After 1900, several tung orchards were planted, particularly in the county's eastern portion. John A. Craig and Emile DuBois grew grapes and made wine. A few farmers derived profits from peanuts, and others predicted that the kudzu vine would be profitable. A limited number of farmers planted tobacco, and several cigar factories were opened in Tallahassee around 1900. Price fluctuations made their stability uncertain.

By the turn of the century, a much-heralded plan was to divide Leon County's land into small plots devoted to pecan orchards. Owners could build homes on their property, and Leon County would become the nation's pecan capital. A few tracts were opened, attracting some immigrants. Success was limited because of the extreme care required by pecan trees, and neither the year-to-year crop nor the price was consistent.

Inadequate transportation remained an obstacle

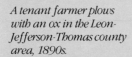
A tenant farmer plows with an ox in the Leon-Jefferson-Thomas county area, 1890s.

The Union Bank, at its original site on the west side of Adams Street between College and Park avenues, in the early 1870s when it was a freedman's bank.

Wagons of cotton were posed on the way to the depot in this previously unpublished view looking north on Monroe Street from College (the Clinton) Avenue, in the early 1870s.

o prosperity. Saint Marks became a sleepy fishing village, losing its importance as a port. Tallahassee had east-west rail connections, but, more importantly, no direct lines to northern markets. Finally, in 1903, a connection with Bainbridge gave access to Georgia railroads and the North.

Success was achieved in the timber and turpentine industries. Leon County's livestock production also increased. Beef cattle and hogs became more numerous and of better quality, but the country's largest profits came from the dairy industry. In 1900, the county led the state in milk production, a rank it still held in 1920. Richard H. Bradford and his son, R. F., descendants of the pioneer Bradford family, were among the leading dairymen. William Cooper, a Scotsman, and Jan Donk, from the Netherlands, also were important in the dairy industry.

In the economically bleak period from the 1870s to the 1890s, civic leaders in Tallahassee formed the Middle Florida Agricultural and Mechanical Society, which sponsored fairs from 1879 to 1885. The association members bought property just north of Tallahassee for a fairgrounds that included a half-mile racetrack and a grandstand. William D. Bloxham and other leaders were pleased with the results of the first fair. Premiums were awarded for the best livestock entries as well as for field crops and vegetables. Events included trotting races, flat races, and—for human competitors—foot and bag races. The patrons marveled at the phonographs and telephones on display. The old ring tournaments of antebellum times were revived and attracted wide interest.

The association's seven fairs featured local militia companies in competitive drill. Railroads reduced their fares for out-of-town patrons. Blacks participated freely, entering the various livestock and crop contests and furnishing an excellent brass band. Occasional bad

weather and waning interest caused the association to disband. In 1887, the Tallahassee Stock Show was held at the grounds, and the Leon County Farmers' Alliance sponsored a fair there in 1890. The fairs were festive events that brought the town and country people together and greatly boosted their morale.

LEON COUNTY'S LAND OWNERSHIP CHANGES

By the 1880s, north Leon County's red hills had changed significantly in land ownership and land use. The small farms, remnants of old plantations, and tracts of forest were transformed into large hunting plantations by affluent northern sportsmen. The northerners had begun to come to southeast Georgia, seeking relief from harsh winters. In addition, the pine-scented lands were thought to aid those suffering from pulmonary ailments. The visitors (prominent among them was the Hanna family of Cleveland, Ohio) quickly discovered the area's attractions for sportsmen. Few regions in America equaled its game-bird terrain.

Soon southerners—burdened by debts, taxes, unproductive soil, and low prices—were selling land to eager Yankee buyers. Inevitably, desirable property became scarce in Georgia, and the purchasers moved into Leon County. A few native Leon countians also developed estates.

The antebellum plantation system was resurrected in the hill country, often on the old plantations themselves—even their names were retained. Yet an important difference existed: the land was taken out of row-crop farming to provide bird life, especially the bobwhite quail, for hunting. Grains, legumes, and various crops were integrated into the plan. The planta-

The flier "Features of the Hill Country, Florida," was written in 1894 by Richard C. Long to encourage immigration to Leon County.

In the 1880s and 1890s, the Florida Railway and Navigation Company was Tallahassee's rail link to the east and west. This photograph of a 4-4-0 engine dates from 1885.

tions employed large staffs, including sharecroppers who operated on a limited scale.

Two Scotsmen, Edmund H. Ronalds and his brother Tennent Ronalds, purchased Leon County's old Live Oak plantation and changed it into a hunting preserve. Their example was duplicated by Edward Beadel of New York City and later by his nephew, Henry L. Beadel, who pieced together several tracts along the shore of Lake Iamonia. Their property eventually became Tall Timbers, today an important center for environmental research. Dr. Edward A. Bradford's prewar Horseshoe plantation and land around it were bought by the Philadelphia industrialist Clement A. Griscom and were developed by his daughter Frances Griscom. Others who developed plantations included Udo M. Fleischmann at Welaunee plantation and Lewis S. Thompson at Sunny Hill.

The plantations were the center of an active social life during the fall and winter hunting season. Dinner parties, small hunts, and field trials enjoyed—and continue to enjoy—wide popularity. Although the "Yankee" visitors remained a colony unto themselves, some local people participated in their activities. More importantly, they furnished a badly needed payroll for many Leon countians, and contributed significantly to the county's tax base. In addition, the owners expanded beyond the sporting aspects of their plantations to combine reforestation, conservation, and scientific experimentation.

Northern plantation owners voluntarily removed

Leon County land from agricultural production, but many native farmers were forced to abandon their fields. They could not make a living by farming. By 1910 Leon was no longer Florida's banner agricultural county. The sharecropping system held its victims in thralldom, and King Cotton was an ailing monarch. Between 1900 and 1910, Leon County lost population, but Tallahassee gained. Some farmers were moving away from the county, but more were moving in to Tallahassee. They were not being replaced by immigrants.

BLACKS STRUGGLE FOR EQUALITY

At the end of the Civil War, Leon County's more than 9,000 slaves were freed. The new citizens occupied a special place: apart from and yet an important part of white-dominated society. Their status as free persons, citizens, and voters was established by the Thirteenth, Fourteenth, and Fifteenth amendments, all ratified between 1865 and 1870. After Reconstruction ended, blacks were not disfranchised, although their votes were manipulated and controlled. In time, the voting rights guaranteed by the United States Constitution were circumvented by local and state laws and by the Florida constitution of 1885, which legalized property and literacy requirements, the poll tax, and the white primary. Between 1876 and 1920, blacks in Leon County, like blacks elsewhere, were relegated to second-class citizenship.

Local blacks faced discrimination in housing and education. In the county's limited industrial sector, blacks accepted inferior jobs. In an economy dominated by agriculture, a number of black farmers became landowners, but most worked as sharecroppers. They soon were joined in their misery by increasing numbers of white tenant farmers.

Around the turn of the century, extreme "Jim Crow" laws were enacted at the state and local levels. The measures established segregation in public transportation, restaurants, theatres, parks and other facilities. Southern blacks were often the victims of lynch law, but Leon County and Tallahassee experienced far less racial violence than other counties in the region. Between 1889 and 1918, of the 160 lynchings of blacks recorded in Florida, two were in Leon County. Ironically, while blacks did not control their own fate, in 1920 they comprised a majority of the population of 18,059—about two-thirds.

It is important to remember that the strict letter of the law was not always carried out. Blacks and whites had daily contacts—casual, social, and business. Relations were often cordial and based on mutual respect and friendship. Blacks worked hard to open businesses, buy farms, own homes, and obtain educations. They developed a strong community based on family relationships and largely formed around their town and country churches. Under adverse conditions, they achieved remarkable progress.

The Freedmen's Bureau and northern-based religious and philanthropic groups operated schools for blacks in Leon County as early as 1865. John Wallace, a black, established a school in 1866 on William D. Bloxham's plantation. The Republican legislature of 1869 passed a law providing for public education, and the Lincoln Academy of Tallahassee soon qualified as one of the state's few black high schools (the building was burned in 1872). From the first, public schools were segregated, a separation made mandatory by the state constitution of 1885. Even so, that document required the operation of a public-school system. After the United States Supreme Court issued its "separate-but-equal" doctrine in the case of Plessy vs. Ferguson (1896), the South conformed to the first part of the phrase while ignoring the second. For example, the highest-paid teacher in the county in 1900 was a white male who received $85 a month; the lowest-paid teacher was a black woman whose salary was $15 a month. Consolidation of schools increased by 1920, but not much progress had been made. Despite 2,082 more black schoolchildren than white, the county spent $66,663.38 on white schools and $12,819.78 on black schools.

In 1887, the Tallahassee State Normal College for Colored Students was established by state law. Thomas De Saille Tucker—a native of Sierra Leone, West Africa, who had been educated in the United States—became the first president. Finally located on an impressive campus in the hills south of the capital, the institution struggled for state funds and recognition. By 1900, 153

THE "WRESTLESS," HUSTLING CAPITAL

A contest was held in 1915 to select a slogan which would convey Tallahassee's special appeal and attract new residents and investors. The contest was sponsored by the Boosters' Club, with W. L. Moor, George W. Saxon, G. P. McCord, J. P. Clarkson, and P. T. Mickler serving as judges. More than 50 slogans were submitted, reflecting not only the attributes of the city but also the public-relations skills of some of its citizens.

Some suggested mottoes emphasized Tallahassee's natural beauty:

"The city beautiful"
"The garden city of the land of flowers"
"The key to the land of flowers"
"The city of health, beauty, and plenty"

Others pointed out the geographical features so prominent in the area:

"The queen of the hills"
"Tallahassee: 'Mid fertile hills and valleys"
"Tallahassee on the crest o' the hills"
"The mecca of the hills"

Some slogans obviously were aimed at the businessman:

"The key city to success"

"The city of all opportunities"
"El Dorado city"
"Greater Florida's greater city"

Some seemed to fit no particular category:

"The conqueror city"
"The capital of celerity"
"Florida's Canaan"
"The totally different city"
"Be sure to see Talla-has-see"
"The Athens of Florida"

A few entries reflected contempt for the whole scheme:

"The boosters' paradise"
"City of irrepressible booster"
"The sleepless, wrestless [sic], hustling Capital"

students were enrolled, although 73 were in the college's preparatory school. The name was changed to the Florida State Normal and Industrial School in 1901, and in 1905 the school was designated the state's land-grant institution for blacks. A name more descriptive of its functions came in 1909: the Florida Agricultural and Mechanical College for Negroes.

Many black churches had developed by 1920; the process had begun early. Slaves had been a large part of Trinity Methodist's congregation. In 1868, the free blacks formed their own congregation, the Saint James Christian Methodist Episcopal Church. Even earlier, in 1866, another group of black Methodists founded the Bethel African Methodist Episcopal Church. Their minister was the Reverend Robert Meacham. Black Baptists followed a similar course. James Page helped form the Missionary Baptist Church on Bel Aire Road in 1868. By 1869-1870, the Reverend Page was involved in establishing the Bethel Baptist Church in Tallahassee. Phillip A. Davis filled the pulpit at Saint Mary's Primitive

Baptist Church on Call Street, also founded in the late 1860s. For both black and white communities, religion was an important part of life.

TALLAHASSEE REMAINS THE CAPITAL

Between 1876 and 1920, Tallahassee experienced inevitable change, but no radical transformation. Each successive census during the period showed an increase in population, but in 1920 the capital was still a small town of 5,637 people. Although their town had been designed to serve as the seat of government, Tallahasseeans had to struggle to keep the capital. They well knew that if the capital were removed, Tallahassee would decline into obscurity. In the end they won, but the contest was not always easy.

In the antebellum period, people complained that Tallahassee was remote, unhealthy, and too small,

lacking in hotels and restaurants. The dissatisfaction led to the introduction—but ultimate defeat—of several bills to remove the capital. The most serious challenge came in 1854 in a statewide referendum. By a fairly close majority, the voters decided to leave the capital where it was.

The Civil War interrupted the efforts to remove the capital, but in 1881 a bill was introduced to establish the capital at Gainesville or elsewhere. Fortunately for Tallahassee, William D. Bloxham was governor. A Leon countian and the first native Floridian to serve as governor, Bloxham vetoed the measure and was upheld by the legislature. After a first term in 1881 to 1885, Bloxham returned to politics and served a second term from 1897 to 1901. Once more, Tallahassee was the beneficiary. Agitation for removal of the capital had become so intense that the issue became part of the general election of 1900. Florida voters chose from Tallahassee, Jacksonville, Ocala, and Saint Augustine. Led by Governor Bloxham, Leon countians cam-

paigned hard and prevailed once more. Future attempts were made to remove the capital—rarely was a legislative session held without at least the introduction of a removal bill. But no threat was so serious as that of 1900.

Part of Tallahassee's trouble lay with the dilapidated condition of the capitol building. The structure had remained unchanged from 1845 until 1891, when a cupola was added. Once the decision was made to keep the capital, the legislature appropriated funds for extensive enlargement. That came in 1902 and 1903, when east and west wings were added.

EDUCATION BATTLES THE ODDS

Public education in the South to 1920 generally was inadequate. Tallahassee and Leon County were no exceptions. Revenue sources were limited, and the educational program was under-

The Bloxham Guards, shown on the steps of the capitol in 1899, marched in drill competition with other local militia companies at early Leon County fairs.

Governor William D. Bloxham is shown with two ladies on the north porch of his home at 410 North Calhoun in the early 1900s.

funded, understaffed, and burdened by the expense of maintaining a dual system. The school-age population in 1900 was 7,416. To educate the black and white students, the system employed 81 teachers to serve 71 schools. The average school term was 103 days. By 1920, the school-age population had declined to 6,477 and the number of schools to 67. In that year, only 1,167 books were in all public-school libraries—and all were in white schools. Yet in Tallahassee, Leon High School developed into a fine institution, comparable to the best in the state. But educational improvements were badly needed for both races, particularly blacks.

Tallahasseeans managed to keep the West Florida Seminary open during the Civil War and the economically depressed decades that followed. In 1883, the name was changed to the Literary College of Florida, but in 1886 the old name was readopted. In 1901 the coeducational institution was named the Florida State College. In 1900-1901, FSC had an enrollment of 207, yet only 55 young men and women were taking college-level courses. Eighty were enrolled in Teachers' Training School and 101 in the preparatory department for students over twelve.

In 1905, the Florida legislature passed an

important law relating to higher education. Representative Henry H. Buckman of Duval County authored an act locating an all-male University of Florida at Gainesville. The Buckman Act named the Florida State Normal and Industrial School as the state's land-grant school for blacks. The measure limited Florida State College to women students and renamed it the Florida Female College. The name raised so many protests that it was changed in 1909 to the Florida State College for Women. Tallahasseeans were not happy about the decision, but they accepted it. Dr. A. A. Murphree, the first president, supervised a campus of not quite thirteen acres, three buildings, and a makeshift gymnasium. Murphree hired a young Ph.D named Edward Conradi as his dean. In 1909, Murphree became president of the University of Florida, and Conradi succeeded him at Tallahassee. Dr. Conradi remained president of the college until he retired in 1941.

TALLAHASSEE ENTERS THE TWENTIETH CENTURY

Extensive building in the 1870s and 1880s was proof that Tallahasseeans had pride and were not completely poor. Alexander Gallie built a two-story red brick building on the northeast corner of Adams and Jefferson. Completed in 1873-1874, the building was a retail store at street level, but the upper floor—reached by stairs from the outside—became known as Gallie's Opera House. Later, it was known as Munro's. Minstrel shows, dramas, concerts, lectures, variety programs, graduation exercises and other events were held there. In the twentieth century, competition from the movies caused the opera house to close.

Despite the "Great Fire" of 1843, no lessons had been learned. Tallahassee did not have an adequate fire department. Fires raged unchecked in the 1870s, accounting for much of the building and rebuilding that occurred. The old Planters Hotel on the northeast corner of Pensacola and Adams burned in 1867. A similar fate befell the county courthouse in 1879. Located on Park Avenue at the site of the present federal courthouse, the building dated from 1838. It was rebuilt and opened in 1882 at a different site—Washington Square with its public well. The new location had been the site of Peres Brokaw's livery and blacksmith shop. As late as 1906, Tallahassee's fire department had three paid firemen and twenty volunteers who manned a hose wagon (drawn by two stalwart but venerable steeds named Tom and Jerry) and a hook-and-ladder wagon.

William P. Slusser's City Hotel, a beloved prewar hostelry that was rickety but still standing, had a monopoly when the 1870s began. The dire need for more commercial housing was soon supplied. First, the three-story Saint James (later the Broward) was built on the east side of Monroe. Impressive but not elegant, the Saint James had an observatory on the roof that afforded an excellent view of the town and countryside. On January 1, 1883, the Leon Hotel opened its doors. The capital city finally had a hotel it could be proud of. Owned by the Tallahassee Hotel Company, it was built by Alexander McDougall. Located on Park Avenue at the site of the old courthouse, the Leon had an aesthetic appeal from the first. The upper floors could accommodate 60 guests, and the first floor became, in the truest sense, the social center of Tallahassee.

The brief economic upswing of the 1880s was followed by a financial depression in the 1890s. Out of economic discontent, the angry Populists formed a political party and challenged Democratic supremacy. Their revolt failed. Better times returned, and in 1898 the Spanish-American War eased lingering sectional tensions as the former wearers of the blue and the gray united in a common cause against the Spanish. The people of Tallahassee and Leon County followed such events, but they were more concerned with local affairs. For instance, the theme of the year's May Party always was discussed with interest. The first May Party may have been held as early as 1833. The celebration of spring varied from year to year, but the format featured young people dressed in costumes. The whole town turned out. After some experimentation, the location was set on the green of Park Avenue under a venerable live oak, which ultimately fell in 1986.

Tallahassee in the 1880s was not a fiercely competitive city of hustle and bustle. No better proof could be found than the town's mule-drawn streetcar. The track's northern end was the midsection of Monroe and Brevard. From there it followed a zigzag route through town to its terminus at the railroad station. No turnaround existed. The mules were unhitched from one end of the car and hitched up at the other, and the route was retraced. A black man named "Uncle" Jim Alexander and his small mules, Bucephalus and Napoleon, became famous locally. The fare was only five cents, and Alexander did not mind waiting when his women passengers ran into various stores to shop. Critics argued that the line, which operated from 1889 to 1896, did not make any money. Supporters replied that it did not lose any either.

The main house of Tall Timbers plantation as it looked when it was purchased by Edward Beadel in 1895.

A break for refreshments during a hunt in 1932 at Welaunee plantation

COMMENCEMENT DAY AT
WEST FLORIDA SEMINARY, 1880

*T*allahassee's *West Florida Seminary, the ancestor of Florida State University, opened its doors in 1857 as a coeducational institution. Although it remained open through the Civil War and afterwards, it was not until 1880 that degrees were conferred in a formal graduation ceremony.*

The event, carefully planned by Principal James D. Wade and college officials, was scheduled for Thursday evening, June 24, at Gallie's Hall on Adams Street. Gallie's, completed in 1874, served as Tallahassee's opera house and civic center. Things got off to a bad start Thursday morning when rain began. It increased through the day, reducing attendance and delaying the start of the festivities.

Dignitaries seated on the stage as the commencement program began included members of the board of education, the state cabinet, Principal Wade, the graduating class, and two undergraduates who were participating in the exercises. Unfortunately, that left no room for the three assistant teachers—two women and a man. The remaining students sat in the front row before the stage, and were reported to have been "attentive and well-behaved."

The Tallahassee Brass Band entertained the audience, followed by the Reverend Dr. W. H. Carter of Saint John's Episcopal Church, who offered the opening prayer. Several students welcomed the guests with speeches. Senior Eugenia "Jennie" C. Tatum read the class valedictory, then "gracefully retired."

Following the student's remarks, Principal Wade rose to address the crowd. Wade, who had been at the school's helm for seven years, got the attention of everyone present when he announced his resignation and delivered some complaints which evidently had been

burdening him for some time. Wade claimed that during his tenure, not one mother had visited the school or shown any interest in it. Few fathers had been on the campus, he added, except as members of the board. Wade urged parents to encourage their children to study and to become more involved in the institution themselves.

The audience hardly could have been surprised to learn that the commencement speaker, R. H. M. Davidson of Quincy, was unable to appear because of illness in his family. R. C. Long of Tallahassee delivered an impromptu speech, encompassing almost the entire history of education, and calling for reforms close to home. Long's words were well received by his appreciative audience.

Awards for outstanding achievement were distributed by Captain Patrick Houston, president of the board of education. Women students received books of poems for their efforts in rhetoric, philosophy, English composition, and arithmetic. The male designees were given more unusual gifts. One scholar was awarded a gold pen, two others were presented pocketknives, and another was given a baseball. Two young men honored for deportment and punctuality were favored with baseball bats.

The unorthodox graduation exercises closed with a benediction by the Reverend C. A. Fulwood, presiding elder of the Methodist Church. Later that evening, any ruffled feelings were undoubtedly soothed when Mrs. S. S. Williams, a faculty member, entertained the "larger pupils and their friends" at a commencement ball in her home. The class of 1880 had enjoyed a unique graduation.

Eugenia "Jenny" Tatum, shown here in the graduation dress made for her by her grandmother, completed the English course of studies and was awarded "diploma number one" at West Florida Seminary on June 24, 1880, during commencement ceremonies at Gallie's Opera House on Adams Street.

A woman on the steps of her Leon County cabin, late 1880s

The Winthrop family employed Mary Merritt to care for their sons Francis and Guy (on pony). Mathew Merritt was the coachman, and the Merritt's son Eddie tagged along.

As the twentieth century opened, Tallahassee still did not have quite 3,000 people, and the county had less than 20,000 with blacks comprising about 80 percent of the total. Yet the small town could withstand adversity because of its institutions of higher education and its role as the center of trade and professional services for Leon and other counties.

The years 1900 to 1910 brought several "firsts" to Tallahassee. Electric lights illuminated the city in 1903, the same year street signs went up and buildings and houses were numbered. A sewage system was completed in 1904. Telephones became fairly commonplace, and the art of conversation was given wider application when long-distance service became available in 1905. Also in 1905, the city's two journals, the *Capital* and the *Tallahasseean*, were consolidated by John G. Collins into the *True Democrat*. Collins shortened its title later to *Democrat*, and the paper has remained in publication to the present.

Tallahassee still had somewhat limited accommodations for visitors. Several boardinghouses were in operation as well as the elegant Leon Hotel and the Bloxham Hotel. The town's inadequacies were evident, however, especially every two years when the legislature met. Even more embarrassing was the absence of a state-owned residence for the governor. The deficiency was rectified in 1905 by a state law. Construction began that year, and the mansion, on the north end of Adams Street, was completed in 1906. The rambling multi-columned mansion housed Governor Napoleon Bonaparte Broward as its first resident. Broward's large family needed all eight bedrooms on the second floor.

Out-of-town visitors still found railroad service the most reliable means of reaching the capital city. Although train service was available for those who wished to travel east and west, north-south connections were non-existent or took some maneuvering. Few

Willis Jiles, a Tuskegee-trained cobbler, was said to be one of the first blacks to own a business in Tallahassee.

Susie Rebecca Baker Jiles was a teacher at Kirsey Community School No. 69 near Bakertown, Leon County.

John Gilmore Riley, Leon County's first black principal, poses with four Lincoln School students in the 1900s.

Gibbs Hall, Florida State Normal Industrial School, later Florida A & M, 1909

people were overly concerned about the limited rail service because of that amazing new machine, the automobile. The first car in Tallahassee made its appearance in November 1900, and in 1907 the Tallahassee Automobile Company was organized. Proudly selling Fords, it was probably the capital's first automobile agency. It became clear that more cars and trucks would require more and better roads and highways. Still, few people would have predicted that in 1920 Florida would issue registration forms for 80,163 vehicles.

TALLAHASSEEANS ENJOY RECREATION AND CULTURE

Most Tallahasseeans liked the easygoing pace of their capital and could not understand nonresidents' complaints about the town's lack of "action." Surely, the defenders said, no one could fault the unrivaled hunting opportunities for game birds as well as rabbits, squirrels, opossums, and deer. Such relatively safe types of hunting always held the added possibility of encountering rattlesnakes, water moccasins, and alligators. Truly adventurous sportsmen also could try their skills at hunting bear and wildcats. A large number of locals—without regard to age, sex, race, education, or socioeconomic status—loved to fish. No need, they mused, to defend the joys of the county's lakes, ponds, creeks, and rivers. If pressed, they would cite the Ochlocknee River as a favored place. The anglers did become concerned in 1909 when Lakes Iamonia, Jackson, and Miccosukee

went dry. Strict defenders of the Puritan work ethic saw the Lord's hand in the phenomenon (one that occurred every twenty years or so); it was punishment, they said, to those who lingered too long and indulged too often in pursuit of the finny tribe. The fishermen gave such arguments little consideration.

Tallahassee offered things to do, if one sought them out. Blacks and whites could choose (separately) from a number of clubs and fraternal orders. Churches remained important, and Sunday schools saw their rolls soar. Summer revivals or "protracted meetings" attracted the "saved" and saved the "sinners." Many citizens considered the legal sale of alcohol morally reprehensible. In 1904, church leaders, along with a large and active Women's Christian Temperance Union chapter, won a public referendum that closed the town's bars and saloons.

Cultural activities included lectures and performances sponsored and staged by the colleges. The Tallahassee brass band always seemed to be folding or reviving. Several private music teachers survived, even if they did not prosper. The David S. Walker Library on Park Avenue (now the headquarters of the Springtime Tallahassee Association) was built in 1903 in memory of the former governor, who had started a private subscription library in 1883. A fine line separated culture seekers from those avowedly in pursuit of pleasure. R. J. Phillips, who had taken over the Munro Opera House, booked plays and minstrel shows. In 1910, some enterprising businessmen rented the armory (a frame building on the southeast corner of Monroe and Pensacola) and began to show silent movies. The Bloxham Electric Theatre operated on a limited basis;

The second Bethel African Methodist Episcopal Church was on the northwest corner of Duval and Virginia streets in the 1880s.

Thomas De Saille Tucker, first president of Tallahassee State Normal College for Colored Students.

The Reverend James Page was the first pastor of Bethel Missionary Baptist Church at Bel Aire, and in 1868 helped to form Bethel Baptist Church in Tallahassee.

it was Tallahassee's first commercial theatre. Young, middle-aged, and old flocked to Fisher's Green to see John Robinson's Circus. Andrew Jackson Fish owned a city block near the Seaboard Railway Station, and his green was used for various outdoor attractions. (In less happy days, the young Susan Bradford Eppes had witnessed the execution by firing squad of two Confederate deserters there.)

Bridge began to replace whist as the most popular card game. The citizenry attended parties and dances, and hay rides (or "straw" rides) were especially popular among the young. Cane grindings and parties that featured "pulling" syrup candy appealed to all ages. The social event of the year continued to be the May Party. In 1908, for example, the spectators enjoyed the presentation, and privately tested their memories for the lyrics to the hit songs "The Blue Moon" and "I'll Marry You to Make a Home for Mother."

Spring, summer, and sometimes fall were the favorite times for boarding a train, singly or in groups, and going to the Gulf coast. Outings to Panacea Springs, Lanark, Saint Teresa, and the barrier islands were enjoyed by those who could afford the trip. Organized sports were popular, and watching a high-scoring baseball game was a good way to get through a long summer afternoon. The Tallahassee Country Club, probably the capital's first, was organized at the Grove in 1908. The club proved to be short-lived, however.

Football became popular in the first decade of the twentieth century. At the collegiate level, it became a permanent sport for black fans and participants. For white patrons and players, football came, went, returned, and left—the hiatus would last almost 40 years. Intramural football at Florida State Normal and Industrial School (now FAMU) began in 1901. A so-called varsity played a mixed team of faculty members and "scrubs." The first intercollegiate games were played in

1906, when the team went to Alabama and played Tuskegee and Alabama State College (Montgomery) in the same week. In 1913, the school joined the Southern Intercollegiate Athletic Conference.

Florida State College took its step up from intramural games in 1902. On November 21, its "eleven" played the South Georgia Military Institute from Bainbridge, Georgia. The Purple and Gold of FSC prevailed 5-0. Teams were fielded in 1903 and 1904, but the Buckman Act of 1905 spelled the elimination of football. Even so, in 1909 football-hungry Tallahasseeans formed a town team, the Athletics, and played several games. They scored some victories, but disbanded after being defeated humiliatingly at home by the University of Florida. Not until 1947, when Florida State University played the Stetson University Hatters, would fans see a home college football game between opposing white schools.

Most citizens, especially the members of the Anna Jackson Chapter of the United Daughters of the Confederacy—the "Daughters"—were pleased in 1905 when the state's Civil War flags, captured on various battlefields, were returned. If the memory of the "lost cause" was perpetuated, it was also heartening to many people that in 1907 the Fourth of July was celebrated on a scale not seen since the antebellum period.

TALLAHASSEE UNDERGOES GAINS AND LOSSES

The 1900-1910 decade offered successes and disappointments for Tallahasseeans and Leon countians. A financial panic in 1907 sent shock waves through the country's economy, and tremors were felt in Tallahassee. Near the decade's close, the city experienced the violence that was so tragically a part of the South. Leon County Sheriff

William D. Bloxham (second from right), Florida's first native-born governor, is shown with family and friends in the parlor of his Calhoun Street home.

William W. Langston was murdered in 1909. The crime was followed by the arrest and conviction of a black turpentine worker named Mick Morris. Scheduled to hang, Morris was taken from his cell and lynched by a mob in the jail yard. The shame of the lynching lingered for years.

Locals did not like—and many did not believe—what the 1910 census revealed. The county had lost population since 1900 and stood at 19,427. Even so, a reason for optimism existed. The colleges were growing (Chi Omega sorority was founded at FSCW in 1908), and in 1909 a chamber of commerce was organized. As the county's population declined, Tallahassee's grew, and urban expansion would continue. The *Democrat* claimed, "Tallahassee is no longer a sleepy dull town but is wide awake."

From 1910 to 1920, Tallahassee became more definitely a city under the leadership of Mayor Dexter M. Lowry. The city limits were expanded, voters approved bonds to pave the downtown sidewalks and streets, and in 1916 Clinton Street was renamed College Avenue. Car owners rejoiced at the paved streets. More cars could be seen, as the local Ford dealer had to compete with new franchises: Studebaker, Buick, and Cadillac. Next came agencies that sold Dodges, Kings, and Hudsons. In 1914, Fred Levy established the city's first taxi service, and Tallahassee's speed limit was set at ten miles per hour.

Trade and commerce picked up noticeably until 1914, when World War I broke out in Europe. Cotton prices and shipments were threatened as the conflict disrupted world trade. By 1915, business revived, then prospered as the war boosted the area's economy. The war would be followed by a recession, but Tallahassee and Leon County would enter the Jazz Age with great expectations.

Nursemaids and their charges on the grounds of the capitol, between 1891 and 1901

POLITICS MAKE TALLAHASSEE TICK

In the large view, politics and politicians enabled Tallahassee to function. It was small wonder that the citizens took their politics seriously. Albert W. Gilchrist took over as governor in 1909. A bachelor, he was the object of constant but unsuccessful match-making attempts by local society people.

The national election of 1912 raised the normally high level of political interest. Leon County helped to elect Woodrow Wilson, the first southerner elected to the White House since Zachary Taylor in 1848. Democrat Park Trammell was elected governor in a routine race. The focus of public interest was reversed in 1916. With little deliberation, Tallahasseeans chose Wilson for a second term over Charles Evans Hughes, the Republican candidate. It was the governor's race that captured the excitement. The flamboyant Baptist minister, Sidney J. Catts of De Funiak Springs by way of Alabama, waged a controversial campaign marked by anti-Catholic rhetoric. The local favorite was William V. Knott, resident of Tallahassee and incumbent state comptroller.

Complicated voting laws and uncertain returns resulted in a challenged election. Knott finally was awarded the Democratic nomination, usually tantamount to victory in the solidly Democratic South. Catts refused to quit the race, however. He ran as the candidate for the Prohibition party in the general election, and won. Leon County voters gave Knott a majority of their ballots. In January 1917, the capital was treated to an exuberant Andrew Jackson-like inauguration.

Politics seemed to return to normal in 1920. The Republicans regained the White House, and Florida Democrats claimed the statehouse. Warren G. Harding did not owe his victory to Leon County voters, who expressed their preference for James G. Cox, the Democrat from Ohio. At the state level, Cary A. Hardee a banker and farmer from Live Oak, was elected governor.

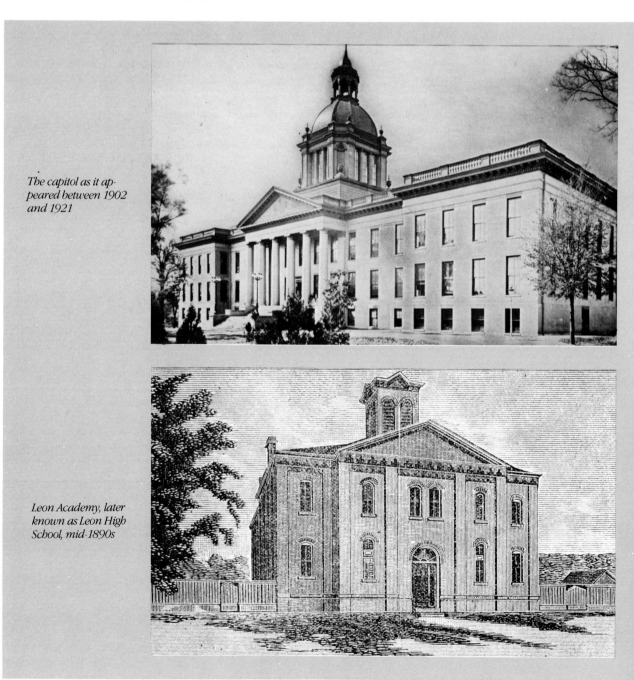

The capitol as it appeared between 1902 and 1921

Leon Academy, later known as Leon High School, mid-1890s

The legislators who passed the "Buckman Bill," which designated Tallahassee's Florida State Normal and Industrial School as the state's land-grant school for blacks, May 20, 1905

The dormitory residents are shown in front of College Hall at the Florida Female College, 1908

The second Leon County Courthouse was built in 1882 on the east side of Monroe Street at Jefferson. This building, and most of its additions, was demolished in 1985.

T. P. Coe drives the fire department's two-horse hose wagon, pulled by Tom and Jerry, circa late 1900s.

Built in 1873-74 by Alexander Gallie on the northeast corner of Adams and Jefferson streets, Gallie's and later Munro's opera house was the site of minstrel shows, dramas, concerts, lectures and graduations on the second floor while general merchandise was sold below.

SOCIAL LIFE BLOOMS IN THE 'TEENS'

Prosperity from 1910 to 1915 was visually evident. Considerable private construction occurred; the Elks Club built a large meeting hall; and two new money managers, the Citizens Bank and the Exchange Bank, opened their doors. So much happened in 1912, in addition to political affairs, that citizens barely could keep up with events. The Tallahassee Chautauqua Association was formed, the first local troop of Boy Scouts was organized, and Tallahassee voted to remain dry. The opponents of whiskey won the election with a solid majority. Former saloon owners and their potential patrons lamented the results. Meaning no disrespect, they likened the event to the recent tragic sinking of the *Titanic*. Many took it as a sign of improving race relations when a mixed audience—the largest crowd in Tallahassee's history—heard Booker T. Washington, famed president of Tuskegee Institute, speak at Fisher's Green.

For some citizens, *the* event of 1912 was the opening of C. E. Daffin's Capital City Theatre on College Avenue between Monroe and Adams. The Munro Opera House had continued its live stage productions, and by 1911 offered occasional movies to meet the Bloxham Theatre's competition. Bloxham's had moved from the armory to a site near the courthouse. Still another cinema, the Electric Theatre, showed films in the new Leon High School when the building was not in academic use. Still, it was the Capital City Theatre (usually called Daffin's) that captured the trade and became Tallahassee's first permanent picture show.

For a minority of the citizens, the early years of the century's second decade offered escapism. They enjoyed the John H. Sparks Circus when it came to town, and kept up with the latest fads and trends. In 1914, the sophisticated crowd adopted the "Hesitation," the newest dance, but some still preferred the craze of 1913, the "Castle Polka." Among the popular songs were "Rag Time Soldier Man," "I Want My Baby Grand," and "You're Just as Sweet at Sixty as at Sweet Sixteen." Any one who pretended to keep up with the times already had bought, or soon would buy, the necessary status symbol, a victrola.

THE REALITY OF WAR PREVAILS

Life was far more grim for the county's farmers and for businesses dependent on their trade. Throughout 1914 and much of 1915, the war's opposing Allies and Central powers attempted to enforce blockades and monopolize neutral trade. Cotton shipments dropped, and so did prices for Leon County farmers. The Allies gradually won control of the seas, and as submarine attacks lessened, trade rose and soon reached unprecedented heights. Cotton prices soared. It was little wonder that in 1915, Tallahassee businessmen formed a Boosters' Club. That year the sinking of the *Lusitania* shocked Floridians into thinking of the United States' possible involvement in the Great War.

In the meantime, the United States reaped the profits of remaining neutral. Agricultural prosperity was a way of life in 1916, although the boll weevil finally arrived in Leon County. Some fields were ruined, but the total cotton crop was large. Putting aside thoughts of war, the people organized the Leon County Fair Association. They turned out to watch Leon High School field what was perhaps its first football team. In 1916, Mrs. D. F. Gramling of Centerville was chosen district school supervisor by the county school board, with general approval. The times were changing: Mrs. Gramling was Leon County's first woman to hold public office.

By 1917, the United States broke off diplomatic relations with Germany, and on April 6 declared war, joining forces with the Allied powers. Leon countians and other Americans responded with great outbursts of patriotism. Locals questioned the logic of daylight savings time, but adopted it to aid the war effort. Women in Tallahassee's newly formed Red Cross organized a sewing circle that met at the Elks Club on Monroe Street. Dressed in full white aprons and regulation Red Cross veils, they rolled bandages and made garments. Numerous patriotic groups, including the Leon County Canning Club, were organized. Servicemen were admitted free to Daffin's Theatre, where they enjoyed such movies as *The Love Hermit* starring William Russell. The Leon County Fair was postponed

Postcard view of Monroe Street looking north, with streetlight, 1910

Gentry's Famous Dog and Pony Show wagons on Monroe Street, in front of Leon Hotel, 1901.

Saint James Hotel, 1880s

In this February 1894 photo "Uncle" Jim Alexander's small mules, Bucephalas and Napoleon have help from a third unidentified white mule.

May Party, 1906

Construction of governor's mansion, 1906. The building was razed in 1955.

Governor's mansion, showing south side of entrance hall, with Governor Gilchrist and three ladies reflected in mirror, circa 1909-1913

Ada Yawn Brown and John P. Brown in front seat of one of Tallahassee's first cars, a Panhard. Brown sold Overland and Ford autos.

Walker Library, 1921

A 1912 postcard view of Lake Miccosukee

"Mr. Jacobs' bar," 1890s. Note the little dog lounging on the bar.

Performers in David Garrick, *May 29, 1908, at Gallie/Munro Opera House*

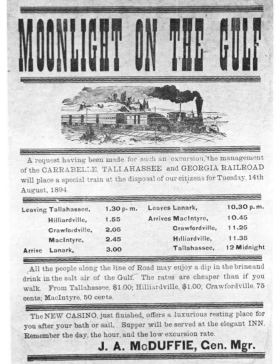

MOONLIGHT ON THE GULF

A request having been made for such an excursion, the management of the CARRABELLE, TALLAHASSEE and GEORGIA RAILROAD will place a special train at the disposal of our citizens for Tuesday, 14th August, 1894.

Leaving Tallahassee,	1.30 p.m.	Leaves Lanark,	10.30 p.m.
Hilliardville,	1.55	Arrives MacIntyre,	10.45
Crawfordville,	2.05	Crawfordville,	11.25
MacIntyre,	2.45	Hilliardville,	11.35
Arrive Lanark,	3.00	Tallahassee,	12 Midnight

All the people along the line of Road may enjoy a dip in the brine and drink in the salt air of the Gulf. The rates are cheaper than if you walk. From Tallahassee, $1.00; Hilliardville, $1.00; Crawfordville, 75 cents; MacIntyre, 50 cents.

The NEW CASINO, just finished, offers a luxurious resting place for you after your bath or sail. Supper will be served at the elegant INN. Remember the day, the hour, and the low excursion rate.

J. A. McDUFFIE, Gen. Mgr.

An ad for a railway excursion to Lanark

The 1907 Tallahassee baseball club

until after victory. The rousing war songs were popular, but so was the plaintive ballad "Juanita," ragtime tunes, and Hawaiian melodies such as "Aloha Oe." A uniformed cadet corps was organized at Leon High.

Tallahasseeans accepted a number of wartime taxes with little protest. Two Liberty Loan drives of 1917 were followed by two more in 1918 and a Victory Loan drive in 1919. The county exceeded its assigned quotas each time. The greatest home-front danger came late in the war with the outbreak of the Spanish influenza. People improvised "flu masks" to ward off the epidemic, and for brief periods schools closed and churches canceled Sunday services.

The state guard, subject to be called into national service, was represented locally by Company B (formerly the Leon County Guards), First Infantry Regiment. The unit was called to service in August 1918. A full week of farewell parties and picnics followed, ending with embraces and tears at the depot. When the men left, Company B, comprised of older volunteers, was formed as a home guard. The company was sent to Camp Wheeler in Georgia for additional training. Later, the men were transferred to machine-gun battalions

and to the field artillery and infantry. Men for the armed forces also were conscripted. The Selective Service Act of May 18, 1917, was amplified by other legislation. Across America, more than three million men were inducted. Florida furnished 42,030 men to the military, of whom 1,046 were killed in combat. Parker Houston of Chaires was the first man drafted in Leon County in 1918. Whenever draftees left the county, they were given parades and patriotic send-offs. Most of the black servicemen from the region took their basic training in the North, while the whites usually remained in the South. In all, Leon County furnished 615 men: 356 blacks and 259 whites.

The county's first casualties came in November and December 1917, when two men died from illnesses contracted in training at Camp Wheeler. Corporal Claude L. Sauls, Company C, Sixth Infantry, Fifth Division, was the first local man killed in action. The young volunteer was killed by enemy machine-gun fire while fighting in France on September 14, 1918. After the war, the Tallahassee post of the American Legion was named in his honor. The young soldier's body was returned to Florida in 1921, lay in

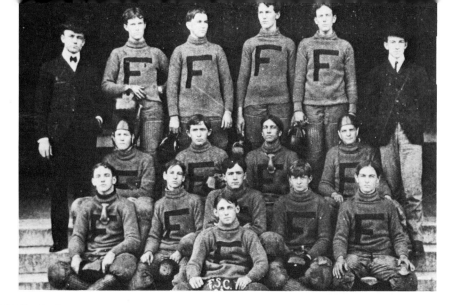

The 1902 Florida State College football team

Governor Park Trammell served from 1913 1917.

In an April 1905 ceremony, the Confederate flags captured from Florida troops during the Civil War were returned to the state.

KUDZU—BLESSING OR CURSE?

"*Crown Kudzu King in Leon County*" urged the headline in a 1913 Tallahassee Daily Democrat. E. B. Eppes, farmer and former school superintendent, was convinced that kudzu would dethrone King Cotton. A few years earlier he had planted several acres in the rapid-growing vine, imported from Asia as a cattle food. Eppes and local experts predicted that if "one half of the cultivable land [in Leon County] were set to this plant, it would bring us $15,000,000 to $35,000,000 instead of the measly little pittance we now get from King (?) Cotton."

Kudzu eventually proved to be more of a curse than a blessing, but some agricultural innovations were of great value in the pre-World War I era. Infestations of the cattle-fever tick lowered the value of the animals and often resulted in government quarantines of entire counties. The Leon County Live Stock Association sponsored a demonstration of cattle dipping in April 1913. The event took place in McDougall's pasture off Miccosukee Road (where Leon High School now is located), and hundreds of Tallahasseans attended the demonstration. Businesses closed and the state legislature adjourned for the afternoon so everyone could witness the experiment. Thirty cows "badly infested" with ticks were dipped, and all the ticks subsequently were pronounced dead. Area farmers were impressed, and "public vats" later were established for cattle dipping.

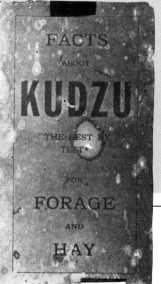

Before 1920, the city had a ten-mile-per-hour speed limit and some directional signs, such as the one in this view of Monroe and College.

Sidney J. Catts waged a controversial anti-Catholic Prohibitionist campaign for governor in 1916 from his Ford auto. He credited his mobility for the victory, as seen by the sign on his inaugural-parade car.

Comptroller W. V. Knott who won the Democratic nomination for governor in 1916, but lost the election to Sidney J. Catts. Knott is shown here with his staff, about 1914.

Governor Cary A. Hardee is shown in his office with legislators, circa 1923.

The Daffin Theatre, which opened in 1912 as the Capital City Theatre, is shown in this 1920s photograph.

Tallahassee's first Boy Scout troop was formed in 1912. The scouts are shown on a camping trip.

John P. Brown, in this decorated car, campaigned to keep the city dry.

state at the capitol, and was given a military funeral at Oakland Cemetary. At war's end, Leon County's war casualties were thirteen whites killed and seven wounded, and five blacks killed and none wounded.

The bitter war of attrition finally ended with the signing of the armistice on November 11, 1918. The news reached Tallahassee at about 9:00 p.m. Working furiously, Editor John G. Collins put out an extra edition of the *Democrat*.

The paper hit the streets at about 2:30 a.m., and people began to gather downtown. As dawn broke, the joyous crowd built a large bonfire at the center of College and Adams. In a crescendo of noise, nobody seemed to mind being unable to hear the speakers, who barely could hear themselves. Some innovative celebrants concocted a dummy of Kaiser Wilhelm II, appropriated a coffin, and placed the effigy inside. The flames then became a funeral pyre for the last of the Hohenzollern princes. The celebrations—parades, speeches, unrehearsed and unregulated cries of victory—went into the following day. The city's youth

The auditorium of Leon High School was rented occasionally by the Electric Theatre for use as a "movie house."

Tallahassee Elks Club, early 1910s

seemed especially appreciative of the holiday from school. The Great War—the war to end wars—was over.

TALLAHASSEANS FACE A CHANGING WORLD

The servicemen returned from stateside camps and from overseas. In 1919 and 1920, they and the civilians adjusted to a peacetime economy. The war-fueled prosperity was followed by a post-war slump. In time the economy would rebound, although bitter disappointment was felt when it was learned that Leon County's population had dropped by seven percent. Tallahassee increased in size, but its growth rate could not match that of other Florida cities, favored by northern railroads and an expanding highway system.

In 1919, groups gathered at the revived Leon County Fair. Along with socializing, the more philosophical pondered the future. Some doubted that the Eighteenth Amendment would be any more effective in stamping out liquor than local option had been. If that amendment appealed to one's sense of morality, the Nineteenth Amendment appealed to one's sense of justice—on August 26, 1920, women gained the right to vote. A number of Leon County women would exercise that right in the election of 1920.

Automobiles had become so commonplace that no one questioned their importance. More at issue was the uncertain role of the airplane. By about 1915, a crude "lighting place" had been marked off east of Tallahassee at Magnolia Heights. Located in the general area of present Governor's Square, it was little more than a pasture marked by a flag. Occasionally, a barnstormer would fly in and charge admission for taking the bolder citizens for a ride in the air. Some people predicted that was only the beginning. Editor Milton A. Smith saw the future: "The air plane is coming. What the auto did for the horse and buggy, the air plane is going to do for the auto, only in a milder way. Most of us will live to see aviation as common and useful as automobiling is today, and it won't be so very far off either."

Members of the Home Demonstration Club display canned goods in 1912.

The Tallahassee depot was the site of many tearful farewells to World War I soldiers.

A cotton wagon waits its turn at the Tallahassee gin near the depot.

View of Monroe Street at the time of the United States entry into World War I, 1917

C. W. Cleveland flew
into Tallahassee in a
Ryan monoplane, sister
craft to Charles Lind-
bergh's Spirit of St. Louis.
The camera on the
ground was used in an
aerial survey of Leon
County.

FEAST AND FAMINE

In the early twentieth century, H. Johnson Jr.'s Jersey herd at Leon Dairy Farm, on Micco-sukee Road, was part of Leon County's profitable dairy industry.

5.

The 1920s were years of change for Tallahassee, as they were for much of the nation. Agriculture and rural life remained vital to the area's economy and culture, but urbanization became more dominant. In 1923, the newly chartered Kiwanis Club invited farmers to a luncheon meeting to aid in "fostering a closer spirit of cooperation between the farmers of the county and the business men of the city."

In the early 1920s, new "miracle" money crops included Bermuda onions, figs, and satsumas. Onion advocates argued that every thousand acres planted in that pungent crop would return a quarter of a million dollars. Another Leon countian pled the cause of sugarcane. Besides making $1,800 per acre, he sold cane to local merchants for three cents a stalk "for chewing which is a distinctively southern habit, but which would be indulged in by . . . the entire country if they only knew of its delights." If Yankees "were apprised of this delicacy we could ship and sell to them not only car loads but train loads."

Over 3,500 milk cows made the dairy industry profitable, and the Leon County Dairy Association was an active and effective organization. Truck farming and fruit crops continued to be significant. In 1923, the Pullman Company served guava jelly made in Leon County in its dining cars. Mules still were used to power farm machinery and for transportation. One livestock dealer advertised his "good Tennessee mules" as well as "good second hand mules that we can sell cheap."

The 4-H Club was organized in Leon County in 1929. Before that, other farm clubs had existed for boys and girls, directed by the county agent and the home-demonstration agent. Black 4-H clubs presented an exhibit at the county courthouse in 1929, under the direction of Alice Poole, black home-demonstration agent for Leon County. The two-day event emphasized thrift and featured ways to fashion necessities from inexpensive objects.

Rascal Yard, the public market, was on the west side of Adams at Jefferson, now the site of city hall, 1922.

BOOSTERISM USHERS IN THE ROARING TWENTIES

The chamber of commerce and various civic clubs made "boosterism" an untainted and preferred word in the 1920s. The Kiwanis and Exchange clubs received their charters in 1923, a year after the Rotary. With the chamber of commerce, Woman's Club, and Tallahassee Garden Club, they worked to publicize the city, improve its appearance, and encourage growth and prosperity. The service clubs and area churches sponsored "International Boys' Week" under the slogan "Boys—The Nation's Greatest Asset." The chamber of commerce raised $20,000 to publicize Tallahassee and sponsored an automobile club affiliated with the American Automobile Association because "a live motor club can be a great power for good."

Woman's Club, Los Robles, 1929

In November 1924, Tallahassee celebrated its centennial with a week of gala days. Churches held special Sunday services followed by a communitywide service on the grounds of the Grove. Locals and visitors enjoyed concerts, athletic events, speeches, street dances, a costume ball, and at least three parades. Reinette Long Hunt's historical pageant recounting local events was presented as a "living tableau." The hometown cast was costumed as Indians, Andrew Jackson, early settlers, Prince Murat, and others.

Although excluded from "mainline" civic and social clubs, blacks contributed to the city's cultural life. The Tallahassee Development Club was organized to "cooperate with the Chamber of Commerce [and others] in development of the city and county." W. E. Clark, an insurance agent, and John G. Riley and W. A. Armwood, both of FAMC, were among its leaders.

Community bands gave summer concerts at Leon Park on Park Avenue between Adams and Monroe streets. There the Capital City Band, the Junior Band,

and the Beginners Band gave alternating performances. Director Frank Fitch became a familiar and innovative figure (his charges held "musical bouts"). The well-known bands performed in nearby communities. FAMC staged concerts of vocal and instrumental music during its "Sunday-evening music hour." Separate seating was available for white Tallahasseeans. In 1929, the FAMC quartet with financial help from the chamber of commerce, traveled to Gainesville for a special two-hour broadcast on WRUF, the University of Florida's radio station. The program also featured two violin solos and a talk about the college itself.

Daffin's theatre continued to be Tallahassee's entertainment center. Daffin brought live shows to town—*Lasses White's All Star Minstrels* and *No, No, Nannette*. Still, movies were the Daffin's main fare. As the decade ended, residents were excited about the prospect of seeing "talkies." After extensive remodeling (new "aircushioned seats, dignified in appearance"), Daffin presented Tallahassee's first talking picture, *Broadway Melody,* in April 1929. Later that year, *The Dance of Life* was the first movie to have sound and color.

Historic Goodwood plantation became a social center under the generous ownership of state Senator and Mrs. W. C. Hodges (it was purchased from Fannie L. Tiers of New Jersey). The Hodges permitted girls from FSCW to use Goodwood's cottages and swimming pool for weekend house parties. Ever the politician, Hodges had his wife invite students according to their senatorial districts.

Tallahasseeans loved to give receptions, teas, and bridge parties. One bride was honored with four bridge parties and a dinner in less than a week. The parties were held in private homes and in such favored spots as the Ponce de León Grill, the Colonial Tea Room at the Cherokee Hotel (opened for business in 1923), and the Seminole Grill. The Three Torches Grill was also popular for bridge parties, while Joe Nahoom's Liberty Delicatessen drew crowds of young people.

Dances were held at the Woman's Club. At the Sunset Inn on the Jacksonville highway, couples danced to the Black Diamond orchestra's "entrancing"

The All-Florida Boys' Band tour was announced by (from left) Lorenzo Wilson, Nathan Mayo, Edward Ball, Earl Brown, Senator W. C. Hodges, and an unidentified man.

Card notice of the November 1924 Tallahassee centennial

music and enjoyed "refreshments." The Lake Bradford Country Club reopened each spring with dancing, boating, and swimming.

Women of the Tallahassee Literary Club met to discuss writing, and sometimes listened to Victrola music. Beginning in 1926, the flower show became an annual spring event. The Capital City Rod and Gun Club attracted some of the town's most influential men. Competitors from Georgia and Alabama came to the club's trapshooting grounds at Lake Jackson. The usual prizes were hams and bacon.

Tallahassee's Boy Scouts were active in the 1920s. The scouts were given ten acres of land by Herman C. Fleitman, a large plantation owner, and established a camp at Orchard Pond. In 1927, a parade honoring aviator Charles Lindbergh was held in Jacksonville. Sixty-five local scouts made the trip, camping in the Jacksonville armory and forming part of the parade's honor guard (Tallahassee had a float). The Tallahassee Girl Scouts received their official charter in 1929, although the organization had been active in the area since 1918.

Christmas was Tallahassee's and Leon County's favorite holiday. A town Christmas tree was lighted every night on the courthouse square. Residents began a new tradition in the late 1920s by decorating trees in their yards and on their porches with electric lights. In 1927, Santa Claus arrived in an airplane for the first

The black community marked the centennial with separate parades, pageants, and speeches.

Negro Activities

IN THE

Fla. Centennial Celebration

PAGEANT

Friday, Nov. 14, 8:15 P. M.

PARADE

Saturday, Nov. 15, 11:00 A. M.

PATRIOTIC ADDRESS

Saturday, Nov. 15, 3:30 P. M.

NEGRO MUSIC

BAND   ORCHESTRA   VOICES

PAGEANT: "THE SPIRIT OF FREEDOM." The story of a Climbing race in Song and Pantomine. A century's growth of a struggling people depicted in a series of pictures, strikingly dramatic and powerful in their simplicity. FRIDAY EVENING, NOVEMBER 14, 8:15 o'clock. OUT-DOOR THEATRE on the HUNT ESTATE, The Home of the Tallahassee Girl.

GENERAL ADMISSION - 25c

Watch for the other announcements

time. Abandoning his reindeer at Albany, Georgia, Santa headed for Tallahassee with stunt pilots Doug Davis and Mable Cody, niece of Buffalo Bill. Although "forced down" at Pelham briefly, the flying Santa did not disappoint local children. Miss Cody appeared in person at the Daffin (which had sponsored the event) to greet moviegoers, who then watched her in the movie, *Fireman Save My Child!* with Wallace Beery. Tallahassee even had a Ku Klux Klan Christmas tree and service. Camouflaging its real motives, the Klan held its festivities at the local Klavern. Santa Claus was present, and the program included patriotic songs, hymns, speeches, and a manger scene. The gifts distributed by Santa subsequently were packed up to give to needy children in the area, as were a number of food boxes.

Besides movies and home entertainment, Tallahasseeans had a range of recreational choices. Lakes, ponds, and streams offered fishing and swimming, and hunting remained a favored seasonal activity. FAMC and Leon High football and basketball teams played at the new Centennial Field. In 1928, the city commission permitted construction of a "high board fence" around the field, paid for by the sale of advertising space on the fence.

Neither football, basketball, nor local boxing matches equaled the popularity of baseball. Tallahassee's team in the late 1920s, organized by the T. J. Appleyard printing firm, was known variously as the "Red Apples" or the "Inkslingers." In 1928, the team led the north Florida league because of its talented pitcher, the appropriately named Ralph Swatts.

The more affluent sports fans watched or participated in golf tournaments at the Tallahassee Country Club. Occasional motorboat races were held on Lake Bradford. Scheduled on Sunday afternoons, the races

troubled some citizens. After one such event, 57 prominent women objected in the local newspaper. Entitled, ironically or not, "Whither are we drifting," their statement denounced the trend towards "Sunday sports." The women wondered if the promoters "realized they were breaking one of God's commandments 'Remember the Sabbath day and keep it holy.' . . . Inevitably the fruits will be disloyalty, corruption, crime and vice of the lowest nature."

RELIGION AND POLITICS KEEP THEIR IMPORTANCE

Religion was of transcendent importance in Tallahassee. Tent revivals and camp meetings were popular, and traveling evangelists made regular appearances at Tallahassee's churches. In 1926, Captain Gipsy Pat Smith drew large crowds at Trinity Methodist Church. His wife, "Mrs. Gipsy Pat," traveled with him and sang for the congregation. In 1925, the Reverend James W. Jackson preached a "book sermon" at the First Presbyterian Church, based on Nathaniel Hawthorne's *Scarlet Letter*.

The Indian Springs Baptist Church in eastern Leon County held a "singing convention" near summer's end in 1927. Families from nearby Jefferson County joined in the all-day sing and picnic. Tallahassee's Bethel A.M.E. church observed men's day on July 14, 1929. Ten girls led 200 men to Sunday School, and men taught all the classes. On the following Sunday, the roles were reversed, as the church women took over. Some black citizens attended "open forums" on Sunday afternoons on West Pensacola Street, where speakers held forth on a variety of topics. Refreshments followed the discussions.

The Methodist Woman's Missionary Conference met at Tallahassee's Trinity Church in 1928. Nearly 400 people attended. Conference guests enjoyed an organ recital by Ella Scoble Opperman, dean of the FSCW School of Music. Drama students at the college presented a pageant, Methodist Womanhood, to critical acclaim.

During the summer, church groups often boarded the train to Lanark-by-the-Gulf for a day of picnicking on the beach. The Tallahassee band usually went along to entertain, and the 6:00 p.m. train got everybody home before dark.

Republican Presidents—Harding, Coolidge, Hoover—ran the nation during the 1920s. Florida, however, (aided by Leon County's voters), had Democratic governors—Cary A. Hardee, John W. Martin, and Doyle E. Carlton.

The national election of 1928 was a difficult one for Tallahasseeans and other southerners. Historic loyalty to the Democratic party was strained severely by the nomination of New York's Governor Alfred E. Smith. An Irish Catholic who opposed Prohibition and was a product of urban machine politics, Al Smith was anathema to the South. Before the Democratic national convention met, prohibitionist editor Milton A. Smith

A flower-covered Cadillac served as centennial-parade float for Mae Johnson's dress shop.

The Lake Bradford Country Club reopened each spring with swimming, boating and dancing in the pavilion on the pier.

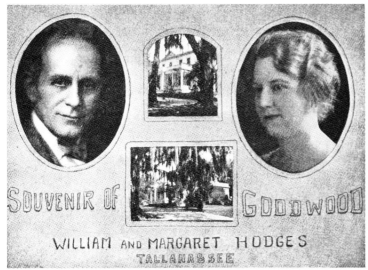

SOUVENIR OF GOODWOOD

WILLIAM AND MARGARET HODGES
TALLAHASSEE

Souvenir card of Goodwood estate, with William and Margaret Hodges

The Cherokee Hotel, south side of Park between Monroe and Calhoun, circa 1930s

Boy Scout Troop 101, 1927

Centennial Field opened for games played by community baseball teams in 1924. In 1928 a high board fence was constructed and paid for by the sale of advertising space and in 1935 the grandstand was built as a Federal Emergency Relief Act project.

Appleyard's Printing Company was built in 1924

A Karl F. Wittman revival, 1928

[Ca]pital City Country [Clu]b, 1929

[c]riticized the "wet" candidates and favored Georgia's [S]enator Walter F. George. Editor Smith finally sup[p]orted the party, but in the November election, Florida [v]oted for the victorious Republican, as thousands of ["]Hoovercrats" deserted (temporarily). Leon County [w]as an exception, returning 1,897 votes for Smith to [9]46 for Hoover. Editor Smith summed up the feelings [o]f many people: "Tallahasseeans are particularly [c]hagrined over Florida's majority for Hoover [and [b]lame it on party leaders], but Leon County should feel [p]roud of the magnificent [D]emocratic majority her [o]wn voters registered." The Ku Klux Klan, a major [p]olitical force in many areas of the country in the [1]920s, supported Hoover. The hooded order kept a [l]ow profile in Tallahassee. Occasional stories of its [r]allies and marches in Florida and other parts of the [U]nited States appeared in the local press, but little [m]ention was made of local Klan activity.

TALLAHASSEE "SPRUCES UP" ITS IMAGE

"Beautification" drives were launched in Tallahassee. The city continued to plant Washingtonia palm trees and offered to plant them free on private property if the [h]ome owners paid for the trees. George B. Perkins, an [e]arly developer, objected that the palms were ill-suited [t]o Leon County's occasional cold weather. Even brief [f]reezes left the fronds damaged and unattractive. [N]orthern visitors might get the wrong idea. Perkins advocated a "comprehensive beautification plan" for streets and sidewalks, rather than reliance on "individual taste." Responding, the city commission appointed a park board, charged with surveying beautification needs. A committee of representatives from various clubs planned a giant cleanup campaign. The committee proposed a city-wide plant day, and talked of establishing a municipal nursery. Other projects included seeding parks, cemeteries, and medians with winter rye grass, and planting oaks and dogwoods.

Blacks, although not included in the original planning bodies, participated in the project. Led by President J. R. E. Lee of FAMC, 500 black citizens held a mass outdoor meeting. The FAMC band and quartet performed, and after Tom Turner of the chamber of commerce outlined the improvement plans, those present pledged cooperation.

During the 1920s, advertisements for opulent new communities in central and south Florida appeared in the local newspaper. Tallahasseeans, however, did not have to look to Coral Gables. New developments were announced right at home. Lots were offered for sale in 1926 in Country Club Estates, Los Robles, and Highland Park (the Lafayette Park area). The Los Robles section attracted city residents longing for suburbia. It had paved streets and, once it came into the city limits, all municipal services were available, including a proposed elementary school.

Transportation improved and provided better contact between Tallahassee and other cities. Two bus lines were in operation. The Blue offered daily runs to Jacksonville and points south, and the Georgia-Florida

Entrance to Los Robles subdivision with The Woman's Club in distance, circa 1940s-1950s

Looking west on College Avenue, circa 1925

Motor Lines linked the capital with south Georgia. The Seaboard Airline Railway ran east and west, while the Georgia, Florida, and Alabama Railway took Tallahasseeans to northern connections.

City travel became easier in 1927 with the arrival of three "genuine" Yellow Cabs. Gradually, dirt streets were surfaced. A white way was installed around the capitol square and on East Park Avenue. Paid for by popular subscription, the lights were turned on in 1923 and 1924. Traffic lights were introduced in 1927, when five lights were installed on posts in the middle of the busiest intersections.

In 1925, the old airport at Magnolia Heights was replaced by one east of town on the Old Saint Augustine Road. It was little used privately, although military planes from the Pensacola training center stopped occasionally. Inspired by Charles A. Lindbergh's record flights (and his flight later over Tallahassee), city and county authorities purchased land west of town. A landing field was constructed, and the facility was in use by the spring of 1929.

Improvements—lights, hangars, paved runways—came later. Watching takeoffs and landings became a favorite community pastime. In the summer, the city commissioners named the airport Dale Mabry Field. The named honored Captain Dale Mabry, a native so who survived World War I only to be killed in 1922 ir the crash of the "Roma," a dirigible he was piloting. Armistice Day 1929 was selected for the formal dedic tion; the colorful event was attended by thousands. Commercial air service began a few weeks later, and Ivan Munroe was appointed manager. The operation most citizens agreed, heralded nothing less than a new era.

A historic enemy, the mosquito, came under attack in 1923 from the town's first "sanitary officer" (h also inspected dairies and supervised garbage collec tion). A massive campaign enlisted Girl Scouts and B Scouts who won movie passes, ice cream, NuGrape drinks, and other prizes by destroying mosquito bree ing sites. Those joining the "Mosquito League" received special buttons to wear as they went about the

During the 1928 national election this banner flew over Monroe Street at Pensacola.

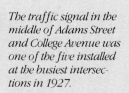

The traffic signal in the middle of Adams Street and College Avenue was one of the five installed at the busiest intersections in 1927.

asks. One effort involved stocking wells infested with mosquito larvae with "top water minnows" to destroy the hatchlings.

New businesses opened during the jazz age and changed the face of Tallahassee. The six-story Exchange Bank building, constructed in 1927 at the southwest corner of Monroe and College, was Tallahassee's first "skyscraper." Commercial buildings along the principal streets were renovated and given modern plate-glass fronts.

An abrupt break with the past came in October 1925 when the venerable Leon Hotel burned. It had been an elegant landmark since the 1880s, and the loss was a severe blow. Except for the Cherokee, the town lacked sufficient hotel facilities. Lawmakers, in town for a special legislative session, and visitors had to be housed. Local citizens filled out forms indicating their willingness to rent (a key question was "Do you have a bath; and lights?"). Senator Hodges offered his colleagues free accommodations at Goodwood.

Members of the chamber of commerce and others launched a drive to build a new hotel; volunteers from civic clubs canvassed the town selling stock in the Tallahassee Hotel Corporation. Work began, and in early May 1927, the Hotel Floridan held its grand opening. Each of 68 rooms had a phone, private bath, and hot and cold water—luxuries which many residents lacked. In December 1929, the Floridan opened a 75-room five-story annex which also housed a banquet hall and ballroom.

TALLAHASSEE REACHES A TURNING POINT

Florida's speculative boom peaked in 1925. The unrestrained real-estate market invited fraud, and soon the state began to receive unfavorable newspaper publicity. Uncertainty existed about the present and impending tax structure. By 1926, land sales slumped. When deposits fell sharply, coupled

Ivan Munroe is shown with "Ole Hon," the city's first locally owned aircraft. The plane, an eight-cylinder Curtiss OX-5, was purchased in 1928.

The municipal airport west of Tallahassee was named for Dale Mabry, who had survived World War I only to be killed in the crash of the dirigible Roma *in 1922.*

Opening day of Dale Mabry Field was November 11, 1929.

with heavy withdrawals, banks began to fail. In Tallahassee, the Lewis State Bank, Capital City Bank, and Exchange Bank were sound, but the Citizens Bank—in existence since 1912—was sold in 1928 to the other three. The negotiation was accomplished quietly, and customers transferred their accounts to the Lewis State Bank, Capital City, and Exchange.

The end of Florida's prosperity came with dramatic fury. In September 1926, a devastating hurricane hit the state's southern regions. Then in 1928 an even more powerful storm raked Florida, and the state's economy tottered. The next year the stock-market crisis plunged the nation into the Great Depression. Tallahassee and Leon County did not experience the frenzied boom of the 1920s and, with a stable economy, the area suffered less during the depression than did most of Florida.

By 1930, the capital and the county had changed considerably. Leon County had grown to 23,476 persons. With 10,700 citizens, Tallahassee had almost doubled in size. Blacks represented 58.7 percent of the population. Agriculture still dominated the economy, but 243 fewer farms existed. Cotton remained the basic money crop. Technological advances enjoyed in the capital were rare in the county. Only 33 tractors were in the county, only 41 farmers had telephones, and only 35 dwellings were lighted by electricity. The county was crisscrossed by 702 miles of unimproved roads.

The people had faced hard times before. Once again, they girded themselves for a troubled and uncertain future.

THE DEPRESSION DECADE BEGINS

Herbert Hoover was president when the Great Depression began, but Leon countians joined with Florida and the rest of the nation in 1932—they installed Franklin D. Roosevelt in the White House and gave the Democrats control of Congress. FDR, as the new president came to be called, inaugurated a vast program known as the New Deal. Enough of its measures were effective to assure Roosevelt's triumphant reelection in 1936, with Leon County's solid support.

The Democrats continued to occupy the governor's mansion on North Adams Street and to control the legislature. Doyle E. Carlton, elected in 1928, yielded in 1932 to David Sholtz. Frederick P. "Old Suwanee" Cone, a lawyer and banker from Lake City, was governor in the late 1930s. Cone excluded floats at his inauguration because of the harsh times. Local elections were contested fiercely—only Sheriff Frank Stoutamire remained unbeatable—and many political rallies were held, some featuring mullet fries.

The Great Depression affected the lives of all citizens (in 1932, Leon County's property valuation dropped $207,000). Hoover's efforts to deal with the crisis through volunteers and local and state agencies proved inadequate. In contrast, the New Deal launched a bewildering variety of boards and commissions to deal with the desperate situation. The most important local agency was the Leon County Welfare Association (LCWA), headed by Jack Simmons. The hard times could be measured in human and statistical terms. Soup kitchens that provided food for transients were operating in Tallahassee by 1930. That year, the LCWA and the local Red Cross led a drive to collect Christmas presents for people in need.

The LCWA exceeded its budget every month. Private citizens contributed food for the poor and unemployed. In 1930, the *Democrat* ran free "Situation Wanted" ads, and by 1932 1,500 people were unemployed and another 2,000 needed part-time employment. Alice Poole, the black home-demonstration agent, gave assistance, and her white counterpart, Ruth Kellum, conducted free public canning demonstrations. The Woman's Club helped collect garments for children unable to attend school because they lacked adequate clothing.

A $700 grant from the Reconstruction Finance Corporation (RFC) was used by the LCWA to finance work by whites and blacks. The men cleared land and cleaned up city property at one dollar a day, and the women were assigned sewing projects. Simmons and local ministers received donations of used but repairable shoes, hired an unemployed man to fix them, and saw to their distribution. "Hoboes," unemployed men and boys drifting through town, were not considered vagrants, but were permitted to "go on through." A patrol hired by the Seaboard Railroad to keep hoboes off its cars was discontinued. Charles Deeb's Humpty-Dumpty Grocery Store maintained a woodyard for transients: a man could earn a meal by chopping wood. The wood later was sold to finance the meals. In 1933, the city contributed $5,581.06 in food and shelter for transient relief, and civic clubs provided a free pint of milk daily to needy white schoolchildren.

The people suffered health problems, but in 1930 local and state efforts, along with those of the United States Public Health Service, brought Leon County and the state's first complete health unit. Mosquito eradication was continued and a campaign was begun to control pellagra, a disease caused by dietary deficiencies. Health authorities were amazed when their examinations revealed that the county's black children were healthier than the whites.

Public moneys were squeezed. In 1931, the legislature reduced state salaries from 5 to 15 percent. Tallahassee cut its budget by $20,000 in 1932, and reduced its electric rates. Nowhere was austerity felt more than in education. In 1933, the superintendent of education absorbed the upkeep of his county car, and Tallahassee schools discontinued their telephones. More seriously, the county school board, in the interest of economy, closed 44 black schools in March, and reduced the academic year to six months. In 1934, the schools resumed their mandatory calendar of eight months.

With one exception, Tallahassee's banks weathered the depression, continued to serve the community, and even prospered. The exception was the Exchange Bank. In August 1932, C. L. Mizell, a well-liked civic leader and president of the Exchange since its founding in 1912, committed suicide. The Florida bank examiner reported later that the Exchange had no shortages. Obviously, the crisis was serious, and

*Exchange Bank, Talla-
hassee's first skyscraper,
a six-story edifice, was
built in 1927 at Monroe
Street and College
Avenue.*

*Tallahassee trash
collector, 1916*

Mizell stipulated in a final note that the bank was to collect his $25,000 life insurance.

THE NEW DEAL OFFERS HELP—AND HOPE

After Roosevelt was inaugurated, one of his first acts was to declare a national banking holiday of five days. Governor Sholtz was authorized to carry out the decree. Lewis State Bank and Capital City Bank officials assured citizens assembled at the courthouse that all was well. They would not use scrip because their institutions were solvent. When the banks resumed business, both reported "twice as many deposits as withdraws."

The New Deal's federal agencies—some short-lived, others lasting into the 1940s—had both a profound temporary and a permanent impact on Talla-hassee and Leon County. In essence, their combined functions provided jobs, brought money into the economy, lifted morale, and added needed improve-ments. The principal agencies were the National Recovery Administration (NRA), Public Works Adminis-tration (PWA), Civil Works Administration (CWA), Civilian Conservation Corps (CCC), and Works Progress Administration (WPA). Federal expenditures, com-bined with those of local, county, and state agencies, literally transformed the face of Tallahassee and Leon County.

Action that followed the Democratic takeover in 1933 can only be summarized. Relief roles declined—

the construction of 99 buildings and the expenditure of $500,000 in federal money meant work. Extensive improvements on the campuses of FAMC and FSCW, as well as the city's secondary schools (both black and white), and the repair of public buildings were under-taken. A canning plant was set up in Chaires, and a mattress factory was established in Tallahassee. In 1935, work was begun on the new post office and federal building, as well as the armory. The building boom resembled that of the 1920s. The extensive remodeling of both banks restored public confidence. With 2,474 citizens still unemployed in the fall of 1935, the various projects continued and new ones were added. A new Leon High School replaced the old one built in 1912 (Lincoln, the county's only black high school, had moved into a new brick facility on West Brevard Street in 1929). A new jail was provided, and an addition was made to the Martin building. Funds were expended to enlarge the Tallahassee Country Club and the owning corporation gave it to the city. Streets were paved, sidewalks constructed, sewer lines laid, and work was begun on a county abattoir (slaughterhouse). It was little wonder that in 1936 Tallahassee celebrated its achievements with a progress parade.

In 1930, Leon County's farmers produced more cotton than in 1929, but after that a dramatic change occurred. Throughout the 1930s, emphasis on live-stock—especially dairy cattle—continued. Govern-ment payments by the AAA (Agricultural Adjustment Administration) persuaded farmers to reduce produc-tion in basic crops. Some distressed farmers received cash grants from the government, while others ob-

A 1927 aerial view looks north at the capitol and business district.

The Floridan Hotel, 1927, at Monroe and Call streets

tained loans from the Federal Land Bank and benefited from the Farm Credit Act of 1933 and the Federal Farm Bankruptcy Act of 1934. Sea Island (long staple) cotton made a minor comeback—federal funds bought the poison for weevil control. A black farm agent was assigned to the county, local farmers set up an agricultural exchange, and a rural sanitation program was begun.

By 1940, Leon County's traditional reliance on agriculture was gone. For the first time, urban residents comprised a majority of the county's citizens. Farm income dropped (the 1940 cotton crop was worth one-sixth that of 1930). The number and size of farms declined, as did the number of farmers, most of whom were blacks. The old order had passed.

THE LANDSCAPE CHANGES

The New Deal did much to change the cutover, nonproductive sandy soil of south Leon County, as well as Jefferson and Wakulla counties. Work by the National Park Service, the CCC, the Resettlement Administration (RA), and other federal and state agencies resulted in transforming more than 300,000 acres into the Saint Marks Wildlife Refuge and the Apalachicola National Forest. Leon County had two CCC camps, one for whites and one for blacks. The black camp near Woodville was successful, experiencing none of the resentment evident in other areas. Members of the CCC and other workers—known as the "tree army"—planted trees, built fire lanes and fire

towers, fashioned recreation areas, and carried out projects involving soil erosion and stream pollution.

Tallahassee's subdivisions resumed their expansion because the Home Owners Loan Corporation (HOLC, 1933) made possible the refinancing of home mortgages, and the National Housing Act of 1934 created the Federal Housing Administration (FHA) to insure construction loans. Another result was that the capital got an active mortgage-loan business in 1934— Tallahassee Federal Savings and Loan Association. It became an instant success as building expenditures in 1936 jumped to $1,741,381, the greatest during the depression.

The NIRA, with its symbolic "Blue Eagle," hoped to restore prosperity with its business codes of fair competition and its guarantees to labor. Locally, "Blue Eagle buying Days" were held with street dances and considerable propaganda. Yet the program, too grandiose and badly administered, floundered and was declared unconstitutional in 1935. Still, the local economy continued to benefit from federal funds in the decade's last years. Projects included the Federal Correctional Institution, completion of the sewer system, playgrounds and parks, and school construction, especially at FSCW, where a dormitory, infirmary, and dining hall were built.

Private business (championed by the chamber of commerce and beginning in 1933, the Junior Chamber of Commerce) also benefited from Washington's largess. At whatever sacrifice, Tallahasseeans still owned cars and trucks—4,760 of them in 1935. Passenger trains still ran, and six bus companies operated

Governor Dave Sholtz, third from left, arriving in the capital city for his inauguration, is greeted by Justice Fred Davis, other members of the state supreme court, and various dignitaries, January 1933.

Girls admire fashions in Vogue's window, 1936.

Johnston's Hospital, built in 1924 at the northeast corner of Gadsden and McDaniel, was the city's only health facility for many years.

from the Union Bus Terminal in 1936. "Kruz Kar" taxi service had its "Shopper's Special" from anywhere in the city to the shopping district for ten cents. By the decade's end, Eastern, National, and Atlantic and Gulf Coast airlines served Dale Mabry Field. To great fanfare, airmail service was inaugurated in 1937. A city bus system was discussed, as was the installation of parking meters downtown.

GOD'S LAW AND MAN'S LAW HOLD SWAY

The depression seemed to deepen the religious convictions of the community's Protestants, Catholics, and Jews. People attended church in greater numbers than ever. In the early 1930s, Trinity Methodist and First Presbyterian celebrated their 100th anniversary; the Presbyterians staged a historical pageant. New churches were formed, older ones grew, and revivals retained their popularity, whether conducted in a sweltering tent on the outskirts of town or in the more sedate and cooler confines of a church sanctuary.

For many years, Tallahassee's Jewish population, too small to support a synagogue, hosted visiting rabbis on important occasions. Finally in 1937, some 30 families organized the Tallahassee Jewish Community Inc., and raised money to construct a place of worship. Temple Israel opened in 1940 and a new temple was built in 1973.

A minority of Tallahasseeans and Leon countians broke the law, committing crimes both minor and major. Some felonies were unusual, as demonstrated by one man who stole an easily recognizable Leon

County school bus, allegedly for its tires (he then stole a car to haul the tires away).

In 1934, Company M of the Florida National Guard (founded in 1924) was called out to help maintain order following a lynching in nearby Marianna. Closer to home, after Captain Hugh Mays was succeeded by Captain Henry W. McMillan, Jr., Company M helped protect the courthouse against possible attack by a mob. A young black from Apalachicola had been indicted for the rape of a white woman, and was tried in Leon County to protect his safety. As he was guarded by Company M with mounted machine guns, the state conducted its case (the verdict was guilty and the punishment was death by electrocution).

The sale of hard liquor continued to be a crime. In February 1933, Congress submitted the Twenty-First Amendment to the states. Pending ratification, Congress passed the Beer-Wine Revenue Act on March 22, permitting the sale of beverages with an alcoholic content of 3.2 percent. The day beer became legal, the Leon County tax collector issued fifteen permits—glad no doubt, to have a new source of revenue. The statewide referendum on ratification came on November 6, but Leon County's commissioners excluded the question of local option from the ballot. Florida voted for repeal, and so did Leon County (1,212 to 1,022). The amendment went into effect on December 5, 1933. The "wets" took heart and forced an election in 1935. Even so, the "drys" did most of the campaigning and won by a majority of 289 votes. The sale of liquor continued to be illegal. Still another election in 1937 resulted in victory for the opponents of rum, and the "wets" surrendered.

*The Rotary Club tours
the Jackson Bluff hydro-
electric plant, circa
1930.*

Lincoln High School, a new black school, 1929

Leon High School under construction, 1937

Leon County courthouse, 1930

Early in the 1930s, Floridians sought to increase local and state revenues by legalizing slot machines and punchboards. The legislature legalized the machines in 1935, and 30 were installed in Tallahassee. The locations were limited to the center of town, excluded from hotels, and kept more than 300 feet from churches and schools. Leon countians held a special election in 1936 and overwhelmingly voted the slot machines out. The state law was repealed in 1937.

The decade's worst crime occurred in 1937, when two blacks were taken from the local jail and lynched. Apprehended during a robbery attempt, the men had stabbed a policeman, who recovered. Despite the resulting furor, the case was dropped for lack of evidence. In 1939, another sensational case involved the arrest and indictment of four local men on charges of "white slavery."

EDUCATION FACES ECONOMIC REALITY

Education suffered at all levels during the depression. In 1931-1932, Leon County had eleven white schools and 45 black schools. Some of the 174 teachers were paid as little as 35 dollars a month. Because the state reduced school funding but required an eight-month term, county officials had to practice strict economy. Both FSCW and FAMC received construction benefits, but faced restrictions on the expansion of faculties and staff and on raising salaries. Private grants helped, and in 1932 blacks honored the contributions of Julius Rosenwald to their race's educational progress. FERA funds were available for some students who worked 30 hours a

week at 30 cents an hour and federal money founded two nursery schools in 1933. Beginning in 1935, the National Youth Administration (NYA) provided jobs for young people no longer in full-time attendance at school.

Lively Vocational School was established in 1931 with one full-time and one part-time instructor, five typewriters, an adding machine, a kerosene stove, and little else. The school met in a building owned by Lewis M. Lively, a Tallahassee businessman and member of a pioneer family. Evelyn K. Messer became the effective longtime director of a program that begun with courses in typing, shorthand, bookkeeping, and accounting. When the new Leon High School opened, Lively moved into the old building.

RECREATION AND ENTERTAINMENT PROVIDE "ESCAPE"

In the early 1930s, the Claude L. Sauls American Legion Post built an open-air arena near its lodge at Lake Ella and sponsored well-attended boxing matches. Whites boxed whites, and blacks boxed blacks. The Legion resumed the fights in 1935 at Recreation Park. Located on South Monroe Street, the park was an amusement center with a skating rink and facilities for boxing, wrestling, dining, dancing, plays, and vaudeville.

The city installed two tennis courts in 1931, and others were added when parks were improved and laid out. Periodically, citywide tennis tournaments were held. Golf remained popular, and several tournaments were held. In 1935, a Georgia-Florida golf league was

"THE GREAT ESCAPE"

Tallahasseeans woke on a Sunday morning in early June 1923 to the discovery that every prisoner in the Leon County jail had escaped the night before. One inmate, Clarence Padgett, pried the lock off his cell door, then helped the other five prisoners do likewise. Unable to break through the locked outer doors, the men used the legs of the jail bathtub to pick a hole in the brick wall of the building. Once outside, the six men fled in two groups. Their freedom was ended abruptly Sunday afternoon when all six were recaptured by Sheriff Frank Stoutamire and his deputies. No doubt the sheriff was especially glad to find Padgett, who had been incarcerated in Leon County's jail for safekeeping after twice breaking out of the Franklin County jail.

Tallahassee post office federal building under construction, 1936

Leon County armory, 1935

Florida capitol, construction in progress on north wing, 1936

organized. When WPA funds were used to improve the Tallahassee Country Club, the city opened it to the public. In 1938, the golf course was increased from nine to eighteen holes. Ralph E. Carter became Tallahassee's first recreation director, a post created by the city commission in 1936.

Interest in football was widespread. Amos P. Godby became coach at Leon High in 1935, the same year nighttime football was begun in the city. Florida High School played six-man football. Florida High had opened in 1920 as a coeducational "laboratory school" for FSCW. Intramural athletics were begun in 1927, and competition with outside opponents followed in 1930. The Rattlers of FAMC fielded strong teams, and under coach William "Big Bill" Bell and his assistant, Alonzo "Jake" Gaither, the Rattlers won the Southern Intercollegiate Athletic Conference championship in 1937. In 1938 they won it again, and then defeated Kentucky

State in the Orange Blossom Classic to earn rights to the national championship.

Baseball was still the most popular team sport. When the University of Florida and Auburn University played a three-game series at Tallahassee in 1935, Governor David Sholtz threw out the first ball. Numerous city leagues played ball. In 1931, an amateur team, the White Sox, was formed, but played most of its games at home. Even more dedicated were the Capitals, an excellent amateur team whose opponents often included colleges and semiprofessional "nines." The Capitals played in a regular Georgia-Florida league. In 1935, the Tallahassee team, retaining the name of Capitals, became the only Florida entry in the Class D professional Georgia-Florida league. Fred Lowry, a local banker, was the force behind the Capitals, whose home park was Centennial Field (night baseball began in 1938). Tallahasseeans also enjoyed watching the

Children play at the nursery school at FSCW, June 28, 1935.

Nashville Volunteers, who came to the capital for spring training.

Hunting and fishing never lost their appeal. The Tallahassee Rod and Gun Club was a formal expression of universal interest, as attested by the lines of people in what was an autumn ritual—buying hunting licenses.

"Summertime!" Tallahasseeans might declare the season started by May, but nobody said the living was easy. One might argue facetiously that unemployment provided plenty of leisure time. In truth, the citizens took whatever entertainment they could get. The careful and not too demanding celebrity watcher had a few exciting moments during the decade. Appearing in town from time to time were Tom Mix, the cowboy star, and his horse Tony; Major Bowes and his "Amateurs on Tour"; the brilliant opera contralto, Marian Anderson; the crooner Rudy Vallee; Sally Rand, the fan dancer (who was not recognized when she appeared fully clothed as the luncheon guest at the Lions Club); the great-grandnephew of Prince Achille Murat; and politicians as different as James A. Farley, FDR's campaign manager and postmaster general, and former United States Senator Thomas Heflin of Alabama.

The Coffee Pot and the Hitchcock Tea Room were popular in 1930—a year that saw the Ponce de León Grill offer Thanksgiving dinner for one dollar. Outside town, supper clubs provided dining and dancing. Some of the clubs were the Casanova, the Grove, Lake Ella Tavern, the Cotton Club, and the Spic and Span. After paying a cover charge of 25 cents at the Capital Gardens, a customer could dance to a live orchestra and, for 75 cents, have an all-you-can-eat chicken or fish dinner.

Christmas, the most important holiday, was when the Elks Club held its annual charity carnival. In 1931, 7,000 pounds of food went to the needy; in 1935, the big winner drove away in a new Terraplane. George Washington would have enjoyed the way Tallahassee celebrated his 200th birthday in 1932. The Fourth of July and Labor Day were usually quiet, and Halloween celebrations were limited to soaping windows and festooning live oaks with toilet paper.

In 1933, some citizens went to the Seaboard Airline Depot to view an embalmed whale, and others attended the Kiwanis Club's dog show. Tallahassee's first, the attraction raised money for needy children. The "mutt division" was the most popular. Jimmie Lyndon and his Death Dodgers thrilled spectators in 1936 with their car and motorcycle show.

The Downey Brothers Circus came to town in 1935 and in 1937, the same year the American Legion sponsored the Leon County Fair. In 1939, the Leon County Fair Association took over the sponsorship. The four-day event (no gambling allowed) was a big success. The Tallahassee Garden Club had its spring flower shows, and expanded them to include garden

Looking south on Adams Street at east side between College and Jefferson, during laying of sewer line, 1930s

Workers from Civilian Conservation Corps and other federal agencies planted many trees such as these at Spring Hill, in southwest Leon County.

tours. The Garden Club also judged the best home and filling-station Christmas decorations. Lasses White Minstrels had a big tent show complete with vaudeville acts in 1938. The May Queen festival continued its tradition.

Tallahassee easily avoided bankruptcy—ownership of utilities prevented that, and the tax rate was kept low. New street markers in 1931 bespoke bravado and pride. Beyond that, "culture," in its best sense, was important. Among the many dances, the President's Birthday Ball became an annual event. The March of Dimes drive evolved from this fund-raising effort. Band concerts in City Park were popular. The Yale Glee Club came to FSCW, and the Civic Music Association was formed in 1939. The Little Theatre continued to present plays; the Tallahassee Historical Society was organized in 1933 and the Arts Society in 1934.

The citizens were glad, finally, to get a radio station. On October 7, 1935, WTAL began to broadcast. Soon, radio dials were turned constantly to 1310. Even so, the single most popular social activity was going to the "picture show." Despite Daffin's monopoly, the possibility of new theatres was discussed. In 1930, E. J. Sparks of Jacksonville built the Ritz. Located on Monroe Street, the Ritz opened December 31 with the movie *Holiday*. In February 1932, Daffin leased his movie house to the Sparks interests, and it reopened as the State. A. P. Talley began a long tenure as manager of the State and the Ritz. A fire destroyed the State and other buildings in 1933, but the theatre was rebuilt near the original site and reopened in September 1934.

Whether to show films on Sunday became a cause célèbre. In May 1932, the largest voter turnout for any election in Tallahassee's history approved Sunday movies by a vote of 871 to 519.

Tallahassee Federal Savings and Loan Association, circa 1942

Aerial view of FSCW, late 1930s

Looking south on Monroe Street from College Avenue, late 1930s

The theatres continued Daffin's practice of presenting live vaudeville shows, especially those featuring women. Examples included The Big Apple Revue and Follies de Paree. The latter's cast was featured in advertisements by various Tallahassee businesses, a photographic venture that worked well enough to be repeated when the Follies Caprecie came to town.

It was a great decade for movies and movie stars. Admission prices were affordable for a people seeking entertainment and escape. America fell in love with Shirley Temple. Sonja Heine glamorized ice-skating, while Fred Astaire and Ginger Rogers danced up a storm. Jeanette MacDonald and Nelson Eddy were the favored singing duo. Few doubted that Johnny Weissmuller was Tarzan or that Edward G. Robinson, James Cagney, and Humphrey Bogart were tough guys. Glamorous was a synonym for Greta Garbo, Jean Harlow, and Carole Lombard. Clark Gable's masculinity

appealed to both sexes, and Robert Taylor emerged as the leading heartthrob. The public flocked to see many other stars, and excellent movies: *Top Hat, Mutiny on the Bounty, Jezebel, The Wizard of Oz,* and *Snow White* were among them.

A SHADOW LIES AHEAD

The long and increasingly dark shadow of foreign affairs did not go unnoticed. Even during the depression, people remembered Mussolini's rise to power in Italy during the 1920s. They knew of Japan's aggressive machinations in Asia, especially in Manchuria and China during the 1930s. More ominously, Hitler had steered his country on a warlike course. The Nazi dictator rearmed Germany, withdrew from the League of Nations, aided Franco in

*Auxiliary forty-foot
fire-lookout tower,
Woodville, Leon County,
1932*

Spain, made common cause with Italy and Japan, an-
nexed Austria, and sliced up Czechoslovakia. Then
Hitler provoked the Polish crisis which brought Great
Britian and France into World War II. And what of
Russia, which appropriated part of Finland in 1940? The
United States had attempted to remain aloof through
neutrality legislation, but by 1940, changes had to be
made, reality had to be faced.

Tallahasseeans and Leon countians were worried,
yet they realized that the worst aspects of the Great
Depression were behind them. Florida's population
had reached almost two million, and Leon County had
31,646, an increase of 8,170 citizens since 1930. Most of
them had moved to Tallahassee, which had 16,240
people, a gain of almost 50 percent in ten years. Whatever the crisis, foreign or domestic, the people were
confident they could handle it.

Eastern Airlines began scheduled flight service to Dale Mabry Field on October 10, 1938. Fourth from Left is Captain Eddie Rickenbacker, president of Eastern Airlines. The aircraft is a DC-3.

Prince and Princess Charles Murat pose beside the tombs of Prince Charles Napoleon Achille Murat and Catherine Willis Gray Murat in June 1932. Charles Murat was the couple's greatgrand-nephew.

Recreation Park on South Monroe Street was an amusement center.

May Party, 1932

Business and Professional Woman's Club members pose beside the tree given to the city to mark the bicentennial of George Washington's birth, February 22, 1932.

NICE PRICE—IF YOU CAN PAY IT

In 1932, five pounds of sugar cost eighteen cents, twelve pounds of flour cost 39 cents, and a pound of butter cost 25 cents. As late as 1936, a silk dress was $2.55 and a Chevrolet truck was $360.

The Ritz Theatre, on the west side of Monroe Street between College and Park, was opened in 1930 by E. J. Sparks of Jacksonville. This photograph, looking north, was taken in the late 1930s.

WTAL, Tallahassee's first radio station, began to broadcast at 1310 on the dial on October 7, 1935.

State Theatre, north side of College between Monroe and Adams, 1930s

*Aerial view of Tallahassee
looking west, 1937*

THE CRISIS OF WAR

When the First Lady visited Tallahassee in 1940 she spoke to a capacity crowd in F.S.C.W.'s Augusta Conradi Theatre, with a larger crowd standing outside and others listening over radio station WTAL. L-R: William L. Moor, Mrs. Franklin Delano (Eleanor) Roosevelt, Mrs. Frank Moor, Bettie Moor.

6.

The winter of 1940 was bitterly cold in Tallahassee and Leon County. The elements seemed matched by the world situation: a lull occurred in the European fighting, but Hitler's submarine wolf packs took a heavy toll of Allied shipping in the Atlantic. American-Japanese relations continued to deteriorate. Roosevelt was leading America out of its isolationist stance and into a belated but extensive program of military preparedness. For all the bad news, the citizens refused to despair. After all, the bitter years of the 1930s were behind them. The new year would be a momentous one, but with time for leisure.

Seldom had there a better year for movies. E. J. Sparks, owner of the Ritz and the more prestigious State (opened in November 1940), inaugurated the 1,100-seat Florida on Monroe Street. Among the usual light fare were some popular and worthwhile films. Among the best were Irene Dunne and Cary Grant in *My Favorite Wife*, and Charles Laughton in The *Hunchback of Notre Dame*. When *Gone With the Wind* came to the State in February, the opening was a genuine "event."

The deluge of war movies that would come later had not yet begun in 1940. The only portent of the future was Charlie Chaplin's comic satire *The Great Dictator*. Besides movies, the State presented *Midnight Scandals of 1940*, a musical revue with a cast of 35, and numerous other live presentations. The movie houses also were used as meeting places for the Popeye Club, an organization of the town's young boys and girls.

Sports fans enjoyed Amos P. Godby's state-championship baseball and basketball teams at Leon, and their counterparts at Florida High. The Tallahassee Capitals remained in the eight-team Georgia-Florida league. The Capitals had the loyalty of their fans even though the team finished sixth to the pennant-winning Waycross Bears. Tallahassee had a sports spirit. Local women's basketball teams existed. The American Legion and Company M of the National Guard sponsored wrestling matches at the Armory and boxing bouts that featured black fighters from the CCC Camp at Woodville and other area camps. Two softball teams held games, golf gained in popularity (Robert Parker was the best local golfer), and the leading hunters

The Florida Theatre was opened in November 1940 on the west side of Monroe between Park and Call. Shown here in January 1947.

The Tallahassee fire department moved to this building on the east side of Adams between College and Park in 1937. Firemen show off equipment and new uniforms in this 1940 photograph.

formed the Leon County Sportsman's Association.

No end of events in 1940 fitted under the broad umbrella of culture. The Little Theatre continued to stage plays. Music was available at every level. Carl Roberts brought his Swing Band from Lake City to play at FDR's 58th birthday ball. Jimmie Browder and his black fifteen-piece orchestra were a hit at the Edgewood Club, "the Coolest Spot in Town." Gladys Swarthout sang at the Leon High School Auditorium, and the brilliant soprano, Dorothy Maynor, gave a concert at FAMC.

The year's outstanding occasion, however, was an appearance by the first lady, Eleanor Roosevelt. Mrs. Frank Moor, president of the Alumnae Association of FSCW, arranged the event with considerable help from Senator Claude Pepper and other politicians. A large crowd, undeterred by a heavy rain, greeted Mrs. Roosevelt's plane when it arrived from Jacksonville. She was taken to the FSCW campus, where she was greeted by Governor Fred P. Cone, and was introduced by Mrs. Moor to a capacity crowd at the Augusta Conradi theatre. Mrs. Roosevelt's speech, conveyed by a public-address system to larger crowds outside, was broadcast by WTAL.

City Manager M. N. Yancey and Wilson Carraway, head of the chamber of commerce, noted with pleasure that 1940 was a good year for growth and business. City policemen and firemen received new uniforms. When the 1941 car models joined the other cars, traffic was so heavy that the new fleet of city buses began to make stops only at street corners. The infusion of WPA and other federal money was matched with local and state funds with good results: the Leon County Health United Building, Rowena Longmire Student Alumnae Union Building at FSCW, a library at FAMC, a municipal building, and improvements at Dale Mabry Field. FHA loans continued to underwrite the construction of homes, and attempts were made to bring Rural Electrification Administration lighting to isolated parts of the county. NYA funds continued to be used at Lively Tech for vocational training.

F. Arlie Rhodes was county superintendent of public instruction, presiding over 56 schools. Ten of them (three in the city) were large white institutions. The remaining 46 were black schools that had not been consolidated.

The big news in 1940 was the Army Air Corps' selection of Dale Mabry Field as a subbase of McDill

Field at Tampa. The impact on the capital was obvious, and the long economic dry spell of the depression seemed over.

THE NATIONAL AND INTERNATIONAL EVENTS CAPTURE TALLAHASSEEANS' ATTENTION

If wars and rumors of wars occupied the public's attention, it was still a presidential-election year. The big question of whether Roosevelt would seek an unprecedented third term was resolved when he did so. A group calling itself Anti-Third Term Democrats of Florida ran extensive advertisements in the local papers, but in November balloting, FDR easily carried Leon County, the state, and the nation.

Spessard L. Holland won a runoff election as governor, with the support of Leon countians. By then the county had 34 voting machines, and the returns from the twelve precincts were read over a public-address system at the *Democrat's* office on Adams Street.

Pro-Allied sentiment mounted as the European situation worsened, especially after the surrender of France in June. Tallahassee's Red Cross chapter collected funds for the relief of Europe's war refugees, and Leon countians contributed to the state's Finnish Relief Fund. Considerable support was given to the national Committee to Defend America by Aiding the Allies. Several local leaders formed the Tallahassee Committee for the Defense of America. The organization was headed by Dr. Harold Richards, chairman of the physics department at FSCW.

FDR urged more aid as the Luftwaffe attempted to destroy its opponent from the air in the Battle of Britian that summer and fall. In the United States, enlistments in the regular armed forces were speeded up. In Tallahassee, a local recruiting office was opened at the post office, but volunteers were few. Then in September, Congress passed the Burke-Wadsworth Act, the first peacetime draft in the nation's history.

In compliance with the act, Governor Holland, like other governors, set up a state system of selective service. The key unit was the local draft board. Leon County's initial registration on October 15, 1940, involved more than 5,000 men, most of whom enlisted at schools while the students took a holiday. Lottery numbers were assigned to prospective draftees, and later, in Washington, Secretary of War Henry L. Stimson drew number 158. Among the men holding that number was Fred Winfred Parker of Tallahassee.

In December, the first men—Harvey Monroe Barnette, John Franklin Herring, and James Lee Turner—left from the Tallahassee bus depot for Camp Albert H. Blanding at Starke, Florida, for their physical examinations and induction. Outgoing Governor Cone and other dignitaries saw them off, and bandmaster Romulus Thompson led his Leon High School musicians in stirring renditions of "Suwannee River" and "God Bless America."

Shortly after Christmas, Company M, the local component of the Florida National Guard, was activated and left by troop train for Camp Blanding. The unit previously had been converted from a machine-gun company to a heavy-weapons company. Led by Captain Henry McMillan, the men had taken part in war games with the United States Third Army in Louisiana, and had drilled extensively at home—Natural Bridge was a favorite practice site.

The Armistice Day festivities and parade took on new meaning in 1940. Although the United States had not yet joined the fighting, people were worried about the future.

THE WAR BEGINS

Governor Holland's inauguration in January 1941 revealed the temper of the times. Besides the usual floats, a heavy military flavor was evident, with members of Company M marching in field uniforms. Young men—black and whites, many of them volunteers—continued the steady process of monthly departures to be sworn in and to begin basic training. The city leased Dale Mabry Field to the government for one dollar a year, although the military installation continued to serve private lines, Eastern and National. Soldiers began to report for duty. Among them was Colonel Jacob W. S. Wuest, the newly assigned base commander, the first of several who would hold that position through the war years.

From left, Mildred Cone, Mary Holland, Governor Frederick Cone, and Governor-elect Spessard Holland pose on the governor's mansion steps before leaving for Holland's inauguration, January 7, 1941.

The extra Sunday edition of the Daily Democrat *on December 7, 1941, tells of the attack on Pearl Harbor and Manila.*

In early 1941, the Red Cross and other groups collected and made clothes for the British. On right is United States Sen. Claude Pepper, now a United States representative.

Leon High School students received wartime production training on actual airplanes in the early 1940s at the old Lively Vocational School on Park and Bronough.

An extensive preparedness program and the imminent possibility of war required planning and organization. The Red Cross and other groups collected and made clothes for the Allies, and fund-raising dances and other activities were held. Official preparedness work was carried out by the Leon County Defense Council (LCDC), supervised by the state council and headed locally by City Manager M. N. Yancey. The LCDC, through its many committees, dealt with almost every aspect of life, including transportation and communication, water supply, labor and personnel, and civic protection. Citizens were asked to register with the LCDC for volunteer work. By November 1941, more than half the county residents, including college students, had enlisted.

Part of the LCDC's work was to establish air-raid observation posts. At least seventeen such posts were set up across the county, with volunteers serving as "plane spotters." Emergency first-aid stations were equipped. After the bombing of Pearl Harbor, the defense council selected 60 air raid wardens, divided the town into districts and blocks and, on December 29, conducted a 30-minute blackout which was considered "mostly successful."

The LCDC and the city made major efforts to entertain the military personnel of Dale Mabry Field, nearby bases, and servicemen home on leave. Early on,

students at FSCW held socials, open houses, and dances for the soldiers. The city commission appropriated money to refit and maintain the auditorium and four rooms in the old Leon High School as a club for enlisted men. The LCDC's Recreation Committee "drafted" 1,000 young women as the "Girls' Defense Club." They served as dates for the servicemen, and soon took the name Victorettes. A Chaperons' Club was organized to divide the Victorettes into teams, issue "cards of approval," and arrange weekend dances at the base and servicemen's club. Later, a similar group of young women known as the Bombardears was organized. Groups such as Charlie Page's orchestra, the Florida Footwarmers, and the Dale Mabry Field Jive Bombers soon had all the bookings they could manage.

The United Service Organization (USO) established a center for servicemen at 403 West College. The hall had a reading room, with books and magazines donated by local people, a game room, and a large dance floor. A number of black soldiers were stationed at Dale Mabry. During off-duty hours, they visited the "colored recreation center" at 433 West Saint Augustine, a far less elaborate facility than that for the whites.

Everywhere were unmistakable signs of excitement, tension, and uncertainty. Soldiers passed through town on troop trains and in truck convoys.

Tallahasseeans enrolled in first-aid courses, as the war in Asia and Europe began to seem less distant. A flurry of activity enlivened Dale Mabry Field. As the base grew, the military service added a chapel, movie theatre, private telephone system, and hospital. Housing units for married noncommissioned men and civilian technicians were built on 21 acres known as Mabry Heights. Athletic teams were organized, and by October 1941, the *Democrat's* Sunday edition contained a section called the *Dale Mabry Observer.* Locals read with regret that a lieutenant from the base was killed when his P-35 plane crashed into the Gulf of Mexico. Deaths from training accidents at Dale Mabry became sad but frequent news stories during the war years.

    A home company was organized to replace Company M. Hugh Mays became the commanding officer of Company 6, Florida State Guard. The company's approximately 50 men were armed with rifles and bayonets, and held regular drills throughout the war.

TALLAHASSEEANS "DO THEIR BIT"

From 1941 to 1945, Tallahasseeans undertook an unending community effort to collect scrap metal, paper, and other items needed by the military. The first collection, for aluminum, came in 1941 and drew a strong response. Pens to hold old aluminum articles were placed at strategic places in town, as Sons of the American Legion and black and white Boy Scout troops went door to door in Tallahassee—a process repeated in the county by black and white 4-H Clubbers. At the governor's mansion, Mrs. Holland donated an old dishpan and double boiler. Free movie passes were given to donors, and the drive was pronounced a success.

    "War" was substituted for "defense" as the word preceding government stamps and bonds in 1942, and the embossed minuteman, gun in hand, became a familiar symbol. The sale of war stamps and bonds continued, as well as great periodic fund drives with monetary quotas assigned to communities. Tallahassee and Leon County responded enthusiastically, oversubscribing throughout the war. Boy Scouts conducted house-to-house campaigns, and stores urged customers to take their change in stamps. Many workers had employers withhold part of their paychecks for the purchase of war bonds. Various businesses, especially the banks, ran advertisements urging people to buy stamps and bonds (one store, the Hub, asked its customers to buy bonds instead of clothes). During 1944 alone, well over $10 million was raised in Leon County. For Tallahasseeans, the highlight of the drive that year came during a football game at FAMC. A black military band from nearby Camp Gordon Johnston participated in halftime ceremonies as fans in the stadium bought large numbers of war bonds.

tion problem, with tire thieves replacing antebellum horse thieves as the most despised of villains. Bus lines—municipal as well as interstate—juggled schedules, patched their equipment, and tried to accommodate tired, impatient travelers. Buses and trains gave priority to military demands—for example, the colleges in Tallahassee frequently rearranged or canceled annual holidays because of transportation problems.

"Keep 'em Rolling" was the cry, and Tallahassee claimed it was the first city in the country to organize "Share Your Car" clubs; by the end of 1942, the capital had 38 such clubs. A national speed limit of 35 miles per hour was established (and often violated), and posters demanded of travelers, "Is this trip necessary?"

Gasoline was rationed under a system which classified drivers according to their needs, allowing doctors and others a greater supply. Black-market trade

Black troops, including the famous 99th Fighter Squadron (pilots under the command of Lieutenant Colonel Benjamin O. Davis, Jr., the nation's first black air force general) trained at Dale Mabry Field.

Citizens found other ways to aid the war effort. Dry cleaners persuaded customers to return bags, hangers, and shirt boards after using them. Garbage collection was reduced to twice a week, and "unnecessary" activities, such as the Trot-a-way Horse Show, sometimes were canceled. As the war—and the draft—continued, the labor problem grew. A number of citizens left Tallahassee for high-paying jobs in the shipyards at Mobile, Alabama, and elsewhere. The Tallahassee area had a severe shortage of municipal workers and farm laborers; in other occupations, relief came with the increased number of women workers who took jobs formerly held by men.

Transportation became an immediate crisis. Early in 1942, the government ordered a halt to the manufacture of cars and trucks for civilian use. Dealers with new cars in stock saw their supply vanish quickly, and the used-car business boomed. Gas and tire rationing for individual car owners complicated the transporta-

in gas stamps took place, but most people struggled as best they could on their allotment. The gas and transportation crisis seemed unending. Gas could not be bought on credit, and many delivery services were reduced. After some filling-station owners sold their monthly gas allotments, they simply closed temporarily and became calendar watchers.

So many people, both military and civilian, were entering and leaving Tallahassee that in 1943 the War Production Board relented and approved the building of a modern bus station at the corner of Adams and Tennessee streets. It was owned by Southern Greyhound, but Florida Motor Lines and Trailways shared its use.

Rationing was not limited to transportation. Early in 1942, sugar became the first food to be rationed, followed in the fall by coffee. In 1943, shoes were rationed, with individuals limited to three pairs a year. The War Production Board decreed "victory" clothing, and women's dresses became shorter and tighter, while men's trousers were pleatless and cuffless. Men's suits with vests and two pairs of pants became relics of the past. By early 1945, even electricity was conserved. The city adopted a "brownout" policy—all outdoor advertising lights had to be turned off to save power.

One by one, the amenities of civilian life disappeared as rationing and shortages continued. Ration books ran out, only to be replaced as people stood in long lines to register for them. Restaurants had to restrict their menus because they could not obtain sufficient food supplies. With food shortages acute, some people found it ironic when the government began to ration stoves.

With food often in short supply or too expensive, Leon countians returned to their agricultural heritage and, like millions of other Americans, began to plant "victory gardens." The 4-H Club boys and girls took the lead, and toward the end of the war, 80 percent of Leon County's 4-H girls were cultivating gardens. The unlikeliest people—including students at FSCW—became amateur farmers, and conversation at parties focused on prospects for a good backyard harvest.

The county operated a free cooperative canning center at Gadsden and Bloxham streets. It was open six days a week for canners, who brought their own containers and supplies. During the 1943 canning season, nearly 4,800 jars of food were processed at the center.

Housing was the biggest problem which wartime Tallahassee faced. City Manager Yancey followed a WPB decree and stopped issuing building permits. Another ruling suspended the installation and extension of utilities for the duration of the war. If the housing shortage was a bad dream most of the time, it became a

Weekend dances at Dale Mabry Field, and this one at Camp Gordon Johnston in Carrabelle, were lively and well attended during the war years.

A serviceman participates in services at Temple Israel, then at the southwest corner of Copeland and St. Augustine streets.

nightmare on weekends. Two thousand or more soldiers descended on Tallahassee looking for diversion—and a place to sleep. It was not uncommon for soldiers (in town from Camp Gordon Johnston and other nearby installations) to spend the night in hotel lobbies, bus and train stations, park benches, and back and front porches, in addition to more conventional places.

LEISURE ACTIVITIES LIGHTEN WARTIME WORRIES

Wartime tensions made escapism more important than ever, and Tallahasseeans turned to their usual pastimes with added intensity. Those seeking culture were rewarded with the singing of Lawrence Tibbett and Ezio Pinza. Those with different musical tastes jammed Centennial Field in 1944 when Grand Ol' Opry star Roy Acuff came to town. Live stage shows at the State continued to draw crowds. Although many of the shows were revues of chorus dancers, some were geared toward general audiences, including an all-army pro-

duction in conjunction with the movie version of Irving Berlin's *This is the Army*.

Movies at the State, the Florida, the Ritz, and the Capital (the theatre for blacks) were well attended. More and more films had war themes, including *Bombardier*, starring Randolph Scott, and John Wayne's *Back to Bataan*. Even so, several nonwar films met with great success as well. *Bambi* and *Casablanca* appeared in 1943, and *National Velvet* in 1945.

Nighttime entertainment was limited, but dining and dancing clubs offered some diversion. The sale of beer was legal, but an ongoing controversy existed over the sale of hard liquor. Repeated referendums—some of them close—on local option had seen the "drys" triumph. Yet federal laws permitted the sale of whisky, and a number of places in Leon County held federal licenses. The result was confusion: as one wag put it "There are two things in Leon County that the public insists upon—one is prohibition and the other is whiskey." In any case, Tallahasseeans could chose from several dancing and eating spots, usually located on highways—the Edgewood, the White Kitchen, Rendezvous, the Silver Slipper, and numerous others had many patrons.

The Victorettes and the Bombardears stayed busy, as did the unpublicized Girls' Service Organization at the black USO. As the war came to an end, funding for various servicemen's clubs declined and disappeared. In September 1945, the city purchased the USO building on West Jefferson and turned it into a "Teen Canteen." It is difficult to exaggerate the contribution of the wartime clubs to soldier morale, nor is it possible to calculate the hours the club women put in without pay or without complaint. Certainly the Chaperons' Club and the young women who staged the dances and parties and listened to the troubles of the soldiers far from home performed a service of major importance.

Sports activities were curtailed somewhat during the war. College and university football teams accepted abbreviated schedules, played against service teams, or sometimes gave up the sport altogether (in 1942, FAMC won the National Negro Football Championship). High-school teams continued to function, while baseball fans in Tallahassee could watch the Knoxville Smokies train or could follow the fortunes of the Capitals as they dropped out of and rejoined the Georgia-Florida League.

The Silver Slipper
PRIDE OF CAPITAL CITY

MINIMUM .80 PERSON

PRIZE WINNING BEEF IS NOW BEING SERVED

APPETIZERS

Pickled Herring and Olives	40c
Roquefort Cheese Canape	30c
Cream Cheese and Anchovies	40c
Filet Anchovies and Olives	35c
Kosher Pickles, Olives, Peppers	35c
Stuffed Egg Plant and Olives	35c
Stuffed Celery	45c
Iced Celery Hearts	30c
Special Silver Slipper Dish	50c
Imported Swiss Cheese	35c

COCKTAILS
Served with Saltines or Cheese Wafers

Jumbo Shrimp Cocktail	35c
Oyster Cocktail	35c
Lobster Cocktail	50c
Fruit Salad Cocktail	35c

SALADS
Served with Our Famous Kum Bak Dressing

Famous Greecian Combination Salad	45c
Head Lettuce	25c
Famous Cole Slaw	20c
Genuine Chicken Salad	50c
Sliced Tomatoes	25c
Lettuce and Tomato Salad	35c
Pineapple and Cheese	35c
Shrimp Salad	50c

SINGLE ORDERS SERVED FOR TWO 35c EXTRA

OUTSTANDING WESTERN MEATS
Served with Waffle Potatoes and the Famous Greecian Salad
Rolls and Butter

ALL STEAKS AND CHOPS CHARCOAL BROILED

U. S. Prime 16-oz. Choice Cut Club Steak	$1.65
U. S. Prime 12-oz. Blue Ribbon Steak	1.25
Filet Mignon, Choice Steer	1.10
Plank Steak for Two, with All Trimmings	3.50
Plank Steak for Four, with All Trimmings	6.00
Genuine Thick Lamb Chops (2)	.90
Thick Loin Pork Chops (2)	.80
Premium Ham Steak, Fried Tomatoes	1.60
Breaded Veal Cutlets, Tomato Sauce	.90
Fried Brown Milk Fat Chicken, half	.90
Half Broiled Milk Fat Chicken	1.00
Chicken Saute a la Catalina with Rice	1.25

FRENCH FRIED SPANISH ONIONS	35c
MUSHROOMS IN BUTTER	35c

FLORIDA SEA FOOD
Served with Waffle Potatoes—Tartar Sauce—Our Famous Greecian Salad
Hot Rolls and Butter

Stuffed Deviled Crabs (original)	75c
Whole Broiled Florida Lobster, Drawn Butter	1.00
Fried Jumbo Shrimps or Pan Broiled	75c
Fried Select Oysters, in Yellow Meal	75c
Cold Diced Lobster on Lettuce, Mayonnaise	75c
Charcoal Broiled Snapper Steak, Parsley Sauce	75c
St. Johns Pompano, Broiled, Special Sauce	1.25
Combination Seafood Platter	1.25

WE RESERVE THE RIGHT TO REFUSE SERVICE TO ANYONE

ITALIAN DISHES
Served with Cheese—Rolls and Butter

Italian Spaghetti with Meat Balls	65c
Italian Spaghetti with Chicken Livers	80c
Italian Spaghetti with Chicken	80c
Spaghetti with Mushrooms	75c

CHINESE DISHES
Served with Butter, Rolls or Saltines

Chinese Chop Suey with Rice	50c
Chop Suey with Mushrooms	75c
Special Chicken Chow Mein with Rice and Noodles	85c

DESSERTS

Fresh Apple Pie, made by us	10c
Apple Pie with Toasted Cheese	20c
Imported Roquefort Cheese	30c
Sliced Hawaiian Pineapple	25c
Cream Cheese and Figs	35c

DRINKS

Coffee or Tea Served in Pots	10c
Canada Dry Ginger Ale	25c
Canada Dry Sparkling Water	25c
Schlitz, Budweiser, Pabst and Ale	20c
Hot Chocolate, made with milk	10c
Sweet Milk, Buttermilk	10c
Iced or Hot Tea	10c
Bowl of Crushed Ice and Set Ups	35c
Tomato Juice	15c

NOT RESPONSIBLE FOR LOSS OF PERSONAL PROPERTY

Menu from the Silver Slipper restaurant, 1943-1945. Note crossed-off pork chops and seafood, both of which were rationed.

Fuel-oil and gasoline ration coupons and savings stamps were a familiar part of Tallahassee life by 1942.

LEON COUNTY MAINTAINS ITS "ONE-PARTY" STATUS

Tallahassee's longtime member of Congress, Millard Caldwell, won a runoff victory for governor of Florida in 1944. Many local races had runoffs that year, and some of the candidates were on active duty overseas. In the presidential race, Leon County aided FDR's fourth-term victory by giving him 3,967 votes to 729 for Republican Thomas E. Dewey.

A decision by the United States Supreme Court in 1944 portended political changes. In a case involving the Texas primary election, the court ruled that the primary was not a private affair and that the party could not control who participated in it. The court held that, as an integral part of the election process, the primary must be open to anyone who registered as a Democrat. In Leon County, Democrats were so numerous and Republicans so few that the outcome of any partisan election was never in doubt—in 1944, less than 50 percent of those eligible bothered to vote.

That year, Leon County had only nineteen blacks on its books as Democrats. One black woman teacher attempted to register to vote, but was refused until her party status became clear. But it was only a question of time before blacks would vote in Democratic primaries. The FSCW student newspaper, the *Flambeau*, heralded the decision and predicted a new day.

*FSCW students in the
College Defense Garden,
1942*

TALLAHASSEE BECOMES A MILITARY TOWN

By 1943, it seemed that everyone was in the service or about to enter it. S. P. Deeb sold everything he possessed of value—from a Dodge car to a nightclub—and announced that his new job with the federal government involved "$50 a month—room and board, medical service and khaki clothes." Tallahassee still had 42 lawyers, but fifteen had enlisted. Several faculty and staff members at FSCW and FAMC joined the service or worked with such agencies as the Red Cross.

Housing remained woefully inadequate, sometimes leading to tension between the townspeople and the military. A Dale Mabry officer once asked that "non-productive" citizens move to make room for working people. Asked who the nonproductive were, he replied, "salesmen, authors, and maybe other groups."

Military and civilian authorities worked to make the service personnel feel welcome and to create diversions for them. Servicemen's clubs were upgraded continually, and the USO hosted the Rocking Chair Club, a group of servicemen's wives. A black USO club was opened on Tennessee Street, and in 1943 an officers' lounge was established on Park Avenue.

Relations between the military and Tallahassee's civilian population were not always smooth. When altercations between soldiers and civilians occurred downtown, a question of authority prevailed: who had jurisdiction, the Tallahassee police or the military

police? In September 1943, Colonel Edmund P. Gaines was assigned as commander at the newly named Dale Mabry Air Base. He immediately became involved in a controversy with city officials.

Alarmed by the increase in venereal disease among his soldiers, Colonel Gaines threatened to declare Tallahassee off limits to his entire command. In the resulting negotiations, prostitutes and their military customers were arrested. Trials and convictions for the women followed in civilian courts, while the soldiers were dealt with by the military. Subsequently, a United States Public Health Service physician was appointed to work with the Leon County Health Department. A massive campaign followed, and many people consented to voluntary examinations. The drive was given drama the following year when the governor, the commander, and the entire membership of the Rotary and Exchange clubs submitted voluntarily for testing. Despite all efforts, the problem continued.

Dale Mabry Air Base continued to carry out its mission. In mid-1943, it became a base of the Third Air Force. The general public became acquainted with base operations as varying commanding officers held open houses, staged parades, and held ceremonies to recognize units such as the WACS.

Besides offering employment to many civilians, Dale Mabry Air Base was something to be proud of. Townspeople liked the personnel, service, and ground units as well as those training to be pilots. Besides Americans, Chinese, French, Brazilian, and Filipino pilot trainees were stationed there. Also present was

INFORMATION FOR SERVICE ME

Mrs. William May and Mrs. P. T. Mickler sit in front of the servicemen's information booth at Park and Monroe.

Baritone Lawrence Tibbett performs as part of the FSCW artist series, 1942.

ne famous 99th Fighter Squadron—black pilots under ne command of Lieutenant Colonel Benjamin O. Davis Jr.—which carved a distinguished record in Africa nd Europe. In 1954, Davis would become the first black general in the air force. Local citizens considered vith envy the base's modern hospital and equipment.

A racial incident occurred in 1944 when a crowd f black soldiers objected to the arrest of five of their llows in Frenchtown, the predominantly black sec- on of Tallahassee. A serious disturbance was averted hen black and white military police and local city olice used riot guns and tear gas. Most of the soldiers nvolved were from Camp Gordon Johnston. A military nvestigation followed, and for a time no black service- nen from the base at Carrabelle were permitted to ome to Tallahassee on weekends.

In April 1945, Tallahassee had its only serious riot nvolving servicemen. The disturbance was not racially riented (black civilians, however, protested against heir treatment on the segregated city bus line). The ot, involving about 200 to 250 black soldiers from ale Mabry and Camp Gordon Johnston, was confined o the Frenchtown section. It lasted from 10:00 p.m. to 2:30 a.m., and before it ended all available military olice, local police, and highway patrolmen were lled out. According to reports, the men simply an- ounced that before their imminent overseas assign- nents took effect, they intended to "take Frenchtown

apart." They roamed the streets throwing bottles, rocks, and anything available. A number of black-owned businesses were damaged. Only the military police made arrests, and no one was injured. A military inves- tigation followed, but its results were not made public.

WORLDWIDE EVENTS AFFECT TALLAHASSEE

On June 6, 1944—D-Day—Operation Over- lord began when Allied forces landed in Normandy in the largest amphibian opera- tion in history. The news reached Talla- hassee at 4:00 a.m. The invasion had been anticipated eagerly, and the citizens knew the meaning of the local signal—the wailing of five sirens from the fire depart- ment. By early fall, France, Belgium, and Luxembourg were liberated, and time began to run out for Hitler's armies.

Events moved swiftly in 1945. The Allied offenses swept into Germany in April, following the Battle of the Bulge. That same month, Mussolini was killed. At home, the most shocking news of the year was the sudden death of President Roosevelt at Warm Springs, Georgia, on April 12. In Tallahassee, stores were closed in tribute. The deeply grieved citizens of the capital city held numerous memorial services. Roosevelt was not

The Capital Theatre on Macomb Street was patronized by blacks.

Young Tallahassee couples at a popular nightspot during World War II.

only the nation's leader, he was the only president many of them had ever known. The people rallied around his successor, Harry S Truman, and were pleased later in the year when the "Goddess of Liberty" was replaced on dimes by FDR's likeness.

In May, a provisional German government announced the death of Adolf Hitler. Berlin fell and German forces capitulated. The long awaited V-E day came with the unconditional surrender of Germany, and the war in Europe formally ended on May 8.

The news was received in Tallahassee with heartfelt relief, but without wild celebrations. Governor Caldwell pleaded for a safe and sane observance, and for 48 hours no intoxicants were sold. Small knots of people gathered in front of stores, where radios were placed outside. Churches rang their bells and opened for prayers, stores closed, and the chimes at FSCW played the national anthem. Families of soldiers stationed in Europe could at last relax. J. Q. Ashmore Jr., who had entered the Royal Canadian Air Force and was captured in 1943, became the first Tallahasseean to be released from a German prison camp.

Peace had come to Europe, but the war continued in the Pacific. For many Tallahassee families, the worried waiting continued. During early spring, costly fighting took place on the island of Iwo Jima, only 750 miles from Tokyo. In a bitter struggle, United States Marines took Mount Suribachi, raising the American flag, and providing a historic photograph for Associated Press photographer Joe Rosenthal. What went unpublicized was that another group of Marines had been photographed raising the flag even earlier. More incredible still was that before either photograph was taken, Platoon Sergeant Ernest Ivy Thomas Jr. of Monticello was part of a platoon that mounted a smaller version of Old Glory on the summit. The young marine was killed a few days later, on his 21st birthday, March

American troops moved closer to the Japanese mainland in the late spring and early summer, meeting stiff resistance. In late July, the Allied demand for unconditional surrender was rejected. However, after atomic bombs were dropped on Hiroshima and Nagasaki, Japan conceded defeat. V-J day was proclaimed August 15. In Tallahassee, the news arrived at 7:00 p.m. Eastern War Time, and a spontaneous response followed. With horns blowing wildly, cars converged downtown. An eyewitness reported "a continuous riot of cheering, singing, and noise making." Chief of

lice Prater kept vigil over domestic tranquility, but
more or less let the people "go the limit." Strangers
nbraced, and no person in uniform was safe from
ng kisses and crunching hugs. People cried openly. It
is too much to believe. The war was over. The next
y, 10,000 people looked on as a giant parade moved
wn Monroe Street. Stores were closed and church
ors opened, and within the next few days signs
oclaimed "Welcome Home, GI's."

With the war over, Dale Mabry's training mission
ded. In October, it became a temporary separation
se, not included in the list of installations to be
ained. In November, the base was placed on the war
partment's inactive list. Twenty-five men were
tioned there, and later the property was returned to
e city. Ivan Munroe became manager once again, and
e runways were open to civilian planes. The locally
ned Wheeler Airport, on the Old Saint Augustine
ad, moved its activities to Dale Mabry, and every-
dy anticipated a boom in aviation.

For the last months of 1945 and into 1946, men
d women were discharged and returned to Talla-
ssee. At first, release from the service was based
points determined by time in service, overseas

duty, and combat action. Finally, it was determined
by time spent in the service, and those whose civilian
lives had been so dramatically interrupted came home
as veterans.

Gas rationing ended in August, and the production of new cars was resumed. The housing situation
gradually eased. Tallahassee needed private dwellings
as well as office space, and the only thing missing was
building material. Still, room was found for the state
legislators, and in October, unregulated building was
permitted. Despite the restrictions, between 1940 and
1945, 410 new dwellings were built in Tallahassee. In
1945, contracts were let to add a south wing to
the capitol. Plans for postwar expansion of the capitol
center, the colleges, and the city were already on
the books.

The previous 25 years had been sharply deli-
neated into the jazz age, the Great Depression, and
the world war. Yet there was little time for reflection.
Ready or not, Tallahassee and Leon County faced the
postwar era.

At the inauguration of Governor Millard F. Caldwell, January 2, 1945, Chief Justice Rivers H. Buford administers the oath of office.

Tallahasseans in service met while in Europe in 1944. Shown here are Syde Deeb (center) and Miller Walston (right).

British, Chinese, and American officers were in training at Dale Mabry Field, 1943.

THE NUMBERS SPEAK FOR THEMSELVES

*S*tatistics are an incomplete means of recording a war, but numbers at least demonstrate the magnitude of World War II. The United States armed forces totaled 12,466,000 men and women. In all theatres of war, the nation lost 322,188 killed and 700,000 wounded. Florida furnished 238,431 military personnel, and 4,712 were killed. In Leon County, almost 8,000 men registered for selective service and 4,009 were inducted. Of those, 2,596 were whites and 1,413 were blacks.

The 124th Infantry, which included Tallahassee's Company M, was deactivated in 1944. After a protest by Governor Spessard Holland, the company was reconstituted and served with distinction in the Pacific. Six men from Company M were killed in action. In all, 56 Leon countians were killed during the war. Company A of the Florida State Guard was disbanded in December 1946.

The Daily Democrat *tells of Germany's surrender.*

Louis Lowery's photograph shows members of the patrol which planted the first United States flag atop Mount Suribachi, Iwo Jima, on February 23, 1945. Facing cameras, rifle in hand, is Sergeant Ernest Thomas of Monticello. Thomas was killed a week later on Iwo Jima.

Aerial view, looking north, shows construction of the south wing of the capitol, 1946.

FROM PAST TO PRESENT

Looking southeast over the Capitol in 1961 before Leon County had reached 100,000 in population.

An anomalous simplification can explain the last half of the twentieth century: it was complex. After World War II, every aspect of society and life became more complicated for Americans, a situation shared by Tallahasseeans and Leon Countians. For one thing, more of them were there to share it. In 1950, Leon County had a population of 51,590, and Tallahassee had grown to 27,237, an increase of 67.7 percent since 1940. During World War II and the five years that followed, important demographic changes occurred. For the first time since the 1830s, Leon County had more whites than blacks. Not only were more people living in Tallahassee, but the county's rural non-farm population outnumbered its rural farm population. The total value of all agricultural production was less than a million dollars, and the ghosts of antebellum planters must have marveled that Leon's nursery and greenhouse products were worth more than the cotton crop.

Florida's population soared in the 1950s, increasing by 79 percent to almost five million. In 1960, Tallahassee's rise to 48,174 people (a 77 percent increase) matched that of the state. Leon County's population climbed to 74,225. By then, only five farms in the county produced cotton. In 1970, the area still was attracting peo-

ple. Leon County passed the 100,000 figure, with 75,525 whites and 26,021 blacks. With 71,897 citizens, Tallahassee contained about two-thirds of the total. In 1970, four times as many teachers lived there as farmers, farm managers, foremen, and laborers combined. The residents worked at a variety of jobs; 11,500 were employed in clerical positions, and another 15,800 were classified as professionals, a reflection of government, education, and directly related services.

Tallahassee began the 1980s with 81,548 people (the county had 148,655). Projections for sustained growth were accepted as certain, but with the knowledge that growth needed regulating. Things had changed dramatically since 1825 when 996 people lived in the county.

GOVERNMENT EXPANDS

With an expanding population, Florida became more important in Washington, D.C. State government, of necessity, was forced to enlarge its functions. As a result, monuments to politics and government—public buildings—rose to meet ongoing and newly created needs. Not the least was the R. A. Gray building, which housed

A 1985 aerial view, looking west, shows the capitol complex, supreme court, R. A. Gray Building, civic center, FSU Law School Buildings, and city hall.

Tallahassee city hall, October 1985

the Florida State Archives and Bureau of Records Management, created in 1967. Modern demands, some people insisted, required a streamlined capitol building. They sought to use precious real estate by demolishing the old capitol, standing since 1845 and renovated periodically. Fortunately, a campaign to save the historic capitol was successful. Architects and builders carefully restored the venerable structure to its proportions of 1902-1903, and it became a museum of Florida government in 1982.

Meantime, directly behind the revitalized seat of government, a gleaming 22-story capitol was constructed. Governor Reubin O'D. Askew oversaw the dedication ceremonies in 1978. In the area adjacent to the capitol buildings, other state buildings—usually painted in "wedding-cake" white—were built, creating an impressive and expanding governmental complex.

Leon countians built a new city hall, a new courthouse, and conducted hotly contested local elections. The results usually were decided by issues and personalities rather than by party affiliation. Sporadic elections to consolidate city and county government met with little success. State elections were followed closely, and the local electorate—as usual—voted Democratic. Blacks, disfranchised throughout the century but now supported by federal

laws, began to register and vote in the 1950s and 1960s. Their political loyalties lay with the Democrats (largely because of FDR's New Deal programs and the efforts of subsequent administrations), and the party kept electing the state's governors. Of the chief executives chosen after World War II, only two, Claude R. Kirk (1966-1970) and Robert Martinez (1986-1990), were Republicans.

Traditional Democratic loyalties prevailed in national elections. Leon County voted for Harry S. Truman in 1948, Adlai E. Stevenson in 1952 and 1956, and John F. Kennedy in 1960. In the latter three elections, Florida went Republican. In 1964, political turmoil resulting from the civil-rights struggles saw Leon County cast a majority vote for Barry Goldwater. The voters supported George C. Wallace's American Independent party in 1968 (although Florida had voted for Lyndon B. Johnson in 1964 and for Richard Nixon in 1968). Leon County and Florida meshed in 1972 to support Nixon and in 1976 to back Jimmy Carter. Florida supported Ronald Reagan in 1980, but Leon County stuck with Carter. In 1984, both Leon County and Florida were in the Reagan column.

Through the years, white Floridians have been conservative on fiscal and racial matters. As the twentieth century wound down, it was apparent that the old

Blacks and whites stand in line at Tallahassee city hall to register to vote in the early 1960s

taunt of "reconstructionist" no longer applied to a person professing Republican sympathies. The Democrats remained in the majority, but the state and Leon County had a viable two-party system at every level.

THE CRISIS IN EDUCATION CONTINUES

After World War II, the chronic "crisis in education" was more acute in Leon County than ever. Public schools lacked physical plants adequate to meet the needs of their growing student bodies. The state labored under the financial burden—social and psychological as well—of administering a segregated school system. Florida State College for Women could serve the state better as a coeducational institution, and Florida Agricultural and Mechanical College for Negroes could demand rightly to expand and upgrade its role in higher education. Another concept needed to be implemented: providing population centers with two-year junior colleges. Such institutions could offer inexpensive education for students during the first two college years, for people seeking specialized training, and for entire communities taking advantage of adult-education programs.

Agitation to change FSCW's role came toward the end of World War II. In 1946, FSCW was crowded, but the all-male University of Florida faced a major crisis, with legions of veterans returning to or beginning college. Using the facilities at Dale Mabry Field, FSCW accommodated some of the male students under the euphemism of Tallahassee Branch of the University of Florida. Beginning in October, men and women were shuttled by bus between the campuses. In 1947, Leon County's legislative delegation and civic leaders pushed for coeducational status for the school. On Ma[...] 7, a law created Florida State University. The University of Florida also became coeducational.

FSU enlarged its faculty and staff, inaugurated a competitive athletic program, and worked to achieve the academic respectability that the women's college had held. In ensuing decades, the institution became oriented toward research as well as teaching, added a law school, and expanded its graduate program to include Ph.D programs. FSU was desegregated in 196[...]

In 1951, "for Negroes" was dropped from the name of the Florida Agricultural and Mechanical College title, and in 1952 the school became Florida Agricultural and Mechanical University. In the post-World War II years, the university's officials and academic leaders maintained their struggle to receive

In 1946, the FSCW campus welcomed its first male students since 1905.

Claude Kirk (right), Florida's first Republican governor since Reconstruction, and United States Senator Ed Gurney greet President Richard Nixon at the Tallahassee Municipal Airport, October, 1970.

an equitable portion of state funds, which traditionally had been denied to them. As the land-grant college for blacks, FAMU benefited from federal money as well. Dr. William H. Gray, who became the school's fifth president in 1944, doubled the physical plant during his aggressive tenure (1944–1949). The expansion included a $2 million university and community hospital, completed in 1951. Besides its undergraduate program—including Florida's first school of nursing—FAMU began to offer graduate instruction at the master's level in 1945. Its band and athletic teams achieved and sustained national prominence. The first white student enrolled at FAMU in 1962.

Florida had a private junior college as early as 1927 and a public one dating to 1933. The system was expanded in 1947, but did not accelerate until a decade later. Tallahassee Junior College opened its doors in 1966 with Dr. Fred W. Turner as president. The temporary home was at Amos P. Godby High School, itself an example of Tallahassee's expanding school system. In 1967, a spacious campus was opened in the capital's western section. Now known as Tallahassee Community College, the institution offers a two-year associate of arts degree, as well as an ever-expanding variety of other programs, and enrollment surpassed 10,000.

Tallahassee and Leon County were in the midst of coping with the growing demands of public education when, in 1954, the United States Supreme Court handed down its historic Brown decision. The ruling overturned *Plessy v. Ferguson* (1896), which had upheld segregation as constitutional provided that "separate" facilities were "equal." Like other Southern school systems, Leon County's white and black schools were never "equal." A year later, the Supreme Court ordered the transition accomplished "with all deliberate speed." In the wake of the court's decision came a variety of protests and delaying tactics from white Southerners, but finally, integration was accomplished. In 1959, a Dade County school became the first in Florida to integrate. The admission of blacks to white classrooms occurred in Tallahassee in September 1962, at FSU and Blessed Sacrament, a Catholic elementary school. Leon County's public schools began to integrate in the fall of 1963. The local process was imperfect and slow, continuing piecemeal until 1970, but it occurred with little violence.

As the twentieth century neared an end, the demands for quality, or even adequate, education had not been met—or funded. Yet the effort continued, and a bewildering number of "schools" offered some form of "educational" training in Tallahassee and Leon

Aerial view shows Florida A & M University in 1957

County. Among them were the public schools, numerous private and church schools and academies, many community and outreach programs, and countless daycare, nursery, and kindergarten schools with religious and sectarian associations. One could obtain training in everything from flying to bartending to massage therapy. The system was nothing if not eclectic.

THE CIVIL-RIGHTS MOVEMENT AFFECTS TALLAHASSEE

During the 1950s and 1960s, southern blacks struggled to end the discrimination and segregation which restricted them to second-class status. The civil-rights movement in Tallahassee began in May 1956 with a boycott of the city buses. The spontaneous action was prompted by the arrest of two FAMU coeds who sat next to a white passenger in the only empty seats. When city commissioners and the holders of the city's transportation franchise refused to yield to black demands, the boycott dragged on for several months. Arrests and harassment of black carpoolers became a common occurrence. In December, blacks resumed using the buses,

sitting where they liked. The economically damaged Cities Transit Company tolerated the move, but the city sued to force the bus company to obey local segregation laws.

Sporadic and increasing acts of violence, aimed at black leaders such as the Reverend C. K. Steele and others, prompted Governor LeRoy Collins to suspend operation of the bus system for a brief cooling-off period in the winter of 1957. City commissioners and protesting blacks never achieved a formal settlement, but gradually the sight of blacks riding at the front of the bus became more common, and the battle moved to another front.

In the early 1960s, FAMU students launched "sit-ins" and peaceful demonstrations against segregated facilities at department-store lunch counters, movie theatres, and public swimming pools. The city reacted by arresting many of the protesters, but lunch counters and theatres eventually were desegregated by agreement between blacks and store managers. Even so, the city commission kept Tallahassee's municipal swimming pools closed for five years.

Black persistence—backed by federal legislation and accompanied by moderating attitudes on the part of many white southerners—worked a gradual and far-reaching change on everyday life in the capital city.

Tallahassee Community College opened on the site of Dale Mabry Field in 1967.

*NAACP march in Talla-
hassee, early 1960s*

*At commencement,
August 12, 1965, FSU
President John E.
Champion presents a
diploma to Max Court-
ney, the first black to
receive a degree at FSU.*

HIGH
EARNINGS
LEON
FEDERAL SAVINGS

THE REVEREND C. K. STEELE

The Reverend C. K. Steele was born on February 17, 1914, in Bluefield, West Virginia.

At age 38, he came to preach at Bethel Baptist Church in Tallahassee. Later, he helped found the Southern Christian Leadership Conference, marched with the Reverend Dr. Martin Luther King and others at Saint Augustine, Florida, Selma, and Montgomery, Alabama.

He also led the Tallahassee bus boycott and took part in the sit-ins at the Woolworth's lunch counter.

The Reverend Steele died August 19, 1980, in Tallahassee. On September 29, 1985, the new municipal bus terminal at Adams and Tennessee was named in his honor.

Between May and December 1956, the Reverend C. K. Steele (next to window) and other black leaders boycotted city bus services to protest relegation of blacks to back seats.

Blacks demonstrate against segregated facilities in a sit-in at Woolworth's lunch counter, March 15, 1960.

Ku Klux Klan rallies, as this one in 1956, were infrequent and seldom violent.

Progress came as new elected officials took office, and in 1964 Tallahassee hired its first black policemen.

TALLAHASSEEANS TAKE THEIR LEISURE SERIOUSLY

People in the Tallahassee area still worked hard, but in the post-war years had more time, more money, and more choices for entertainment and diversion. Sedentary leisure—listening to the radio, watching a movie or television—remained popular. Radio stations, some maintaining both AM and FM units, offered all types of music, as well as other programs. The noncommercial WFSU-FM, which went on the air in 1955, was linked to National Public Radio (NPR). WFSU also added a second station, WFSQ, which offered primarily classical music. FAMU also had a radio station, WAMF-FM.

The ubiquitous television set began to make its appearance in the 1950s, and Tallahassee's first television station was WCTV, which opened on September 15, 1955. Other commercial stations followed. WFSU-TV began operations in September 1961 as the capital's second station. It offered local-interest shows as

"Willie" Ragsdale and Frank Pepper broadcast the weather and news at WCTV, Channel 6, which went on the air September 15, 1955.

well as educational and cultural programs from the Public Broadcasting System and other producers.

Although films made for theatres were broadcast on television and available for rent, the public's traditional habit of "going to the movies" continued. People in Tallahassee had a wide selection of theatres, most with multiple auditoriums. With only an occasional exception, movie theatres were located in shopping centers or malls.

The more intellectual—but still sedentary—had available a public county library which was narrowly approved by popular vote in 1954. Permission from the legislature and county commission followed, and the library opened its doors in the basement of the Columns (at its original location on the corner of Park and Adams) and began to check out books on March 21, 1956.

Local citizens could choose from a broad variety of cultural activities. Throughout the year, the three colleges offered entertainment series and special events. Secondary and elementary schools also had active programs. Building on an earlier tradition, the Tallahassee Little Theatre was organized in 1949, and presented plays in an abandoned theatre at Dale Mabry Field. The LeMoyne

Art Foundation was established in 1963 to display and sell the work of local artists. It did much to promote community awareness and appreciation of fine art. The Tallahassee Civic Ballet, established in 1972, developed local talent, and its members presented well-received performances. The Tallahassee Symphony Orchestra finally took form in 1979 after years of discussion by Tallahasseeans. Its first concert was presented on September 14, 1981, to open the new civic center. A turtle-shell umbrella of concrete and steel, the civic center was host to events ranging from rock concerts to basketball games, from circuses to industrial exhibits.

The Tallahassee Junior Museum, founded in 1957, made a unique contribution to the community. The museum recreated a north Florida farm of the late 1800s. Its nature trails linked a variety of natural wildlife habitats, and its professional staff worked closely with the school system and community to provide educational programs in cultural and natural history.

March, when the capital city moves from its short winter toward its long summer, was the occasion for the Springtime Tallahassee festival. The pageant was begun

The Leon County Library opened in the basement of the Columns on March 21, 1956.

The former Deeb home at the northwest corner of Calhoun and College became the LeMoyne Art Foundation in 1963

The Donald L. Tucker Civic Center, 1984

in 1968 at the urging of Betty McCord, a local civic leader. Tallahassee's natural beauty, especially the dog-woods and azaleas in full bloom, formed an appealing stage. The main attraction among various events was a parade featuring floats with historical themes. "Andrew Jackson," as portrayed by a local citizen, led the procession and presided over activities. Tallahasseeans took strong sides on whether "Old Hickory"—dead since 1845 but still controversial—was an appropriate symbol for the pageant.

From colorfully attired men and women players on lush golf courses to the Tumbling Tots gymnasts, Tallahasseeans pursued an infinite variety of recreational activities. Private swimming pools were commonplace, but public pools were also in use. The more adventurous swam in limestone sink holes (some of them dangerous) in the county's southern area. Tennis courts, fitness centers, gymnasiums, tracks, athletic fields, jogging and biking trails all formed part of Tallahassee and Leon County's kaleidoscope of sport. Beyond that, the traditional pastimes of hunting and fishing endured and flourished.

TALLAHASSEE TACKLES URBAN PROBLEMS

As an expanding city after World War II, Tallahassee was hard pressed to provide facilities for visitors, but the number and quality of restaurants improved. Downtown hotels—by no means relics of the past—yielded in numbers, if not in elegance, to the many motels and

motor hotels that lined the network of roads leading to the capital. The motels varied from spartan accommodations to sophisticated services—a revolutionary change from 1945, when Clark's Deluxe Motor Court was perched in lonely solitude on the Quincy highway.

For those whose choice of a bed away from home was not voluntary, Tallahassee had modern hospital facilities. Such was not always true, however. The Tallahassee Memorial Regional Medical Center, originally a municipally owned hospital, was established in 1945, when the city took over the medical facility at Dale Mabry Field. The hospital moved into a permanent (and frequently expanded) facility in 1949, and became a regional center in 1979. The FAMU hospital closed in 1966, after TMH yielded to federal pressure and accepted black patients and medical personnel. Additional medical services became available in 1979 with the opening of the Tallahassee Community Hospital.

Population shifts in Tallahassee and Leon County since 1945 make clear the importance of urban history. The pattern in the area was a reflection of the nation. Post-war decades saw a historic "double move" to suburbia. Tallahasseeans exited from the city to the suburbs and many county residents migrated to the suburbs. In 1980, more than 40 percent of the nation's population lived in suburbs, more than in cities or rural areas.

The omnipresent automobile eased Tallahassee's residential congestion, making it no longer a "walking city." The suburbs' attractions were increased because they offered private lodging and the opportunity for people to live together as family units in permanent settings. People also could get away from the noise,

The McMillan house was the first home of the Tallahassee Junior Museum. Shown here in 1958 are: Mrs. Robert Fokes, Mrs. Guyte McCord, Mrs. J. L. Cresap and Mrs. John A. Henderson.

sounds, and increasing dangers of downtown city life. After 1945, the government made loans available to veterans. FHA funds remained in effect and per capita income increased, swelling savings accumulated and unspendable during the war. New building techniques made residential construction profitable for builders, attractive to speculators and developers, and affordable for citizens, An added incentive was that federal tax policies favored homeowners over renters. Local citizens became willing participants in the flight to suburbia, as former agricultural and wooded areas around Tallahassee proliferated into subdivisions. In Tallahassee, the most popular areas were north of the city as the exodus to suburbia continued.

Even so, Tallahassee did not experience a frenzied flight of its citizens to the suburbs. The capital was not so large that attractive residential areas were precluded from the city limits, and the city's boundaries were expanded occasionally. Many older sections retained their integrity and commercial value, and areas closer to the town's center were not so

congested that homes, townhouses, and condominiums could not exist. Despite certain advantages, the suburbs were not without their own headaches. Traffic flow was a problem and, while shopping centers offered numerous services, many tended to be characterless, aesthetically unappealing, and crowded.

Long noted for its trees, Tallahassee had taken intermittent action to preserve them. Arvah B. Hopkins, who served as city manager from 1952 to 1974, instituted a program of planting dogwoods free for homeowners. Later, the program was expanded to include other varieties. Evidence of community concern with preserving and enhancing the environment came with zoning laws and protective tree and landscape ordinances. As the end of the century approached, hope existed that a metropolitan area with Tallahassee's historical importance, traditions of culture and education, and natural beauty could survive the ravages of urban blight. Civic organizations, concerned citizens, politicians, and such associations as the Tallahassee Historic Preservation Board (founded in 1970), now the

Tallahassee Trust for Historic Preservation, Inc., certainly could be expected to serve as guardians and preservers of their unique area.

Betty McCord, credited with spurring Springtime Tallahassee, stands with Will McLean and Roy Weissinger at the first Springtime Tallahassee parade in 1968.

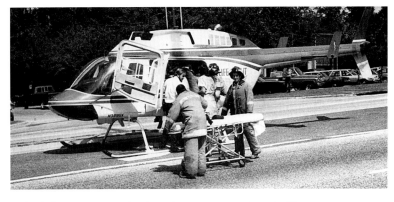

Life Flight crew paramedics have been coming to the aid of Leon County residents with health emergencies since the early 1980s.

183

Bicyclists wheel along
one of Tallahassee's
canopy roads, 1986.

A 1950s photograph of
the Tumbling Tots

A view west toward the capitol shows some of the modern motels built after Apalachee Parkway was 4-laned in the late 1950s.

CLARK'S DE LUXE AUTO COURTS
Tallahassee, Fla.

In the 1940s the Clark family owned two motels in the area, one on North Monroe Street, the other on the Quincy Highway. Their advertisement boasted of 50 modern brick cottages, radios, telephones, fans, and garages.

The nearly completed Tallahassee Memorial Hospital is shown in 1950.

*Apalachee Parkway
Shopping Center, Talla-
hassee's first large mall,
opened in 1959.*

Governor's Square Mall,
the city's largest, 1984

Tallahassee's tree
ordinances failed to
save this huge canopy
oak on Miccosukee Road
in 1985.

Lake Ella Fountain. Photo credit: Florida Department of State, Florida State Archives, Department of Commerce Collection.

The Vietnam Veterans' Memorial was dedicated on November 11, 1985.

Knott House Museum dedication.
Photo credit: Tallahassee Trust for
Historic Preservation.

The Grove. Photo credit: M. Mead.

The Black Archives, Florida Agricultural and Mechanical University.
Photo credit: Florida Department of State, Florida State Archives, Jackson Stevens.

The Union Bank. Photo credit: Tallahassee Trust for Historic Preservation.

Restored Railroad freight depot. Photo credit: Tallahassee Trust for Historic Preservation.

The University Center at Florida State University's Doak Campbell Stadium. Photo credit: Florida State University Photo Lab, Bill Langford.

Bloxham Park in the Park Avenue Chain of Parks. Photo credit: Tallahassee Trust for Historic Presesrvation.

Leon County Courthouse.
Photo credit: Florida
Department of State,
Florida State Archives,
Department of Commerce
Collection, J. L. Gaines.

Springtime Tallahassee
headquarters in the old
Walker Library.
Photo credit: Florida
Department of State,
Florida State Archives,
Department of Commerce
Collection.

Candy stripe awnings on restored 1902 Capitol Building. Photo credit: David E. Ferro.

Great Seal in the Rotunda of the new Capitol.
Photo credit: Tallahasse Trust for Historic Preservation.

Entrance to the Florida House of Represenatives
Photo credit: Florida Department of State, Florida State
Archives, Department of Commerce Collection.

North Florida Christian School's Band in front of the Capitol.
Photo credit: Florida Department of State, Florida State Archives, Department of Commerce Collection.

DeSoto archaeological dig, U.S. Senator Bob and Adele
Graham (center) with State Archaeologist Calvin Jones at right.
Photo credit: Tallahassee Trust for Historic Preservation.

Pioneer farm house at the Tallahassee Museum of History and
Natural Science.
Photo credit: Florida Department of State, Florida State
Archives, Department of Commerce Collection, Ed Fortune.

Reenactment of the Battle of Natural Bridge.
Photo credit: Tallahassee Trust for Historic Preservation.

Bradley's Country Store.
Photo credit: Florida
Department of State,
Florida State Archives,
Department of
Commerce Collection.

Brokaw-McDougall House.
Photo credit: Tallahassee Trust
for Historic Preservation.

The Beadel House, Tall Timbers Research Station.
Photo credit: Florida Department of State, Florida State Archives, Department of Commerce Collection.

The Visitor Center (Messer House), Mission San Luis, state historical and archeological site.
Photo credit: Florida Department of State, Florida State Archives, Department of Commerce Collection.

LeRoy Collins-Leon County Public Library.
Photo credit: Tallahassee Trust for Historic Preservation.

Florida Agricultural & Mechanical University's Marching "100."
Photo credit: Robert Overton.

Hospitality Square, home of the Florida Restaurant Association.
Photo credit: Tallahassee Trust for Historic Preservation.

Leon High School, built in 1937, is now on the U.S. Register of Historic Sites.
Photo credit: Florida Department of State, Florida State Archives, Jackson Stevens.

Tallahassee Tiger Sharks Hockey team.
Photo credit: Robert Overton.

Looking south on Adams Street from College Avenue.
Photo credit: Tallahassee Trust for Historic Preservation.

Canopy road in autumn
Photo credit: Tallahassee Trust for Historic Preservation.

TO THE TWENTY-FIRST CENTURY

Some of the diversity of Tallahassee's population is apparent in this 1985 photograph of the Pledge of Allegiance at the Fourth of July celebration in Tom Brown Park. Photo credit: The Florida Flambeau, Bob O'Lary.

8.

Local citizens thought the limits of communication had been reached in 1904. That year long distance telephone connections were made between Tallahassee and Thomasville, Georgia. Yet, unprecedented technological advances followed, benefitting but confusing the last decades of the twentieth century. It was all a far cry from the Tallahassee of 1916 when businessmen first began to hire secretaries and purchase typewriters—Woodstock was the favorite. By the 1990s Tallahasseeans lived in a high-tech world. People added to the complexity because there were so many of them. The average life span had increased, and although some residents moved away, more moved in. In 1990 the traditional mathematical division of Leon's County's population into whites and blacks acquired new dimensions. There were 500 Native Americans, 3,738 Asians and Pacific Islanders, and 4,715 Hispanics. The last two minority groups increased in numbers and significance as the new millennium approached. By 1996 Florida was the nation's fourth most populous state, and Leon County's population reached 221,621. By 2000 it was well beyond that figure. No further back than 1927 Madelin Jacobs was the first Leon County woman admitted to the Florida bar. In 1928 she became the first woman to handle a case in county court—she got the defendant acquitted. At the end of the century problems related to race and gender remained, but it was clear that Tallahassee and Leon County had moved a great distance from the past. Photographs of city and county officials from mid-century show only the faces of white men. Today the governing bodies, including the court system, reflect to a much greater degree the diversity of the area's residents. It has become commonplace for blacks and women to win seats on the city and county commissions, school board, and in the legislature. They have demonstrated impressive leadership in those positions. A considerable number hold non-elective positions of responsibility. In 1997 city commissioners hired an African-American woman, Anita Favors, to serve as Tallahassee's new city manager. In that same year, Walt McNeil became the first black to serve as the city's chief of police. County Administrator Parwez Alam, hired in 1989, became the first Asian to hold such a prominent post in the region.

GOVERNMENTAL GROWTH AND NEW DEVELOPMENTS

Growth affected every aspect of life in Tallahassee and the county. The Civil Rights movement resulted in a large increase in the number of black voters. That, added to the natural increase in resident whites plus the steady arrival of new citizens, earned Florida more attention in Washington, D.C. Presidents and vice presidents and aspirants for those offices regularly made campaign stops in Tallahassee and elsewhere in the state. Growing importance on the national scene was seen as presidents from Lyndon B. Johnson to Bill Clinton named Floridians to cabinet posts and other high-ranking federal positions. The state's twenty-three House members plus its two U.S. Senators gave Florida a powerful voice in the nation's capital.

As Tallahassee became a focus of national political attention, it served simultaneously as the command post of state politics. State government had become multifaceted. An incident such as one in 1912 that saw the state legislature adjourn so that members could watch a demonstration of cattle dipping in McDougall's pasture seemed as remote as a meeting of parliament in medieval England. In the century's last decades, Florida and Leon County's voting habits underwent dramatic changes. The Southerner Bill Clinton won the county in 1992, although he failed to gain the state's electoral votes, losing to George Bush in a close statewide race. In 1996 the Republicans named Bob Dole to oppose President Clinton, but Florida and Leon County went Democratic. In the gubernatorial race of 1998, Republican Jeb Bush easily carried Florida, but Leon County favored Democrat Buddy MacKay by a vote of 41,153 to 31,455. Before Bush was inaugurated in January 1999, the state was saddened by the death of incumbent democratic Governor Lawton Chiles. The popular governor, who had served two terms, died just before the end of his second term. Chiles was succeeded for a brief interim by Buddy MacKay, the lieutenant governor.

In congressional and senate races in the 1990s both parties in Florida sent their nominees to Washington. The Republicans gained control of both houses of the state legislature in 1996 and

By 1996 Florida was the nation's fourth most populous state and Leon County's population reached 221,621. Christmas shopping at Governor's Square makes it seem as if every one of them is there. Photo credit: The Florida Flambeau, Deborah Thomas.

Janet Reno lived in Tallahassee from 1971 to 1973, serving as staff director of the Judiciary Committee of the Florida House of Representatives and counsel for the Senate's committee to revise Florida's Criminal Code. After serving as state attorney of Dade County for fifteen years she was sworn in as the first woman attorney general of the U.S. in 1993. Photo credit: Department of Justice.

After spending the night in the Mansion as the guest of Governor and Mrs. Chiles, President Bill Clinton was welcomed in the plaza between the Old and new Capitols on March 30, 1995. Photo credit: Donn Dughi

Governor Lawton M. Chiles' official portrait, painted by artist Christopher M. Still and unveiled in early December, contains at least a dozen references to his life and career including: the Federal Glass mirror that hung in his U.S. Senate office. Reflected in the mirror are Rhea Chiles, her painting of the Governor's Mansion, the state flag, his walking shoes, his great-grandfather's Bible, an orange, and the interior of the governor's office. Out the window can be seen the space shuttle, the cracker cabin Chiles used as a getaway, and a raccoon, a reference to Chiles' self description as an old hecoon.

On the afternoon of December 12, 1998, twenty-four days before the end of his second term as governor, Lawton Chiles died at the Florida Governor's Mansion. After one last trip through the panhandle, from Century where he began his 1970 walk for the U.S. Senate to Tallahassee, his body lay in state in the Old Capitol. First Lady Rhea Chiles placed a white rose with baby's breath on her husband's plain pine box casket just prior to the public viewing. Photo credit: Mark Foley.

With his son, John, and wife Anne at his side, Lieutenant Governor Kenneth Hood "Buddy" MacKay, Jr., was administered the oath of office by Supreme Court Justice Charles Wells to become Florida's forty-second governor on December 13, 1998 at 12:30 a.m.
Photo credit: Mark Foley.

With his family, former President George and Barbara Bush, his Texas governor brother George Bush, his wife Columba and children looking on, John Ellis Bush took the oath of office as Florida's forty-third governor from Chief Justice Major B. Harding on the east side of the Old Capitol at high noon on January 5, 1999.
Photo credit: Mark Foley.

won some cabinet seats. At the county and city level each party was successful in electing members of the city commission and the county commission. County and city continued to be governed separately, and all efforts to combine the two were defeated by the voters. There are seven county commissioners, five of them elected by district and two at large. The five city commissioners are chosen in at large elections. One of them is the mayor. Previously the office of mayor was a ceremonial office rotated among the commissioners, but in 1996 a referendum passed that made the position distinct from the other commissioners. In the mayoral election that followed in 1997, Scott Maddox was elected. Both county and state became two-party entities. The outcome of county and city commissioner races often depends more on issues and personalities than on party labels. Independent candidates also seek office.

EDUCATION

The twenty-first century found Tallahassee, and, to a lesser extent, Leon County with many public institutions whose divisions included elementary, middle, and high schools. New schools opened, their location determined by population and geographical balance, but other factors as well. Parents were concerned that their children enrolled in schools of sound academic reputation. Controversies developed over where to place new schools and the effect on the proposed locales and on areas where they were not proposed. The results were lawsuits, public meetings, panels, studies by experts local and imported, agency proposals, regular and special meetings of city commissioners and county commissioners, and so on. The northern and eastern areas were the regions of major growth, and their educational and environmental concerns were intense. No one questioned that education was a matter of citywide and countywide importance, or that questions and answers were complicated and had to be addressed.

Education, in its broadest terms, literally knows no bounds. Florida State University, Florida Agricultural and Mechanical University, and Tallahassee Community College continued to grow in the 1990s. Tallahassee has Keiser

Keiser College, north of I-10 on Capitol Circle includes a culinary school supported in part by local Tallahassee restaurants. Photo credit: Florida Department of State, Florida State Archives, Jackson Stevens.

A former motion picture complex across from Keiser College now houses the Florida News Channel. Tallahassee's first statewide news channel went on the air in 1998. Photo credit: Florida Department of State, Florida State Archives, Jackson Stevens.

College, a regionally accredited private junior college, and a vast number of academic secondary schools that vary in emphasis, scope, excellence, and price. There are private schools that are church sponsored, as well as private schools that are secular. They attract large numbers of students. A bewildering mix of schools, academies, and institutes answer specialty training needs from the commonplace to the esoteric. As a sampling, they include schools of dance, insurance, business, cooking, esthetics and nail technology, real estate, travel, contracting, aviation, and massage therapy and structural bodywork. As needs and demands develop in the new century, they, no doubt, will be answered by resourceful and innovative teachers and experts.

Bobby Bowden's Florida State University Seminoles have won at l̲ ning a national title in 1993. Photo credit: Ryals Lee, Jr.

LEISURE

The amorphous word "leisure" has different meanings and applications. Sports, one part of leisure, offer pleasure to both participants and to spectators. Whatever one's preferences, they can be fulfilled in Tallahassee. The city's universities, junior college, high schools, and secondary schools offer a wide variety of sports. Local universities had remarkable sports years in the 1990s: Florida State University won the national championship in football in 1993 and Florida Agricultural and Mechanical University achieved the same distinction for historically black universities in 1998. The capital's widespread recreational programs are popular, well organized, and include all ages— from preschoolers to retirees. The oldest and most democratic sports—hunting and fishing— attract many people whose budgets are large, small, and in between.

Sedentary leisure, various card games, as well as chess and checkers, has always been popular. Readers of every description got a big boost in the 1990s with the opening of the LeRoy Collins Leon County Public Library. It came as the result of a long campaign to obtain an adequate building. The new building, designed specifically for the library, was located downtown on West Park Avenue. Several branch libraries were established and a bookmobile continued to serve outlying areas. Museum goers have available the Capital

year since 1987 and finished ranked in the top five every year, win-

The Robert A. Gray building, on the southwest corner of Bronough and Pensacola Streets, is the home of the Museum of Florida History, the Florida State Archives, and the State Library of Florida.
Photo credit: Florida Department of State, Florida State Archives, Joanna Norman.

Goodwood Plantation on Miccosukee Road, one of Florida's oldest plantations, will be opened to the public as a museum after restoration is completed by the Margaret Hodges Hood Foundation. Photo credit: Florida Department of State, Florida State Archives, Jackson Stevens.

The Winter festival, with the Jingle Bell Run, the lighting of the downtown lights and the children's wonderland in the Historic Park Avenue Chain of Parks starts Tallahassee's holiday season. Photo credit: The Tallahassee Democrat, Phil Sears.

Kleman Plaza, just west of City Hall and named for former city manager Dan Kleman, includes an underground parking facility, an office complex on the northwest corner, the Capital Cultural Center on the southeast corner that houses the Odyssey Science Center, which opened in October 1998, and the Museum of Art/Tallahassee which opened in January 1999, along with fountains, benches and open park areas used for the Shakespeare festival and other events. Photo credit: Florida Department of State, Florida State Archives, Jackson Stevens.

Cultural Center, the Tallahassee Museum of Art, and the Museum of Fine Arts (the latter is at Florida State University). There are also the Museum of Florida History in the R. A. Gray building, the Old Capitol, San Luis Archaeological and Historic Site, the Tallahassee Museum of History & Natural Science (affectionately known by its original name, the Tallahassee Junior Museum), Goodwood Museum and Garden Center, and the Union Bank. The Brokaw-McDougall House and Knott House are frequently visited public-owned buildings.

Growing in popularity are the Shakespeare Festival, the Winter Festival and parade, and the Caribbean Festival. Such celebrations complement Springtime Tallahassee, help advertise the capital, and bring attention to downtown. The Kleman Plaza, which opened in 1995 and is named for former city manager Dan Kleman, serves as the central point for these festivals.

URBAN PROBLEMS

In 1903 Tallahasseeans declared themselves urbanites and offered their new city lights as proof. By 2000 the capital's residents could not deny that they lived in an urban area, one growing more citified every day. Shopping malls were so ubiquitous that the inauguration of one drew less attention than P. W. Woolworth's gala opening in 1917 as the city's first dime store. When Piggly Wiggly began in 1922, it became the first local chain grocery store (they were almost beyond enumeration at the century's end). In July of that year Mae's Shop opened, and it remained the capital's most stylish women's store for years. Mae's Shop was the prelude to an unimagined future.

The demands of an ever-increasing population had become so important that in 1974 the legislature passed the Growth Management Act. It mandated that local governments develop plans to manage future needs. The intent was to regulate urban sprawl, protect the water supply, provide for storm-water runoff, and ensure that necessary infrastructure was in place prior to the demands of future development. The Tallahassee-Leon County Comprehensive Plan for Growth Management, adopted in 1990, was laboriously developed during the 1980s with considerable participation from citizens and from experts. The "comp plan" was criticized by some as too restrictive of land use and future development. It was welcomed by others as a necessary framework providing protection from the unrestrained growth so common in post–World War II Florida. For some, growth is a curse, for a few it is an unmixed blessing, but for most it is historical evolution. It is inevitable.

Unrestrained growth is also a threat to the survival of the few remaining historic resources in this community. With the adoption of the Historic

Preservation Element in the 1990 Tallahassee-Leon County Comprehensive Plan, Leon County is now required by law to give historic resources further consideration and protection. Today, because of the elimination of the Historic Tallahassee Preservation Board (HTPB) by the Florida Legislature in 1997, the work that was once being performed by the HTPB is now being performed by the Tallahassee Trust for Historic Preservation, Inc.

The most significant prospect for desirable expansion began in the late 1980s when the St. Joe Paper Company announced plans to begin development of a portion of its massive land holdings in Leon County: some eight thousand acres in the southeastern section. The project was to include residential communities, schools, golf courses, apartments, and retail, office, and industrial areas. St. Joe's proposal seemed to provide an answer to the ongoing problem of shifting growth and development from the county's congested areas in the north and east to the underdeveloped south.

Yet, there were concerns about the impact of such a large development. For months representatives of the city and county conferred with St. Joe officials, and citizens offered comment. The city insisted that "affordable" housing be included in the planned residential areas and that the company mitigate damage to the St. Augustine Canopy Road by building an overpass. There was also the broad issue of whether the development would lie within or outside the city limits. The important point affected provision of utility services, density of development, and similar issues. Negotiations continued, but in the summer of 1989 St. Joe balked at the city's requirements, and suddenly withdrew its proposal. An effort to resume talks in 1990 failed, but in the meantime

The look of the entire block bounded by Monroe Street, Park Avenue, Adams and Call Streets changed in the late 1990s. The Florida Education Association United added to and completely changed the look of the old Florida Theater building, on Monroe Street. Photo credit: Florida Department of State, Florida State Archives, Jackson Stevens.

The Courthouse Square building on Monroe Street, the buildings along Call Street that once housed the Chamber of Commerce and Wyatt's Business Machines and the building occupied by Chez Pierre on Adams Street were all demolished by 1998 for this addition to the Federal Courthouse. Photo credit: Florida Department of State, Florida State Archives Jackson Stevens.

Three decades of change to Tallahassee's skyline, the hotel on the southeast corner of Adams Street and Park Avenue that replaced the old post office/City Hall building in the 1960s (R), the new Capitol built in the 1970s (L), and Highpoint Tower that replaced the old State Theatre in the 1980s. Photo credit: Florida Department of State, Florida State Archives, Jackson Stevens.

St. Joe donated a 255-acre office site to the state. The state then built an enormous "Satellite Office" complex, and relocated various agencies and approximately two thousand employees there.

The relationship between St. Joe Paper Company and local government changed in the late 1990s. Under new management, the company sought a new direction and more profitable use of its land holdings across northern Florida. A name change, to St. Joe Corporation, and the leadership of former Disney executive Peter Rummell and others experienced in real estate development, moved the company away from its piney-woods and paper mill traditions. Just a decade after the first plans fell victim to the conflict over managed growth, a transformed St. Joe announced plans to revive the moribund Southwood Plantation project. Company officials proposed a large, high quality development and were eager to work with local and state officials as well as the two universities to complete the plans in the years ahead.

Traffic, a necessary evil, is graphic evidence of growth. Commercial traffic—trains, buses, planes—aside, it is privately owned vehicles that challenge the mental and physical health of the citizenry. Too much traffic is the everyday cry from drivers who try to get to and from their work or other destinations through a tangle of more vehicles than ever. In 1908 Clement A. Griscom, a wealthy Northerner, owned the only registered automobile in Leon County. The city did not have a taxi cab until 1915 when the appropriately named James Horn used his Ford to transport residents in what he called his "car for hire." That year Tallahassee's speed limit for cars was ten miles per hour. Some people wondered as late as 1922 if Walker Brown was not being overly speculative when he opened the initial carwash in Tallahassee. Yet, in 1999 Tallahassee and Leon County had 184,242 registered vehicles. The difficulties of traffic remain, although partial remedies—more streets, more lanes, one-way streets, left turn lanes, right on red after a complete stop, speed bumps, and even a flyover—have been added. No permanent solution to the problems emerged, and perhaps there is none. Traffic control professionals address the issue on a daily basis.

An increase in crime has been a concomitance of growth. In 1923 crime was an important problem, but had not reached epic proportions. Tallahassee's police got new uniforms that year, but it was the first time their regalia was prescribed. Today the Police Department and the Sheriff's Department, together with other state and federal law officials, work hard at their business of protecting the public. They are aided by sophisticated technical equipment and aided, as well, by volunteer neighborhood watch associations. Weapons used by criminals have become increasingly lethal, and the last decades of the twentieth century saw law enforcement officials challenged by new categories of crime—especially drugs. Urban living has created a situation that requires and receives ongoing attention and constant vigilance. At the century's end crime rates, nationally and locally, were dropping.

John Birch's chain saw art gives new life to trees cut down for road widening. This porpoise sculpture is on Old St. Augustine Road. Photo credit: Florida Department of State, Florida State Archives, Jackson Stevens.

The state built an enormous Satellite Office complex in the southeast section of the county on 255 acres donated by St. Joe Paper Company in 1989. Photo credit: The Tallahassee Democrat, Phil Sears.

Trying to improve the flow of traffic along Thomasville road has been ongoing for more than twenty years, as this August 1978 photograph of the stretch just north of the Meridian/Thomasville split attests.
Photo credit: Florida Department of State, Florida State Archives, Joan Morris.

Such are the problems posed as a new century unfolds. Solutions lie with government (at various levels) and private agencies, with groups (official and unofficial) and individuals. No realist expects miracles. Still, only pessimists wring their hands in despair and declare that nothing good has happened since the city limits were extended north of Park Avenue. Compromise, cooperation, planning, hard work, accepting delays and set-

In 1999 Tallahassee and Leon County had 184,242 registered vehicles. Photo credit: The Tallahassee Democrat, Mike Ewen.

luted streams and lakes. The beauty of Maclay Gardens can inspire modified applications throughout the city and county. The twenty-first century can be a time of fulfillment for a county and a capital city that was a frontier region in the 1820s. Contemporary residents have an unrivaled natural setting to protect and enjoy and hand down. Theirs is a past that was hardly perfect, but it is a decent and good legacy. Tallahasseeans and Leon Countians can use that bequest with profit as they assume the task of writing their own history in the twenty-first century.

This flyover, opened in 1997, to ease the traffic moving south from the Killearn area, is still controversial.
Photo credit: The Tallahassee Democrat, Mike Ewen.

backs but setting goals—these are not empty flag-waving words of boosterism. Instead they are necessary to preserve a heritage worth saving and a landscape of green grass and trees and unpol-

The west side of Adams Street between Jefferson and College took on a whole new look in the late 1990s when the Governor's Club altered the north end and Andy Reiss reinvented his restaurant complex, again.
Photo credit: Florida Department of State, Florida State Archives, Jackson Stevens.

227

Partners
in
Progress

Ausley & McMullen

Over 70 Years of Service to Government, Business, and Community

Ausley & McMullen is one of the oldest and largest law firms in the north Florida and Tallahassee area. For over 70 years, the Ausley firm has been synonymous with quality legal service.

The firm was established in Tallahassee in 1930 by Charles Saxon Ausley, who made outstanding contributions to his profession and to the community. He served Tallahassee as municipal judge and mayor, and in 1945, he represented Leon County in the state Senate.

Soon after Ausley established his practice in the Exchange Bank Building at Monroe and College streets, he was joined by LeRoy Collins, and in 1935 by his brother, John Ausley. Although the depression years were difficult for Ausley, Collins, and Ausley, success in litigation earned the three young lawyers a growing reputation. They continued their practice in the Exchange Building, which housed most of the other Tallahassee lawyers, until the early 1940s, when a new building was constructed at Calhoun and Jefferson streets, where the Ausley firm stands today in what is known as the Washington Square Building.

In 1954, LeRoy Collins left the firm to serve as Florida's governor; however, several new lawyers joined the firm, including D. Fred McMullen and E. Martin McGehee.

A new generation of lawyers entered the firm in the 1960s. DuBose Ausley joined his father, Charles, in 1963. Ausley, who is chairman of the firm, served as chairman of the Florida Board of Regents and served longer than any person in the history of the Board. He also is a Fellow of the American College of Trial Lawyers, and served on the 1978 Constitution Revision Commission. Graham Carothers, former assistant attorney general, joined the firm in 1964 and has served as counsel to numerous school boards. Palmer Proctor, son-in-law of LeRoy Collins, joined the firm after a clerkship with the Florida Supreme Court; and J. Marshall Conrad came aboard after several years of trying condemnation cases for the Florida Department of Transportation.

The 1970s brought another member of the Ausley family into the firm when Margaret Ausley joined her father, John, in practice. Other new lawyers included litigator William Smith; Lee Willis, to head a growing public utilities and regulatory department; litigator and Tallahassee Bar president Gary Williams; Jim Beasley; Tim Elliott; Julian Proctor, Jr., former United States Court of Appeals clerk; and state-tax practitioner and litigator Ken Hart, who is now president of the firm. Hart currently serves on the Florida Commission on Ethics and has served on the Second Judicial Circuit Court Nominating Commission and on the Florida Comprehensive Plan Committee.

In the 1980s, new attorneys included Mike Glazer, now a member of the Board of Governors of The Florida Bar; Bob Pierce, former general counsel to the Florida Department of Revenue; Steve Emmanuel; telecommunications expert John Fons; Steve Seymoe; Rob Clarke; and Emily Waugh. Joining the firm in the 1990s were Kevin Carroll; Deborah Stephens Minnis, another former assistant attorney general; Jeff Whalen; and James Harold Thompson, former speaker of the Florida House of Representatives who has recently chaired the Environmental Land Management Study Commission. Thompson also served as a member of the 1998 Constitution Revision Commission. Also joining the firm were John Aurell, former general counsel to the Governor of Florida, and who chaired the Federal Judicial Nominating Commission for Florida; and John

Beranek, a former trial and appellate judge. Aurell and Beranek are Fellows of the American College of Trial Lawyers.

In 1989, the firm joined with 49 other firms to form the State Capital Law Firm Group, a national organization comprised of one firm from each capital city in the United States. The Group has evolved into a dynamic, international organization with nearly 100 member firms across the world. Ausley & McMullen, as Florida's exclusive member, enjoys an extensive network of contacts, as well as the opportunity to share information and expertise about the practice of law with firms in other states and countries.

Although the firm is one of the oldest in the area, it has responded to the growth of Florida and to changing trends in the law. The firm is active in litigation, business and finance, administrative, probate, real estate, partnership, corporate, federal and state tax, health care, employment, and public utility law. All federal-tax lawyers have advanced degrees in tax law, and several litigators and tax attorneys are certified public accountants.

Among the many Tallahassee businesses represented by the Ausley firm are the *Tallahassee Democrat* and the Capital City Bank Group, Tallahassee's largest commercial bank. Other clients have included: the Leon County Civic Center Authority, the Florida Board of Bar Examiners, the Leon County School Board, Sprint Corporation, TECO Energy, CSX Transportation, the Florida Institute of CPAs, R. J. Reynolds, and Procter and Gamble, representing a cross section of major national and statewide corporations. The firm also enjoys the confidence of many individuals, estates, and partnerships.

In addition to memberships already listed, lawyers in the firm have been or are actively involved in professional and community services as members of the First District Court of Appeals Nominating Commission and board members of the Tallahassee Bar. Members have been active in civic organizations, serving as board members or chairmen of the Tallahassee Area Chamber of Commerce, Tallahassee Memorial Healthcare, United Way, Urban League, Tallahassee Symphony, Tallahassee-Leon County Civic Center Authority, Tallahassee Housing Finance Authority, Capital Center Planning Commission, and Legal Services of North Florida.

Ausley & McMullen is proud of its past involvement in the history of Tallahassee, and looks forward to the opportunity to participate in the progress and growth of Florida and its capital city.

From left to right: DuBose Ausley, Palmer Proctor, Lee Willis, Margaret Ausley, and Julian Proctor.

Tallahassee Community College

Leader in Academic Excellence

In 1996, Tallahassee Community College entered its fourth decade of providing educational services to students of the Leon-Gadsden-Wakulla district and beyond. During these years, TCC has consistently provided an instructional program of the highest quality and outstanding service to students.

TCC opened its doors for classes September 21, 1966, in a wing of an also new Godby High School because the Appleyard Drive campus, on the west side of Tallahassee, was still under construction.

The campus moved to its present location in time for the start of the 1967–68 academic year.

Today, TCC's first-year class of 698 students would be hard pressed to recognize the campus, particularly as the enrollment approaches 14,000.

A near-constant building program in the 1990's gave TCC a new Administration Building, Library and Student Union as anchors for a pedestrian mall, and all original buildings were extensively renovated and modernized.

Programs expanded to meet rapid-fire changes in technology, but unchanged are some abiding characteristics—an emphasis on teaching, low administrative costs, a focus on students, attention to meeting community needs, and the success of graduates.

The Faculty

A strong faculty has always been a TCC hallmark. In the Florida community college system, TCC consistently ranks first or among the best in the proportion of faculty holding doctorates, over twice the national average for public two-year colleges.

The Students

Students have always come first at Tallahassee Community College. Instructors take a personal interest in their students; academic, career and personal counseling needs are met with skill and care; the enrollment process is straightforward and efficient; and clubs, student government, intramurals and an athletic program provide a rich and diverse experience in campus life.

TCC ranks at the top among Florida community colleges

A successful graduate, TCC's most important product.

in the important attribute of percentage of graduates who move into the State University System.

In addition, TCC ranks first among Florida community colleges in the enrollment of African-American students and first in the percentage who are A.A. degree completers.

The literary magazine, *The Eyrie*, and the student newspaper, *The Talon,* are consistent state and regional award-winning publications, and students on the Forensics Team sweep competitions in leagues in which universities are predominant.

The Honors Program, the Model United Nations Program and forensics provide educational enhancements that open leadership opportunities for TCC students throughout life.

Presidents of TCC

Dr. Fred W. Turner, Director of Instructional Services in the Department of Education, was chosen as TCC's first President. It was his responsibility to plan the new college from the ground up.

After setting up the general education-transfer program, Dr. Turner turned his attention to developing high-quality programs in occupational areas.

Dr. Turner served until 1979, but returned as Interim President for the 1982–83 academic year. He died in 1987.

Dr. Marm M. Harris became TCC's second President in 1979. During his tenure, a foundation was established, cultural opportunities were expanded through an Artist Series, and the Lifetime Sports Complex was built.

Dr. James H. Hinson, Jr., was named TCC's third president in 1983. During his tenure, the Foundation was expanded and an athletic program was re-established. Major facility additions were made during Dr. Hinson's presidency and campus size increased from 64 acres to nearly 200.

Dr. T.K. Wetherell, who took office in 1995, encouraged faculty in developing innovative instructional delivery methods, vigorously advanced cooperative arrangements with other educational entities and with the business community, initiated an aggressive building and renovation program, instituted a major endowment program for the Foundation, and raised the visibility of the College.

Additions to the curriculum under his leadership reflect the College's commitment to offering instruction that prepares graduates for new jobs created by new technology, and to respond to workplace needs.

Educational Programs

Around 80 percent of TCC's enrollment is in the Associate in Arts transfer program and TCC is one of the top 10 producers of A.A. graduates in the nation. The largest feeder institution to Florida State University, TCC also has an excellent relationship with Florida A&M University and other universities in Florida.

Nearly three-fourths of the College's A.A. graduates transfer into the State University System the next year, the highest percentage in the Florida Community College System. Studies consistently show that these transfer students perform as well as students who start out at a university.

TCC's Technology and Professional Programs Division offers over 30 popular programs for students seeking careers in public service, computer science, business and health.

Graduates of medical programs perform competently in challenging and rewarding careers providing crucial health care services.

The Pat Thomas Law Enforcement Academy provides opportunities for officers from throughout the state to improve their skills to advance in their careers.

Technology and Professional Programs Division graduates have a job placement rate of over 90 percent and 9 out of 10 graduates pass their state examinations for professional licensure on the first try.

The Extended Studies Division offers credit courses at off-campus sites, over television and through independent study. The non-credit program satisfies community interest and occupational needs from professional-development seminars and short courses to personal-enrichment classes responding to lifelong learning needs.

The TCC Foundation

The Foundation, established in 1981, enhances the educational program by encouraging and receiving gifts to advance the College. Thanks to involved community leaders and a spirit of giving, the Foundation has had an outstanding record of success.

Programs and activities supported by the Foundation include the Challenge Scholarship Program, Take Stock in Children Program, endowed scholarships for students and recognition of outstanding student scholarship and leadership. The Foundation also assists the TCC Alumni Association and the Association of Retired Faculty and Staff.

In 1991, the Foundation received its largest single gift, $250,000 from the Tallahassee Memorial Hospital Auxiliary, to be used for allied health programs support. With state matching funds the gift equaled $400,000.

In 1996, the first Challenge Scholarships were awarded to

The TCC Foundation taps a well-spring of a community spirit of giving to provide student scholarships and other enhancements to the educational program.

Students relax outside the TCC Library, a leader among community colleges in the quality of its traditional holding and the extent of its on-line resources.

middle and high school students through the TCC Foundation. These scholarships, donated by numerous individuals, corporations, law firms, civic clubs or governmental entities, will be waiting for the students when they graduate from high school. The students are potentially the first in their families to attend college.

Starting in 1999, gifts of Coca-Cola stock by members of Gretna Presbyterian Church established an endowment to provide Challenge or Take Stock in Children Scholarships for every eligible fifth-grade student at Gretna Elementary School.

Thanks to the generosity of company officials at North Carolina-based Oakwood Homes, the $1,000,000 Oakwood Endowment was established through the TCC Foundation to provide scholarships, the first ones going to engineering students.

In 1999, the Foundation's $1,000,000 Signature Seat campaign began with several pacesetter donors eager to establish scholarships for TCC students in the performing arts.

Athletics

An athletic program with a particularly strong emphasis on academics was re-established at TCC in 1990 after a 20-year absence.

TCC intercollegiate sports include baseball, softball and men's and women's basketball. Softball has won two Panhandle Conference titles and, in 1994, state and national titles. Baseball and women's basketball won Panhandle Conference championships in 1995. Men's basketball finished third in the NJCAA national tournament in 1997 and baseball finished third in the state in 1999.

The four programs have posted excellent records in graduating players, many of whom continue playing on athletic scholarships.

A Commitment to Excellence

Before Tallahassee Community College opened in 1966, the first faculty made a commitment to excellence in teaching. With the support of the District Board of Trustees, the administration and staff, that commitment continues in the College's fourth decade. The outcome, year after year, class after class, is success.

Tallahassee Memorial Cares

Our Past

Today, residents of Tallahassee and the Big Bend rely on Tallahassee Memorial HealthCare to provide sophisticated care for all of their health care needs. But it wasn't always like this.

Back in 1948, Leon County's 51,000 residents had no hospital to care for them. The first public hospital, the two-year-old Baptist Hospital, was closing. Mothers routinely delivered their babies at home, and trauma patients were forced to try to survive the near one-hour trip to the hospital north of town.

All that changed one chilly April morning when six people formed Tallahassee Memorial Hospital. There was no doubt Tallahassee needed a state-of-the-art community health care facility, but little did the hospital's first governing board realize that one day Tallahassee Memorial would serve as the backbone of Tallahassee's $1 billion health care industry.

Since its humble beginnings at Dale Mabry Field, through a polio-like epidemic in 1954, Tallahassee Memorial — now the frosty white, wedding cake of a building sitting at the corner of Magnolia and Miccosukee — offers services and provides care to meet almost every health care need.

"We are a part of this community and its infrastructure, and we have always believed we should put back more than we take out," says Duncan Moore, the hospital's CEO since 1988. "If we don't, then we have real problems. When it's all said and done, we want to have made a difference in the life of the community."

Through numerous renovations and expansions, Tallahassee Memorial has continued to add services with our community's good health in mind. A good example is Tallahassee Memorial's Emergency Medical Services, which was established in 1972 to provide ambulance service to Leon County. By 1973, The Family Practice Residency Program was in place, offering primary care to area residents and training physicians, many of whom have established practices in rural communities surrounding Tallahassee.

Like its counterparts in other cities, Tallahassee Memorial has inevitably experienced societal growing pains. In some cases, the community has looked to TMH and its health care system for guidance and direction in dealing with challenging issues. Tallahassee Memorial has met the challenges. For example, TMH stepped out rather boldly with a community-wide program that educates young people about AIDS.

Internally, TMH practices what it preaches. One of the first corporations in the city to have a diversity management program, TMH also established a GED program, a literacy program, and an on-site child care center. With an on-site kindergarten, TMH is also home to one of Florida's newest partnership schools.

Our Caring Hands

The area's tiniest babies are cared for here, as are those with brain and spinal cord injuries, cancer patients, those who need a new heart or must recover from a stroke.

Tallahassee Memorial has continued to provide state-of-the-art technology even in challenging economic times. But it's the way care is provided at TMH that sets this hospital apart.

"We like to think that people come from miles around to Tallahassee Memorial not because of our fancy equipment but because the people here really do care for them," said Duncan Moore.

The hospital abounds with stories of nurses who buy food for patients' families out of their own pockets; about environmental service technicians, who, long after quitting time, stick around the emergency room to comfort strangers waiting for word on a loved one. Lending a helping hand is all in a day's work for employees at TMH.

Our Caring Hands are evident throughout our patient care areas, too. Cancer patients rely on a high-tech, high-touch approach to individualized care. In the Diabetes Center, families spend special weekends together learning how to manage children's diabetes — to improve their quality of life.

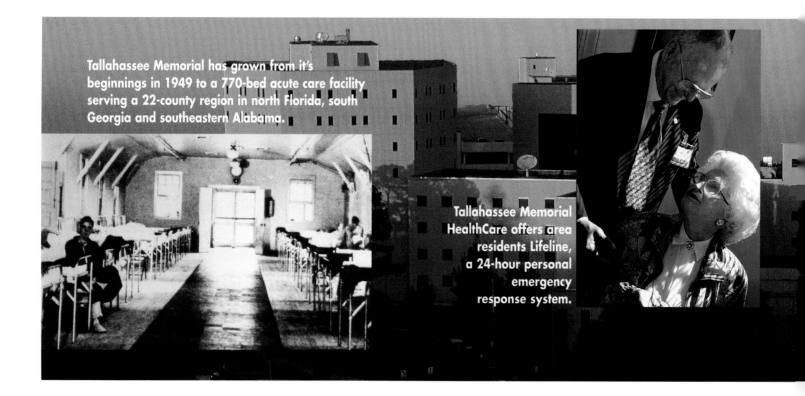

Tallahassee Memorial has grown from it's beginnings in 1949 to a 770-bed acute care facility serving a 22-county region in north Florida, south Georgia and southeastern Alabama.

Tallahassee Memorial HealthCare offers area residents Lifeline, a 24-hour personal emergency response system.

or the Big Bend.

Residents of the Big Bend rely on Tallahassee Memorial for:
• Life Flight, TMH's air ambulance service.
• The region's only newborn intensive care unit.
• Emergency Medical Services for Leon County.
• Five Centers of Excellence, including: the Heart and Vascular Institute, NeuroScience Center, Behavioral Health Center, Women's Pavilion and Diabetes Center.
• The region's only designated brain and spinal cord injury center.
• The region's only heart transplantation program.
• A comprehensive Cancer Care Program.

Outside our walls, however, through patient education and support, we raise public awareness about important health issues. Through the hospital's five Centers of Excellence, we aim to prevent health problems before they occur, and when they do, how to manage the disease and maintain a normal lifestyle.

The hospital's annual prostate screening, offered cooperatively with area urologists, provides nearly 700 free prostate checks each year. Other programs, such as those developed by the NeuroScience Center, provide direct patient care to those suffering from debilitating diseases and disorders — such as Parkinson's, Alzheimer's or memory loss.

In rural communities surrounding Florida's capital city, Tallahassee Memorial's Medical Outreach offers primary care services in family practice offices from Blountstown to Monticello to Eastpoint. Residents of these communities, including Tallahassee, have access to a physician and staff they know and trust.

50 Years of Caring...And Beyond

People helping people. That's what the Tallahassee Memorial HealthCare Foundation is all about. Through their many efforts, the Foundation has successfully reached out to the community and secured financial assistance to fund projects and services which, in our new health care environment, are often unreimbursed.

Through fundraising, endowments and planned giving, the Foundation works with the hospital to support programs and services, as well as staff education and development. A recent project included renovation of the Pediatric Intensive Care Unit, making each room a colorful, bright and cheerful place for little ones in need of special care.

Likewise, the TMH Auxiliary donates over 50,000 hours of time to the hospital annually, and helps fund projects such as an Emergency Department renovation, Perinatal Bereavement Program, and more. The Auxiliary's 27 Service Committees provide greatly needed support by staffing waiting rooms, transporting patients and making favors for meal trays, among other things.

Departments within the hospital take their programs to area schools, churches and community organizations, offering such programs as Think First, Healthy Hearts for Kids and Diabetes Screenings. Think First teaches children the importance of protecting one's brain and spinal cord, while Healthy Hearts for Kids helps children learn the benefits of exercise and a heart healthy diet early in life — to prevent health problems as they grow older.

As the next 50 years unfold, TMH will continue to survive and thrive as the region's leading health care facility. Through a continuum of care — a system that delivers health care to people from birth to old age — one that emphasizes prevention and wellness, TMH welcomes the opportunity to meet the community's ever-changing health care needs.

Regardless of the strides made in technology, the changes in how health care is financed, and the partnerships that may or may not be formed, Tallahassee Memorial will continue to serve its stakeholders, not stockholders, and its mission will remain constant: that we will strive to provide each person with the highest quality health care at the most affordable price.

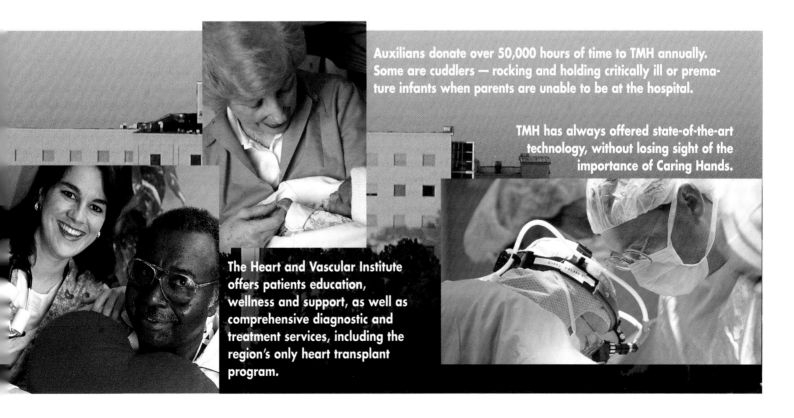

Auxilians donate over 50,000 hours of time to TMH annually. Some are cuddlers — rocking and holding critically ill or premature infants when parents are unable to be at the hospital.

TMH has always offered state-of-the-art technology, without losing sight of the importance of Caring Hands.

The Heart and Vascular Institute offers patients education, wellness and support, as well as comprehensive diagnostic and treatment services, including the region's only heart transplant program.

The Columns

One of the more impressive elements of historic Tallahassee is the preservation and restoration of many of its older homes. Dating back to the mid-nineteenth century and breath-taking to behold, these towering, elegant dwellings enhance the dignified beauty characteristic of the Tallahassee landscape. One of these mansions, built in 1830 and later named "The Columns," enjoys the distinction of being the oldest surviving building in Tallahassee.

Characterized by its four massive white columns, its huge chimneys which rise flush with the gable ends and its weather-beaten yet sturdy appearance, The Columns rises three stories above its foundation. Simple in design, the building is basically a rectangular, red brick box divided by two transverse partitions extending from the finished basement to the second floor ceiling, the attic being a huge open loft running the length and breadth of the basic structure. To this was appended the large front portico, a small porch off the north end, and the small ell projecting from the southwest corner of the basement and first floors. Through the years this stately, majestic edifice that graces the corner of West Park Avenue and North Duval Street has served as host to a wide variety of people and organizations. For the past twenty-eight years, The Columns has been the home of the Tallahassee Area Chamber of Commerce, as well as the Economic Development Council of Tallahassee/Leon County for the past seven years. The Columns also served as the original location for the Tallahassee Area Convention and Visitor's Bureau, the marketing arm of the Leon County Tourist Development Council.

When William Williams, a wealthy banker from Georgia who moved to Tallahassee in the late 1820s, was elected president of the newly chartered Bank of Florida he was in need of a suitable home for his wife Rebecca and their ten children and an adequate facility for his banking business. In November of 1829 he purchased "Lot No. 183" at the southwest corner of Adams Street and Park Avenue from the city commissioners for five dollars. It was here that he built The Columns, complete with banking office and vault room, in 1830. He continued to improve this estate over the next two years, and when he sold it in May, 1833 to the Central Bank of Florida its value was approximately thirty thousand dollars. The Columns was, for the next ten years, the center of banking activity in northern Florida. In addition to the Central Bank of Florida, at times The Columns also housed the Union Bank of Florida.

In the 1840s, economic depression, natural disaster and yellow fever all contributed to the total collapse of the banking business in territorial Florida. In 1847, The Columns was sold at a sheriff's sale to satisfy creditors of the defunct Central Bank. It was purchased by Gen. William Bailey of Monticello and Dr. Isaac Mitchell of Thomas County, Georgia, who leased it to a Mrs. Demilly, who advertised the relocation of her boardinghouse "to the large and commodious brick building next door north of the Union Bank." For a short period of time the boardinghouse served the people of Tallahassee well. During the Civil War, however, the efforts of the building's owners were turned toward aiding the Confederate forces and away from the house's upkeep. Due to wartime neglect, the building deteriorated to the point where extensive repairs to the roof, and probably to other parts of the structure as well, were badly needed. But it was not until the winter of 1867–68 that the needed repairs were made.

After the Civil War The Columns entered its halcyon days as a private home, which lasted for almost sixty years. It was purchased by Dr. Alexander Hawkins, a successful physician, and his wife Martha. Here Hawkins made his home and conducted his medical practice for more than twenty years. In 1897 Hawkins sold The Columns to Thomas J. Roberts, a successful planter, cattleman and businessman, for five thousand dollars. Roberts bought the residence as a wedding gift for his young second wife, Sarah Harley Roberts of Thomasville, Georgia and the deed was recorded in her name. It was Sarah who gave The Columns its name. She adored the home and, after the death of Thomas, she continued to live there with her second husband, Henry Felkel, Clerk of the Leon County Circuit Court. In 1925 the twice-widowed Sarah sold the house to N. D. Suttles and Company Realtors. A variety of business and professional offices again occupied the basement rooms, and the residence was converted into apartments. The most famous tenant during this time was the Dutch Kitchen restaurant, which occupied several basement rooms and served a steady stream of Tallahassee students, residents, and visitors from 1925–1956.

In 1960 The Columns property was sold to the Trustees of the First Baptist Church. In 1961–62, portions of the building were used to house the Leon County Public Library. Later the Church used some of the basement rooms for Sunday school classes and for recreational purposes. In 1970, the Church Trustees announced their intention to clear the land to make room for a building of more modern design and construction to meet their need for additional space and offered The Columns to anyone who would move it. Otherwise, it would be demolished. Following a structural survey to determine its ability to withstand the strain, The Columns was moved to its new location in the early summer of 1971, by Walter Sullivan and Sons of Atlanta, Georgia. The move required about six weeks as the structure was freed from its foundation, inched westward the length of the block and into Duval Street, turned northward along Duval to the north side of Park Avenue, and finally eased into its present position. In 1995 a half million dollar renovation project was completed.

The intent of the Chamber in recent years has been to preserve a sense of the historical significance by retaining its uncomplicated, if somewhat unusual exterior appearance and by decorating and furnishing its interior in authentic period style. By maintaining the old charm and elegance of history and tradition and, at the same time, allowing for the necessary changes and improvements for accommodating the functional needs of a modern-day business, the Columns continues to serve Tallahassee as it has in so many ways for 169 years.

Tallahassee Trust for Historic Preservation, Inc.

Tallahassee and Leon County have a rich heritage. Significant historic resources remain that illuminate that history. From prehistoric ceremonial mounds to Apalachee and Seminole villages, from Hernando de Soto's winter encampment to Spanish missions, from the founding of the Territorial capital and the construction of antebellum plantations to the establishment of institutions of higher learning, many social, economic and cultural changes have occurred throughout the history of this "favored land."

Recognizing the importance of preserving the area's distinctive historical characteristics, the Historic Tallahassee Preservation Board was created by state statute in 1970. This board served the community for 27 years, and successfully carried out its mission to systematically identify, evaluate, protect and interpret the historic resources located in Tallahassee, Leon County and the surrounding area. Since the creation of this board, 150 historic resources and 5 historic districts have been listed on the National Register of Historic Places. Over 4,000 buildings constructed prior to 1947 and many significant archaeological sites and former antebellum and hunting plantations have been documented. The Tallahassee Trust for Historic Preservation, Inc. was established in 1988 as the direct support organization for the preservation board.

The preservation board became instrumental in promoting the area's history by initiating and participating in heritage education programs and by publishing books on the history of Tallahassee and Leon County. The preservation board played a major role in promoting heritage tourism by producing a comprehensive heritage tourism study, by sponsoring and conducting historic tours and by preparing informational brochures about the area's historic resources.

One of this board's most significant contributions to the protection of the community's historic resources was its emphasis on smart growth. The board was actively involved in preparing the Historic Preservation Element that was adopted in the 2010 Tallahassee-Leon County Comprehensive Plan. The board was also instrumental in the drafting and approval of effective local historic preservation legislation including an ordinance to protect Leon County's nationally recognized canopy roads.

In 1997, the Historic Tallahassee Preservation Board was eliminated. The Tallahassee Trust made a commitment to carry on the original mission and activities of the former preservation board. Today, the Tallahassee Trust is a private not-for-profit corporation that receives funding support from the City of Tallahassee, Leon County, private sources, and from various individual and corporate members.

The Tallahassee Trust continues to serve as a clearinghouse for information on historic preservation methods and techniques. It functions as the local historic preservation agency for the City of Tallahassee and Leon County and administers one of its joint advisory commissions, the Tallahassee-Leon County Architectural Review Board. The professional staff of the Tallahassee Trust provide historic preservation technical assistance to owners of historic properties, including information on historic preservation incentives and grants, and maintains and operates a Special Collections and Research Library for public use.

The presence of the Tallahassee Trust, with the continued support of the local governments and its members, will ensure that this community's quality of life and historic treasures will be preserved in and around Florida's Capital City and for generations of Floridians.

"Dedicated to Preserving Our Heritage"

Board of Directors and staff of the Tallahassee Trust for Historic Preservation, Inc. Front row, left to right: Doris Pollock, Stephanie Whitfield, Ann E. Kozeliski (Chairman), Mary Ann Cleveland (Secretary), Serena Moyle, and Mary Casteel. Second row: Wayne Warren, Daniel T. Penton (Vice Chairman), Joe Knetsch, Mark Tarmey, James Culp, Beth J. LaCivita (Executive Director), Barbara Miller (Administrative Assistant), Judy Etemadi, J. Stanley Chapman, and Benjamin K. Phipps (Treasurer). Board of Directors not shown: Jackson Maynard and Don Lanham. Photo credit: Wayne Warren, Communicore.

Tallahassee
Trust for
Historic
Preservation
Inc.

City of Tallahassee

According to the City of Tallahassee's second annual report, dated 1922, "... the cornerstone of the Capitol was laid in 1825 and within seven short years Leon County was home to 6,000 people."

How times have changed! Today approximately 144,000 people live within the city limits of Tallahassee (96 square miles), with an additional 90,000 residing in unincorporated Leon County.

Tallahassee is an old Apalachee Indian word meaning "old fields" or "abandoned villages." Tallahassee not only exemplifies the influence of the Indians, but also that of the Spanish, French, and English who occupied the area in succession.

Tallahassee was incorporated originally in 1825 and again in 1827, 1831, and finally in 1840.

In December 1825, Florida's legislative council provided that Tallahassee would be governed by a mayor and a five-member city council. All were to be elected annually and all were to serve without pay. Following an election in 1826, Dr. Charles Haire became Tallahassee's first mayor. This basic form of government was retained until 1919, when the current form of government (commission/manager) was adopted.

Today, the citizens of Tallahassee elect a city commission, but also separately elect a "leadership" mayor. All five positions are elected at large to serve four-year staggered terms.

The commissioners appoint a city manager, directly responsible to them, who oversees the operation of the government and its staff, and carries out the mandates of the commission.

City government is comprised of numerous departments, and directors of those departments report to the city manager directly or via three assistant city managers. Each of the three assistants oversees the operation of one of three primary service areas of city government, Development and Transportation Services, Safety and Neighborhood Services, and Utility Services. In addition, a fourth service area is comprised of departments performing functions internal to the government, such as human resources, budgeting, and computer services. The Tallahassee City Hall, on a 1.5-acre site at 300 South Adams Street near the Florida Capitol Complex,

opened for business March 28, 1983. The new building was the first in Tallahassee built specifically as a city hall. Previous city halls were "hand-me-down" buildings. The last such city hall, the Martin Building, occupied by the city from 1974 to 1981, was constructed in 1927 for use of and by the state.

City Hall, where most administrative offices are located, has 137,000 square feet of space and houses some 400 city employees. Original construction was completed in twenty months at a cost of $11.6 million.

Five areas with a high volume of public walk-in traffic are located on the first floor of City Hall, which is entirely handicapped accessible. Utility payment cashiers, utility customer account services, licenses and permits, the customer service office, and the city's employment office are within easy reach of Tallahassee's citizens.

The City of Tallahassee offers a full range of municipal services including the distribution of electricity, water, sewer, and natural gas to customers throughout Tallahassee and Leon County.

In addition, the city maintains an extensive network of local streets and the stormwater drainage system, provides community service centers—including a senior citizens' center— and operates the Tallahassee-Leon Community Animal Service Center. Police and fire protection also are provided by

the city. TalTran, the community's mass transit system, is operated by the city, as is the Aviation Department, which oversees the operation of the Tallahassee Regional Airport. The city's nationally recognized Parks and Recreation Department maintains over 1,800 acres of beautiful parklands while also offering a variety of organized recreation programs for youth and adults.

Before 1905, the city's fire services were provided by a volunteer fire department. The city's first fire chief, appointed in 1905, served as supervisor of the gas and water departments as well. In 1915, the fire department retired Tom and Jerry (its iron gray fire wagon horses) and purchased its first gasoline powered vehicle.

The Tallahassee Fire Department's

quality of service enables the department to maintain a Class II fire-insurance rating, as determined by the Insurance Service Office. Tallahassee is one of the few cities in Florida to obtain a Class II rating. The fire department maintains fire and rescue services for all of Tallahassee and unincorporated Leon County, operating 14 stations strategically located throughout the community.

The Tallahassee Police Department was organized by Tallahassee's first mayor in 1840. The TPD was only the thirteenth local law-enforcement agency in the country to receive accreditation by the Commission on Law-Enforcement Agencies. This award certifies and gives national recognition to the Tallahassee Police Department as a modern, progressive, and professional law-enforcement agency.

The city's first airport was built in 1929 on the present Jackson Bluff Road. It was dedicated as Dale Mabry Field in honor of a Tallahasseean who lost his life at the controls of the United States dirigible Roma on the last voyage of that ill-fated ship.

In 1961, a new airport was constructed at its current site on the west side of Tallahassee. A modern passenger terminal

was opened to the public in 1989, built to serve Tallahassee's expanding aviation needs well into the future.

The city's transit system, Tallahassee Transit (TalTran), functions effectively and efficiently in its transfer facility, the C. K. Steele Plaza, on the corner of Adams and Tennessee Streets. TalTran provides dependable transportation daily by carrying thousands of Tallahasseeans over nearly 40 routes in its system.

The bus system was established in 1937 and was privately owned and operated. The City of Tallahassee purchased the system in December, 1973, naming it TalTran.

Electricity is something almost everyone in this country has come to rely on for daily living and convenience. The City of Tallahassee ventured into generating and distributing electricity on September 11, 1902, when the city commission approved the sale of bonds for building a power plant. The plant was completed in December 1902, and in 1903, the Capital City Light and Fuel Company began the conversion of lights from gas to electricity. The plant consisted of a steam-powered unit which generated 87.5 kilowatts of power.

During the 1930s, because of high operating costs, the city closed its power plant and began purchasing power from Florida Power Corporation. In 1948, the commission again decided to enter the power generation business, and the Sam O. Purdom Generating Plant went into operation in 1949. The Arvah B. Hopkins Generating Plant, the city's largest, began generating power in 1970. The city also owns and operates the Clem Corn Hydroelectric Plant on Lake Talquin.

Profits from the city's Electric Operations fund nearly one third of the city's annual operating budget, including important services such as fire and police protection, recreation programs, and street maintenance.

In 1971, Governor Reubin Askew signed into law a bill giving responsibility to the newly formed Downtown Improvement Authority to revamp a 31-block area in the central business district, bounded on the north by Tennessee Street, on the east by Gadsden, on the south by Pensacola, and on the west by Bronough Street. Property owners in that area voted to impose a one-mill tax on themselves to fund the DIA. The DIA was formed in response to what was viewed then as a crisis situation—the exodus of longtime merchants to new malls and shopping centers. The abandonment of downtown led to vacant and deteriorating buildings, an overall rundown appearance, and parking and transportation problems.

Today, downtown Tallahassee's revitalization is evident by the Kleman Plaza facility, a multi-use two-block complex behind City Hall that includes the Odyssey Science Center and Museum of Art/Tallahassee, the Florida League of Cities office building, a beautiful landscaped plaza, a performing arts bandshell, and underground parking for over 1,100 vehicles. The landscaped plaza has become the venue of choice for cultural offerings throughout the years, including the widely acclaimed Southern Shakespeare Festival.

Tallahasseeans are proud of their beautiful north Florida city, gentle rolling hills, and stately trees. The people are protective of their environment, their trees, their history, and their community.

The City of Tallahassee realizes this, and strives to meet its goal of providing its citizens with what they deserve—a continuously and consistently high level of quality service and a safe, productive, and enjoyable community.

Many Tallahasseeans will agree—Tallahassee is truly a special place to live. And this year, its even more special, as Tallahassee was named as one of ten All-America Cities for 1999 by the National Civic League. This prestigious award goes to cities that show a willingness to deal with pressing issues by having different segments of the community work together to solve significant problems.

Watkins Engineers and Constructors

For more than half a century, Watkins Engineers and Constructors has served its clients with integrity, diligence, and careful attention to their individual needs. This client oriented approach to business enables Watkins to focus on individual needs and requirements of their clients, and has contributed to an impressive record of company growth. A majority of projects are completed for repeat clients, which has resulted in the establishment and continued development of many working partnerships with *Fortune 500* companies. Watkins develops and maintains long-term relationships by focusing on executive attention, communication, safe operation, trust, cost savings, and quality performance. Serving as an extension of each client's organization, they are able to achieve long-term cost savings, make continuous improvements, and keep facilities operating at peak efficiency.

Watkins' clients expect quality, and they should know it when they see it. They're the giants of the industry: Procter and Gamble, Air Products and Chemicals, Buckeye, Dupont, Georgia-Pacific, International Paper, and Mitsubishi just to name a few. Watkins' Commercial Division has been a major player in the local con-

struction market too. They have built many projects at Florida State University, FAMU, and the State of Florida and have most recently worked on the remodeling of the Civic Center and the Florida Capitol building.

E. M. Watkins and Company was formed in 1944 by Buck Watkins to provide design and construction services to North Florida and Alabama's emerging wood products and pulp and paper industries. Early client relationships forged remarkable partnerships, and over time, Watkins has been retained for the long term to provide maintenance and retrofit services for plants. Watkins began its first site based service agreement with Procter & Gamble more than 45 years ago. Today, because of a strong commitment to quality service, Watkins continues to serve this site (now Buckeye Cellulose) and many other sites throughout North America.

In 1983, Watkins was acquired by San Francisco-based Dillingham Construction Corp., the 15th largest domestic construction firm. In addition to removing all bonding limits, this merger gained Watkins access to extensive expertise and resources in industrial and heavy construction.

Under the leadership of Eddie Aaron since 1998, Watkins has diversified into construction management and design/build projects and has continued geographic expansion. Watkins has experienced a phenomenal 16 percent average growth per year and boasts an excellent safety record, which is significantly better than the national average. Safety is of key concern to Watkins, whose company culture is safety focused. Each Watkins employee attends intensive company sponsored safety training programs and is empowered to make changes in work processes that enhance safety.

Watkins provides a full range of engineering, construction, and maintenance services for clients in a variety of markets including: pulp and paper, food and beverage, consumer products, specialty chemicals, power, and rock products. Services include planning and feasibility studies, engineering and construction services, and a full range of start up program options tailored to client's individual needs. Through these programs and others like them, Watkins helps clients enhance overall performance, scheduled incremental improvements, and keep their facilities operating at peak efficiency year after year. Watkins also provides long-term contract maintenance, special

project development, and professional construction management through continuing-service agreements at industrial plant sites in manufacturing facilities. Watkins works extensively in the process and manufacturing industries and has additional experience in the public and commercial sectors.

Headquartered in Tallahassee, Watkins currently employs over 3,500 employees nationwide and has ten offices throughout the U.S. to serve clients regionally. Watkins has made a significant commitment to hiring, training, and retaining one of the most long-term and highly skilled work forces in the industry. Watkins formally implemented a company-wide Craft Training Program that is fully accredited by the National Center for construction education and research. Watkins offers a variety of training and development programs, provides fair employment practices and industry-competitive compensation, and actively seeks opportunities to upgrade and promote deserving employees.

Barnett and Fronczak Architects

Injecting New Life in the Heart of Tallahassee

Rick Barnett and Dave Fronczak arrived in Tallahassee in the winter of 1979 to open a new architectural firm. Responding to their own need for office space and to the needs of a growing community whose emphasis was on preservation and restoration of the downtown core, they successfully rehabilitated their own development project, Gallie's Hall Office Building. This project, completed in 1982 and strategically located across from Florida's State Capitol, was the first major renovation project downtown, and as such, captured a great deal of attention for the company. Since then, Barnett and Fronczak have participated in the design and development of many historic buildings on Tallahassee's Main Street and the Adams Street Commons. Projects such as the Governors Club, the law offices of Greenberg Traurig, and Florida Association of Realtors and the renovations to the Florida Hotel & Motel Association further exemplify their sensitivity to the downtown historic urban fabric. Most recently, the completion of the renovations to the Supreme Court Building, the Florida League of Cities Building and Kleman Plaza further the development of the downtown and the firm's growing list of significant projects.

Since the establishment of the firm, the two men have expanded their practice to include the offering of a wide range of architectural, interior design, and planning services for a variety of building types and clients.

The firm has provided services on the high-tech College of Engineering in Innovation Park, and is currently designing other major building projects on the campuses of Florida State and Florida A&M Universities. Most notable of these projects is the Academic Center/University Center located on the Florida State University campus. This 60,000 square foot facility is reshaping the master plan of the campus by becoming the new focus of student and community activities.

Barnett and Fronczak's sensitivity to the characteristics that make Tallahassee unique has been a primary reason for their successes. Throughout the life of the firm they have maintained an active involvement in downtown design. In addition, both have strengthened their commitment through continued involvement in civic and community affairs. Barnett has served on the Tallahassee Downtown Improvement for three terms and is active in the Chamber of Commerce and local United Way campaigns. Fronczak, past chairman of the Tallahassee/Leon County Planning Commission and Florida State Board of Architecture continues his involvement with statewide and national design issues.

Gallie's Hall was known as the Tallahassee Opera House in 1892.

Academic Center/University Center, FSU

Renovations to the Supreme Court Building, Downtown

Florida League of Cities Building, Kleman Plaza Downtown Tallahassee

FAMU/FSU College of Engineering

Mad Dog Design and Construction Company, Inc.

The Mad Dog Story:
WE'RE BUILDING MORE THAN BUILDINGS

As founding members of the Miccosukee Land Co-op our first design/build projects were our own homes. Early collective works included heavy timber residential construction, custom millwork packages, architectural stairs, prefabricated hot tub kits, and a geodesic dome. So different were the designs, materials, and methods that in 1974 the Leon County chief building official changed the original name of MD Construction on a building permit to "Mad Dog" saying, "Only a Mad Dog would do it that way." Over the objections of friends and family, in 1977 we incorporated the name Mad Dog Design and Construction Company. The rest is history. . . .

By 1980 Mad Dog had begun creating communities. We designed and built over 250 homes within our award-winning residential neighborhoods, Blairstone Forest, Sunrise Community, and Twin Lakes. We literally had a stable (a converted barn on the Twin Lakes property) of designers and draftsmen working daily on new models for immediate construction. (Acquiring building permits was different back then!)

Chuck Mitchell, Kelly Dozier, and Laurie Dozier visit the Gazebo at Lake Ella donated by Mad Dog to the City of Tallahassee.

Our house-raising work parties at the Co-op were the forerunners for much of our community work. The Chairs Elementary School playground, a house for WFSU Public Television's auction, the Miccosukee Land Co-op's community center and swimming pool, a gazebo at Tallahassee's Lake Ella, a house for troubled youth at Disc Village, the dining hall at the YMCA's Camp Indian Springs, a maintenance facility at the Tallahassee Museum and many Housing Foundation volunteer projects and Habitat Builds have all involved our coordination—most often with many eager volunteers, tools in hand, awaiting instructions!

Interspersed among the hundreds of homes in our residential communities were scores of custom homes we designed and then constructed on our clients' land. Among them were Betty Barber's Earth Shelter/Berm House which was featured in *Mother Earth News* and *Fine Home Building's* compilation of twenty-four top solar designs. Tom Barr's Onion home and Chuck Mitchell's passive solar home were featured articles in *Rodale's New Shelter* magazine. Additionally, as part of our alternative energy explorations, Mad Dog received a federal grant to design and construct a solar-heated, wood-drying kiln.

Beginning in 1984 with converting the old Joe's Spaghetti House/Seafox Lounge into an office building, commercial construction projects gained more and more of Mad Dog's attention. Although initially we were not providing commercial construction documents, we were frequently becoming the owner's chosen representative. It soon became evident that our clients were looking for a single ally to coordinate their entire projects.

Soon after we began providing commercial clients with complete design/build services we joined in the development of two commercial office parks, Governors' Park followed by Commonwealth Office Park. Mad Dog's venture into commercial development afforded Mad Dog an opportunity to demonstrate our vital interest in the preservation of Tallahassee's cultural history, as demonstrated through its treatment of the discovery of Hernando de Soto's 1539 encampment on a site where Mad Dog had begun the development of a six-acre commercial office park.

When the discovery was made, Mad Dog immediately stopped development activity. Over the next several months, the company worked with state archaeologists to help excavate and preserve the site where Europeans celebrated the first Christmas in North America. Through the cooperation of Mad Dog and Tallahassee Development Corporation, nearly five acres of the site were preserved and conveyed to the Trust for Public Land. The property was transferred to the state of Florida for the creation of a state park and museum to display the thousands of artifacts found on the site. In recognition of Mad Dog's efforts, the Florida governor and cabinet commended the company for its historic sensitivity and its cooperation, and for demonstrating that commercial development can be compatible with sensitive historic preservation. In addition, the firm received proclamations of appreciation from the National Park Service, the U.S. Department of the Interior and the Florida Archaeological Council for a key role in the discovery and preservation of De Soto's winter encampment at the Governors' Park site.

Today, whether as the general contractor or the design/builder, our name is associated with projects as far away as Charlotte, North Carolina, and as diverse as The Moon Musical Hall and the Tallahassee General Aviation Terminal. With each new project, we meet the challenge of providing innovative, efficient methods to deliver a quality product.

Although the foundation of Mad Dog's reputation is directly related to our responsive service to our clients, Mad Dog and its associates are recognized as community leaders and contributors. Mad Dog's selection as the first Tallahassee business to be recognized as a "Volunteer of the Year" by the Tallahassee Chamber of Commerce is indicative of our belief in the integration of business success with civic responsibility. Mad Dog Design and Construction Company's commitment to work to enhance our community and its quality of life is "the tail that wags the dog."

We look forward to many more years of quality responsive service to our clients as—

WE'RE BUILDING MORE THAN BUILDINGS.

BIBLIOGRAPHY

This bibliography mentions a few general works and monographs valuable to understanding the rich and complicated history of Florida. Books about and related to Tallahassee are listed separately. Space limitations preclude to listing of articles, but the reader should consult Michael H. Harris, *Florida History: A Bibliography* (Metuchen, New Jersey, 1972). Also valuable is Allen Morris and Joan Perry Morris (Compilers), *The Florida Handbook 1999–2000* (Tallahassee, 2000, see ongoing and past editions). The best general history of Florida is Michael Gannon (Editor), *The New History of Florida* (Gainesville, 1996). Articles relating to Tallahassee and Leon County appear regularly in scholarly journals, especially the *Florida Historical Quarterly*. The Tallahassee Historical Society, founded in 1933, published four volumes of the *Tallahassee Historical Society Annual* in the 1930s and beginning in 1944, *Apalachee*, a publication that continues. Both journals contain articles related to the area. There is no complete general history of the region. For published and unpublished materials including theses and dissertations, see Mary Louise Ellis and William Warren Rogers, *Tallahassee and Leon County: A History and Bibliography* (Tallahassee, 1986).

General Works

Akerman, Joe A., Jr. *Florida Cowman.* Kissimmee, Fla.: Florida Cattlemen's Association, 1976.

Blake, Nelson M. *Land Into Water—Water Into Land.* Tallahassee: Florida State University Press, 1980.

Buker, George E. *Swamp Sailors.* Gainesville: University of Florida Press, 1975.

Bullen, Adelaide K. *Florida Indians of Past and Present.* New York and London: Kendall Books, 1974.

Cabeza de Vaca, Alvar Nunez. *The Power Within Us. Cabeza de Vaca's Relation of His Journey From Florida to the Pacific 1528–1536.* New York: Sloan and Peace, 1944.

Coker, William S., and Watson, Thomas D. *Indian Traders of the Southeastern Spanish and Borderlands: Panton, Leslie & Company and John Forbes & Company, 1783–1847.* Pensacola: University of West Florida Press, 1986.

Covington, James W. *The Billy Bowlegs War, 1855–1858.* Chuluota, Fla.: Mickler House, 1982.

Davis, William Watson. *Civil War and Reconstruction in Florida.* Gainesville: University of Florida Press, 1964.

Gannon, Michael V. *The Cross in the Sand.* Gainesville: University of Florida Press, 1967.

Johns, John E. *Florida During the Civil War.* Gainesville: University of Florida Press, 1963.

Lanier, Sidney. *Florida: Its Scenery, Climate, and History.* Facsimile reproduction of the 1875 edition. Gainesville: University of Florida Press, 1959.

Laumer, Frank. *Massacre.* Gainesville: University of Florida Press, 1968.

Ley, John C. *Fifty-two Years in Florida.* Nashville: Methodist-Episcopal Church South, 1899.

Mahon, John D. *History of the Second Seminole War, 1835–1842.* Gainesville: University of Florida Press, 1968.

Manucy, Albert. *Florida's Menendez.* St. Augustine: St. Augustine Historical Society, 1965.

Martin, Sidney Walter. *Florida During the Territorial Days.* Athens: University of Georgia Press, 1944.

Milanich, Jerald T., and Charles H. Fairbanks. *Florida Archaeology.* New York: New York Academic Press, 1980.

Pettingill, George R. *Story of Florida Railroads, 1835–1903.* Boston: 1952.

Pyburn, Nita J. *A History of the Development of a Single System of Education in Florida, 1822–1903.* Tallahassee: Florida State University Press, 1954.

Richardson, Joe M. *The Negro in the Reconstruction of Florida, 1865–1877.* Tallahassee: Florida State University Press, 1965.

Rogers, William Warren. *Outposts on the Gulf: Saint George Island & Apalachicola from Early Exploration to World War II.* Pensacola: University of West Florida Press, 1986.

Romans, Bernard. *A Concise Natural History of East and West Florida.* Facsimile reproduction of the 1775 edition. Gainesville: University of Florida Press, 1962.

Shofner, Jerrell H. *Nor Is It Over Yet: Florida During the Era of Reconstruction, 1863–1877.* Gainesville: University of Florida Press, 1974.

Tebeau, Charlton W. *A History of Florida.* Coral Gables, Fla.: University of Miami Press, 1971.

Williams, John Lee. *The Territory of Florida.* Facsimile reproduction of the 1837 edition. Gainesville: University of Florida Press, 1964.

Williamson, Edward C. *Florida Politics in the Golden Age.* Gainesville: University of Florida Press, 1976.

Wright, J. Leitch, Jr. *Florida in the American Revolution.* Gainesville: University Presses of Florida, 1975.

Wright, J. Leitch, Jr. *William Augustus Bowles: Director General of the Creek Nation.* Athens: University of Georgia Press, 1967.

Special Works

Avant, Fenton Garnett Davis. *My Tallahassee.* Edited by David A. Avant, Jr. Tallahassee: L'Avant Studios, 1983.

Bettinger, Julie S. *Tallahassee: Tradition, Technology, and Teamwork.* Montgomery, Ala.: Community Communications, 1995.

Boyd, Mark F., Smith, Hale G., and Griffin, John W. *Here They Once Stood: The Tragic End of the Apalachee Missions.* Gainesville: University of Florida Press, 1951.

Bryant, James C. *Indian Springs: The Story of a Pioneer Church in Leon County, Florida.* Tallahassee: Privately published, 1971.

Campbell, Doak S. *A University in Transition: Florida State University, 1941–1947.* Tallahassee: Florida State University Studies, 1964.

Collins, Thomas Leroy. *Forerunners Courageous; Stories of Frontier Florida.* Tallahassee: Colcade Publishers, 1971.

Dodd, William G. *History of West Florida Seminary, 1857–1901; Florida State College, 1901–1905.* Tallahassee: Florida State University, 1952.

Doherty, Herbert J. *Richard Keith Call, Southern Unionist.* Gainesville: University of Florida Press, 1961.

Eppes, Susan Bradford (Mrs. Nicholas Ware Eppes). *The Negro of the Old South: A Bit of Period History.* Chicago: Joseph G. Branch, 1925.

Eppes, Susan Bradford (Mrs. Nicholas Ware Eppes). *Through Some Eventful Years.* Facsimile reproduction of the 1926 edition, Gainesville: University of Florida Press, 1968.

Ewen, Charles Robin. *Hernando de Soto Among the Apalachee: the Archaeology of the First Winter Encampment.* Gainesville: University Press of Florida, 1998.

Fisher, Barbara Jean. *Meridian Markers.* Great Neck, New York: Todd and Honeywell, 1984.

Florida Hill Country or Agricultural Attractions of Leon County, Florida. Tallahassee: Board of Commissioners of Leon County, 1898.

Groene, Bertram H. *Ante-Bellum Tallahassee.* Tallahassee: Florida Heritage Foundation, 1971.

Hann, John H. and McEwan, Bonnie G. *The Apalachee Indians and Mission San Luis.* Gainesville: University Press of Florida, 1998.

Hann, John H. *Apalachee Land Between the Rivers.* Gainesville: University of Florida Press, 1988.

Hanna, A. J. *A Prince in Their Midst: The Adventurous Life of Achille Murat on the American Frontier.* Norman: University of Oklahoma Press, 1946.

Hutto, Joe. *Illumination in the Flatwoods: A Season with the Wild Turkey.* New York: Lyons and Burford, 1995.

Jahoda, Gloria. *The Other Florida.* New York: Charles Scribner's Sons, 1968.

Johnson, Malcolm B. *Red, White and Bluebloods in Frontier Florida.* Tallahassee: Rotary Club of Tallahassee, 1976.

Jones, James Pickett. *F.S.U. One Time! A History of Seminole Football.* Tallahassee: Sentry Press, 1973.

Ketchum, Eleanor. *Tales of Tallahassee.* Tallahassee: J. Dye, 1976.

Long, Ellen Call. *Florida Breezes: or, Florida New and Old.* Facsimile reproduction of the 1882 edition. Gainesville: University of Florida Press, 1962.

Memoirs of Edward Conradi: President of the Florida State College for Women 1909–1941. Tallahassee: Florida State College for Women, 1946. [?]

Menton, Jane Aurell. *The Grove: A Florida Home Through Seven Generations.* Tallahassee: Sentry Press, 1998.

Mickler, Delia Appleyard, and O'Bryan, Carolyde Phillips. *The Colonel's Inn Caterers' Tallahassee Historical Cookbook.* Tallahassee: Rose Printing Company, 1984.

Morris, Joan Perry, and Warner, Lee H. (Editors). *The Photographs of Alvan S. Harper Tallahassee, 1885–1910.* Tallahassee: Florida State University Press, 1983.

Neyland, Leedell W., and Riley, John W. *The History of Florida Agricultural and Mechanical University.* Gainesville: University of Florida Press, 1963.

Nunez, Kay, and Grissett, Helen P. *A Tale Worth Telling: The First Twenty Years of the Tallahassee Junior Museum 1956–1976.* Tallahassee: Tallahassee Junior Museum Pioneers, 1998.

Paisley, Clifton L. *From Cotton to Quail: An Agricultural Chronicle of Leon County, Florida, 1860–1967.* Gainesville: University of Florida Press, 1968.

Paisley, Clifton. *The Red Hills of Florida, 1528–1865.* Tuscaloosa: University of Alabama Press, 1989.

Paisley, Joy Smith (Compiler and Editor). *The Cemeteries of Leon County. . . .* Tallahassee: Colonial Dames XVII Century, 1978.

Phillips, Ulrich Bonnell, and Glunt, James David (Editors). *Florida Plantation Records from the Papers of George Noble Jones.* St. Louis: Missouri Historical Society, 1927.

Rhodes, Barbara. *At First: the Presbyterian Church in Tallahassee.* Tallahassee: First Presbyterian Church, 1994.

Rogers, William Warren, and Clark, Erica R. *The Croom Family and Goodwood Plantation: Land, Litigation, and Southern Lives.* Athens: University of Georgia Press, 1999.

Ruth, Marion Ursula. *The Tallahassee Years of Ernst von Dohnanyi.* Tallahassee: Florida State University Press, 1962.

Sellers, Robin. *Femina Perfecta: the Genesis of Florida State University.* Tallahassee: FSU Foundation, 1995.

Shofner, Jerrell H. *Daniel Ladd Merchant Prince of Frontier Florida.* Gainesville: University of Florida Press, 1978.

Shofner, Jerrell H. *History of Jefferson County.* Tallahassee: Sentry Press, 1976.

Smith, Charles U., and Killian, Lewis M. *The Tallahassee Bus Protest.* New York: Anti-Defamation League of B'nai B'rith, 1958.

Smith, Elizabeth F. *Tom Brown's Tallahassee Days, 1825–1850.* Crawfordville, Florida: Magnolia Monthly Press, 1971.

Smith, Julia Floyd. *Slavery and Plantation Growth in Ante-Bellum Florida 1821–1860.* Gainesville: University of Florida Press, 1973.

Stauffer, Carl. *God Willing: A History of St. John's Episcopal Church 1829–1979.* Tallahassee: St. John's Episcopal Church, 1984.

Thompson, (James) Maurice. *A Tallahassee Girl.* Boston: Houghton Mifflin, 1881.

Wagy, Thomas R. *Governor LeRoy Collins of Florida: Statesman of the New South.* University of Alabama Press, 1985.

Warner, Lee H. *Free Men in an Age of Servitude: Three Generations of a Black Family.* Lexington: University Press of Kentucky, 1992.

Wills, Martee, and Morris, Joan Perry. *Seminole History.* Jacksonville, Fla.: South Star, 1987.

Womack, Miles Kennan, Jr. *Gadsden A Florida County in Word and Picture.* Quincy: [privately published], 1976.

Yaeger, Jack Jr. (as told to Darren Hoyt). *Smiling Jack Yaeger.* Tallahassee: [privately published], 1997.

PHOTO CREDITS

Abbot, Ann: 96 middle, 145.
American Past, Simon & Schuster, 1947: 28.
Annual Report, City of Tallahassee, 1924: 102 middle left.
Annual Report, City of Tallahassee, 1924: 36 upper.
Annual Report, City of Tallahassee, 1928: 122 right, 123 left, 123 right.
Annual Report, City of Tallahassee, 1930: 120 upper, 128 upper, 129.
Annual Report, City of Tallahassee, 1932: 138, upper.
Annual Report, City of Tallahassee, 1935: 116 lower.
Annual Report, City of Tallahassee, 1937: 131 lower, 142.
Annual Report, City of Tallahassee, 1939: 136-137.
Avant, David A.: 57 right, 88.
Avant, Fenton G. Davis: 95 lower.
Bibliotheque Nationale: 22 left.
Biennial Report, Superintendent of Public Instruction of the State of Florida, 1896: 94 lower.
Bishop, Jean Thomas: 163 lower.
Brevis Narratio Eorum Quae in Florida Americae Provincia Gallis Acciderunt, by Theodor de Bry, 1591: 21 upper, 21 lower.
Bussard, Kathryn Brown: 102 upper, 106 lower, 139 upper.
Carter, Mrs. William H.: 106 upper, 111.
Cauthen, Robert: 41 lower right.
Collins, Mrs. LeRoy: 59 lower right, 97 upper.
Conoly, Mrs. George: 92 middle.
Dictionary of American Portraits, Dover 1968: 35 upper right.
Dixon, Coleman: 102 lower.
Flannery, Margaret: 132.
Florida Agricultural & Mechanical University, Black Archives: 72 right.
Florida Department of Natural Resources, Division of Recreation and Parks: 66 right, 67.
Florida Department of State, Division of Historical Resources: 23 right.
Florida Department of State, Division of Library and Information Services, Florida State Library, Florida Collection: 73, 97 lower, 104 middle.
Florida Department of State, Florida State Archives: 24 right, 35 middle right, 37 lower right, 40 lower middle, 40 lower right, 48 middle, 48 right, 52 lower, 53 upper, 55, 56 left, 57 left, 59 left, 61 lower, 64-65, 68 lower, 70 upper left, 71 left, 74, 79 right, 84 upper, 91, 95, upper, 96-97, 102 middle right, 107 upper, 108

upper, 112 right, 117 lower left, 148.
Florida Department of State, Florida State Archives, Benjamin "Red" Kerce Collection: 178 lower.
Florida Department of State, Florida State Archives, Department of Agriculture, Division of Forestry: 133 lower, 135.
Florida Department of State, Florida State Archives, Department of Commerce, Division of Tourism Collection: 18 upper, 18 lower, 160-161, 167, 171 upper, 171 lower, 172.
Florida Department of State, Florida State Archives, Department of Commerce, Division of Tourism Collection, photo by Carl Holland: 189.
Florida Department of State, Florida State Archives, gift of:
   Boyd, Mark; 70 lower left, 80 upper, 97 middle.
   Byrd, Bernard; 66 left, 80 lower, 81, 89, 94, upper.
   Carter, Mrs. William H.; 105 upper, 108 lower, 126 lower.
   Cawthon, Bender; 105 middle.
   Connolly, Esther; 61 upper.
   Diamond, Ruby; 42 upper right.
   Dixon, Coleman; 39, 96 upper, 103 upper left.
   Granger, Forest; 144, 158 lower, 159, 165, 188.
   Guy, Gladys; 40 middle, 52 middle, 59 upper right.
   Harrison, Agnes; 42 left, 42 lower right, 44, 45 right, 54 right, 79 left.
   Holland, Senator and Mrs. Spessard Holland; 147 upper, 153.
   Johnson, Malcolm B.; 77, 92 upper, 120 lower, 127.
   Langford, Mrs. George; 154 lower.
   Moor, Mr. & Mrs. Frank; 83, 143.
   O'Bryan, Carolyde; 45 left.
   Parramore, Catherine; 117 upper left.
   Pepper, Congressman Claude; 146-147.
   Robinson, Robert; 107 lower.
   Shores, Venila; 112 left, 118 lower.
   Tilden family; 113 right.
   White, J. Edwin; 134 upper.
   Winthrop family; 93 upper.
Florida Department of State, Florida State Archives, *Tallahassee Democrat* collection: 176-177, 178 upper, 180 upper, 182, 183, 186.
Florida Department of State, Florida State Archives, *Tallahassee Democrat,* photo by Dan Stainer: 174-175.
Florida Department of State, Museum of Florida History: 20 upper left, 53 lower, 56 right, 71 upper right, 71 lower right.

Florida Flambeau, photo by Bob O'Lary: 191, 192.
Florida Flambeau, photo by Deborah Thomas: 169, 181, 185, 190.
Florida Flambeau, photo by Ed O'Connor: 173.
Florida Handbook, The, by Allen Morris, 1987: 58.
Florida State College, *Argo,* 1903: 104, upper left.
Florida State College for Women annual, *Flastacowo,* 1936: 126 upper.
Florida State College for Women annual, *Flastacowo,* 1942: 157.
Florida State University, Commencement program, June 1950: 41 left.
Florida State University, Photographic Laboratory, photo by Gilbert Lawhon: 168.
Florida State University, Robert M. Strozier Library, Maps Division: 25 upper, 29 lower, 37 upper right.
Florida State University, Robert M. Strozier Library, Special Collections: 114, 134-135, 155, 174, 184.
Florida State University, Robert M. Strozier Library, Special Collections: R. A. Gray scrapbook: 104 upper right.
Florida State University, Robert M. Strozier Library, Special Collections: Schwalmeyer scrapbook: 139 lower.
Florida Supreme Court Historical Society: 124-125.
Florida Supreme Court Historical Society, Caldwell Collection: 147 lower, 163 upper, 164.
Florida the Land of Enchantment, by Nevin O. Winters, 1918: 17, 109 lower.
Florida Times Union, February 10, 1924: 40 lower left.
Gwynn, John: 40 upper.
Hamilton, E. K.: 74-75.
Harper's Weekly, 1862: 68 upper.
Harrison, Mrs. Graham: 103 lower left.
Heiskell, Mrs. Samuel G.: 36 lower.
History of the Indian Tribes of North America, McKenny & Hall: 33 right, 48 left.
Holloway, Mrs. Frank: 101 (insert).
Hood, Mrs. Thomas: 84 lower, 113 left, 119 upper.
Indians of the Southeastern United States, The, by John R. Swanton, 1946: 20 lower left.
Jiles family: 90 upper left and upper right.
Jones, Mrs. George: 115 upper.
Knott, Charles: 103 right, 105 lower.
La Florida, by Ruidiaz, 1883: 20 right, 22 right.
Le Moyne Art Foundation: 180 lower.
Leslie's Illustrated Newspaper, 1862: 60-61, 62-63.
Leslie's Illustrated Newspaper, 1868: 69 lower.

Library of Congress: 26, 31, 72.
Marks, Sally: 115 middle left.
May, William H.: 156.
McKinnon, Jean Walston: 162 upper.
Mettler, John W., Jr.: 86-87.
Miller, Mrs. J. Frank: 96 lower.
National Archives: 24 left, 25 lower, 41 upper right.
National Cyclopedia of American Biography: 51 left, 69 upper, 70 upper right.
Norman, Olive: 149, 151.
O'Bryan, Carolyde: 43.
Parker, Robert C.: 100-101.
Peggy Eaton, by Pollack, 1931: 51 right.
Phillips, Lynn: 106 center.
Pictorial Life of Andrew Jackson, by John Frost, 1848: 29 upper, 33 left.
Plant, Janet Byrd: 98-99.
Pollock, Phillip: 118 upper, 187.
Proctor, Ralph, Jr.: 116 upper.
Ragsdale, Mrs. William: 179.
Recueil D'Estampes, Représentant Les Différents Événments De La Guerre Qui A Procure L'Independance Aux Estats-Unis De L'Amerique 1784: 27.
Riley, Emlin: 90 lower.
Robert Butler Masonic Lodge No. 305: 35 lower right.
Sandridge, Dorothy: 93 lower.
Scribners Monthly, November 1874: 23 left.
Silver Slipper Restaurant: 154 upper.
Skelton, Betty Ann Munroe: 104 lower, 120-121.
State Historical Society of Wisconsin: 71 middle right.
Stout, George: 109 upper, 110, 115 middle right, 122 left.
Tall Timbers Research Station: 85.
Tallahassee City Hall: 115 lower, 119 lower, 128 lower, 130, 131 upper, 134 lower, 140, 141 upper, 141 lower, 148, 158 upper, 170.
Tallahassee City Hall, *Pictorial Review of Dale Mabry Field:* 150, 152-153, 162 lower.
Tallahassee Junior Museum: 92 lower.
Temple Israel: 152.
Thomas County Historical Society: 78.
Thomas Jefferson Memorial Foundation: 54 left.
Tomicich, Alice Blount: 117 right.
University of Florida: P. K. Yonge Library, Florida Collection: 47.
Vues et Souvenirs L'Amerique Du Nord, 1842: 34, 35 left, 37 left, 46.
Walker, Charles P.: 49.
Watson, Mrs. Alban: 30.
Webb Memorial Library, St. Augustine: 52 upper.

Whiddon, Shorty: 138 lower.
Wright, Wilson: 133 upper.

INDEX

SUPPLEMENTAL INDEX

FOR THE REVISED AND EXPANDED 2ND EDITION

ABOUT THE AUTHORS

Mary Louise Ellis, a Mississippi native and longtime resident of Tallahassee, teaches history at Tallahassee Community College. She earned her Ph.D. at Florida State University, and has published and lectured on a variety of topics related to Florida and Southern history.

William Warren Rogers is Distinguished Teaching Professor of History, Emeritus at Florida State University. He was born in Alabama and received his undergraduate and master's degrees at Auburn University and his Ph.D. at the University of North Carolina at Chapel Hill. Professor Rogers has published numerous articles and books on Southern history.

Joan Morris has been the supervisor of the Florida Photographic Collection in the Bureau of Archives and Record Management since 1970. She received both her bachelor's and master's degrees from Florida State University.

She has frequently lectured to historical associations, genealogy societies, librarians, curators, archivists, and students on the history of photography and the acquisition, conservation, organization, and use of photographs. She is widely known as a newspaper columnist and co-author and editor of several books on history and photography.